Minimizing Marriage

Marriage, Morality, and the Law

Elizabeth Brake

OXFORD
UNIVERSITY PRESS

OXFORD
UNIVERSITY PRESS

Oxford University Press, Inc., publishes works that further
Oxford University's objective of excellence
in research, scholarship, and education.

Oxford New York
Auckland   Cape Town   Dar es Salaam   Hong Kong   Karachi
Kuala Lumpur   Madrid   Melbourne   Mexico City   Nairobi
New Delhi   Shanghai   Taipei   Toronto

With offices in
Argentina   Austria   Brazil   Chile   Czech Republic   France   Greece
Guatemala   Hungary   Italy   Japan   Poland   Portugal   Singapore
South Korea   Switzerland   Thailand   Turkey   Ukraine   Vietnam

Published by Oxford University Press, Inc.
198 Madison Avenue, New York, New York 10016
www.oup.com

Oxford is a registered trademark of Oxford University Press

Library of Congress Cataloging-in-Publication Data
Brake, Elizabeth.
Minimizing marriage : marriage, morality, and the law / Elizabeth Brake.
p. cm.—(Studies in feminist philosophy)
ISBN 978-0-19-977413-5 (pbk. : alk. paper)—ISBN 978-0-19-977414-2
(hardcover : alk. paper)
1. Marriage—Philosophy.   2. Marriage—Moral and ethical aspects.
3. Marriage law. I. Title.
HQ734.B785 2012
173—dc23
2011029589

1 3 5 7 9 8 6 4 2
Printed in the United States of America
on acid-free paper

Minimizing Marriage

Studies in Feminist Philosophy is designed to showcase cutting-edge monographs and collections that display the full range of feminist approaches to philosophy, that push feminist thought in important new directions, and that display the outstanding quality of feminist philosophical thought.

For all the same-sex partners and diverse care networks, urban tribes, best friends, quirkyalones, polyamorists, and revolutionary parents who have suffered legal penalty or social exclusion.

And for my parents, with deep gratitude.

CONTENTS

PREFACE

As a little girl growing up in the south of the United States in the 1970s and 1980s, I learned that a woman could do anything. I saw the first female astronaut on TV, and I met the first female Episcopalian priest in Virginia. At the same time, I learned from nursery rhymes and TV shows, young adult fiction and adult gossip, that the normal form of adult life was in married families and that a child's normal trajectory to adulthood would bring him or her, eventually, to this goal, which also happened to be where fairy stories conveniently ended. I gleaned, too, that unmarried female adults were somehow to be pitied in a way that their male counterparts weren't and that there was an extra urgency for a young woman to marry, that it had a significance that went beyond "happily ever after." But it seemed to me that the women presented in my shows and books divided neatly into two groups: the single career woman or adventurer—whose adventures typically ended in, and with, marriage—and the married woman, who usually provided dependable support to other characters but whose own story was, in some way, over. Marriage had an inescapably special place in society, but it seemed to threaten women's independence. It also seemed to require leaving best friends behind, or relegating them to the sidelines, something I wasn't sure about either. Across the street lived two elderly widows, cohabiting for companionship; these women—an endless source of good food and stories—seemed to have it right: Why couldn't adulthood involve domestic cohabitation with a best friend, rather than requiring postponement of such a household until widowhood? Why couldn't someone just live with her friends, in an arrangement allowing all of them to retain their distinctive identities and take on the domestic tasks that suited them best, rather than taking on the curiously impersonal and prescriptive roles of husband and wife? Why was marriage so important, and what was wrong with the alternatives?

This book is a critical investigation into the often-proclaimed special value of marriage, and its connection to morality. To some readers, such attributions of value might seem antiquated, but they are by no means obsolete: In the United States, the state promotes marriage, and its special value is inscribed in the Social Security Act; and everywhere, it seems, the wedding industry capitalizes on the significance of marriage. Even for those already sceptical of the value of marriage, Part One of this book should prompt a reconsideration of what we can promise to one another and of what we owe to one another in intimate relationships, and of how far privileging the *couple*, married or unmarried, sustains a distinctive type of discrimination. This book examines the costs imposed by the special value attributed to marriage, and to marriage-like cohabitation, in society and law. The privileging of marriage marginalizes the unpartnered and those in nontraditional relationships—quirkyalones, urban tribes, care networks, polyamorists—and same-sex partners, where they are prohibited from marriage. This privileging also brings special costs to women. This book is an attempt to bring those costs to light and suggest solutions.

This book began more than a decade ago in my graduate studies at the University of St. Andrews, and my debts begin there: especially to David Archard, who supervised my dissertation, and to John Skorupski, who introduced me to philosophical ethics. My colleagues at the University of Calgary have provided invaluable comments on my written work and in conversation: thanks especially to Allen Habib, Ali Kazmi, Ann Levey, Dennis McKerlie, Mark Migotti, Nicole Wyatt, Richard Zach, Joshua Goldstein, and Michael Taylor. Many others have generously read and commented on my work: Scott Anderson, Lisa Bortolotti, Bruce Brower, Rachel Buddeberg, Cheshire Calhoun, Eric Cave, Clare Chambers, Jody Graham, Christie Hartley, Laurence Houlgate, Joyce Jenkins, Chad Kerst, Don LePan, Roderick Long, Susan Mendus, David Shoemaker, Laurie Shrage, Lawrence Torcello, Steven Wall, Laurie Shrage, Lori Watson, and Ralph Wedgwood, as well as many participants in an online discussion on the PEA Soup blog. For research assistance, I am grateful to Teresa Kouri, Rodrigo Morales, and Tina Strasbourg. For institutional support, I am indebted to the University of Calgary, the Center for Ethics and Public Affairs at the Murphy Institute at Tulane University, and the Social Sciences and Humanities Research Council of Canada. Finally, many helpful suggestions came from audiences at conferences hosted by the American Philosophical Association, the Canadian Philosophical Association, the Canadian Society for the Study of Practical Ethics, the North American Society for Social Philosophy, the Society for Applied Philosophy, and the Cal Poly Pomona Ethics Conference, the New Orleans Invitational Seminar on Ethics, and the Rocky Mountain Ethics Congress.

For boundless support over the years, including philosophical discussion, lovingly cooked meals, and special treatment of various kinds, I am deeply grateful to Ellen Shreve, Bill and Jeannie Brake, Matthew Brake, Jupiter Brake, David Boutillier, Gur Hirshberg, Ann Levey, Roderick Long, Zayne Reeves, Darlene Rigo, Brad and Magdalena Stewart, Tina Strasbourg, and Richard Zach.

Finally, I should thank two journals for permission to reprint material published elsewhere; Chapter 1 is a revised version of an article published first in *Ethical Theory and Moral Practice*, and some material in Part Two is drawn from an article in *Ethics*, with many revisions and additions responding to the helpful comments I have received.

INTRODUCTION
MARRIAGE AND PHILOSOPHY

Marriage is philosophically undertheorized. This is not because it lacks philosophical interest. For the moral philosopher, it raises key issues of the possibilities of interpersonal moral obligations and their bounds—not to mention the question of a good human life. Secular moralists often assume that marriage morally transforms a relationship, yet contemporary philosophers have paid little attention to the question of how such a transformation could be effected. For the political philosopher, the question of how—or whether—society and the state should organize sex, love, and intimacy is urgent, but recent attention has focused mainly on a set of narrow questions surrounding marriage law: same-sex marriage, or not; polygamy, or not, abolition, or not. A greater variety of reconfigurations should at least be contemplated.

This book attempts to shed some philosophical light on these questions. It has three main theses. The first is that marriage should be de-moralized—that it does not have a *sui generis* moral status or a transformative moral power. The second is that the great social and legal importance accorded marriage and marriage-like relationships is unjustified, and that this privilege harms, sometimes unjustly, those not oriented toward monogamous, central relationships. Those harmed include members of multiple significant overlapping friendships such as adult care networks or urban tribes, the asexual and solitudinous, and the polyamorous. The third thesis is that a truly politically liberal law of marriage would expand the legal category of marriage in surprising ways, minimizing special restrictions on entry, exit, and what transpires between.

These arguments target features of marriage seldom interrogated—its central and dyadic relationship, its association with romance, its one-size-fits-all legal structure. Marriage is so pervasive that many of its features are accepted without question. Some aspects are glaringly foregrounded, while its fundamental structure disappears into the background. Debates over same-sex marriage make headlines, weddings are big business, and marriage promotion is U.S. policy. But is there good reason for marriage to be structured as it is—monogamous, central, permanent (or aspiring to permanence), with its dense bundle of legal rights and responsibilities? Is such an arrangement really part of the good life, and should it be privileged in the just society? From a secular perspective, does it have any moral significance? Are marriages morally distinct from otherwise similar unmarried relationships? Religious doctrines give theological answers to some of these questions. But the value of marriage is affirmed in countless secular contexts that provide no such ready answers. Philosophy has something to contribute to making visible assumptions about marriage, as a social and legal institution.

The starting point of this study is the widely held belief that marriage has a *sui generis* moral significance, one that otherwise similar unmarried relationships lack. In the United States, this value is written into the Social Security Act and taught in schools, and a politician who openly questioned its value could give up hope of election. Many people who do not hold religious views or believe that marriage is the only permissible context for sex nevertheless associate marriage with a special moral status and with goods like stability, love, and trust. Some defenders of same-sex marriage proclaim its moral value just as forcefully as their "traditionalist" opponents. (Many features of so-called traditional marriage are historically vari-able or recently constructed, hence the quotation marks.) Belief in the moral value of marriage bridges political and religious chasms. Such belief invites philosophical articulation and assessment. In turn, this examination raises philosophical issues of wider application. What can we promise, and under what circumstances are we released from our promises? What is commitment, and is it valuable? Are there any involuntary special obligations (obligations to particular others not derived from our general moral duties), and if so, how do we acquire them?

This investigation brings the tools of moral philosophy to bear on claims that marriage has a special moral significance. Analysis of this kind can be complicated by familiarity. Many of us are married or have good friends who are, or, at least, have been touched by a wedding ceremony. Or we may move in circles where marriage is considered an aberration. Either way, marriage may appear beyond the pale of serious philosophical discussion. To some, its value is self-evident. To others, what is self-evident is its obsolescence. But such presumptions should be examined with the same careful and open-minded analysis brought to other philosophical topics.

Part One articulates and assesses secular accounts of the moral significance of marriage. It reviews morally salient features commonly attributed to marriage: prom-ise, commitment, basic human goods, virtues, and care. It concludes by *de-moralizing* marriage: Marriage is neither necessary nor sufficient for the goods often associated with it, it creates no *sui generis* moral status, and it produces harms and injustices that must be weighed against its goods. While there may be special goods in caring relationships, they do not depend on marriage—and, indeed, the special value attributed to marriage has penalized caring relationships that fail to fit the marital norm. The discussion assumes a broad moral framework, one that accommodates talk of obligations and of virtues, of care and of justice.

There are three salient secular elements of marriage that may carry special moral significance: the contractual exchange of rights and responsibilities in legal marriage, social recognition of the marital relationship, and the ideal relationship type associated with marriage (for example, a loving, trusting, and caring relationship). The first two—contract and social recognition—attach to legal and social institutions of marriage, enduring impersonal structures that define roles, rights, and responsibilities for the particular relationships that enter them. The third feature, though, concerns the relationship itself, the ongoing daily interaction between particular parties. Drawing on this distinction, there are two distinct ways in which a unique moral significance could attach to marriage. First, entry into the social or legal institutional structure, through the wedding vows or the exchange of legal rights, could morally transform the relationship. Chapters 1 and 3 address arguments that the institution itself has transformative power. Second, it could be that the ideal type of relationship is valuable and that the institution of marriage has an instrumental value in promoting it. Chapters 2 and 4 address this possibility.

Entry into marriage commonly takes place through an exchange of vows. It might thus be thought that this voluntary undertaking of obligations works a moral transformation, and so, in Chapter 1, I begin by examining the marriage promise. What is this promise? Under what conditions might one be excused from it? The answers to these questions have implications for the morality of divorce, as well as sexual exclusivity and other marital obligations. Here I emphasize the diversity of marriages, arguing that the promise made in marriage depends on spouses' intentions—but not all intentions are promises. A vow sometimes taken as central to marriage—to love, honor, and cherish—is not a possible object of promise at all. Likewise, promises to take on spousal roles presuppose a robust and shared understanding of the moral content of that role—something many modern spouses may lack. Many wedding vows are thus not promises but failed attempts at promising. This casts doubt upon the idea that the distinctive moral significance of marriage is promissory. This is compatible with the de-moralization of marriage, but not sufficient for it, as rival views of marriage hold that its moral content is not promissory at all.

Marriage is often said to involve commitment, as distinct from promise. Chapter 2 begins by clarifying this concept. Commitment, as an internal psychological disposition, is not created in the wedding ceremony: One may publicly profess commitment without actually having it, and being committed requires a temporal duration longer than a wedding. Rather than creating commitments, marriage provides a social form for their expression and provokes pressure to keep them. But does this make marriage valuable? Institutions that encourage keeping commitments are only as valuable as the objects of commitment—or as the alleged virtue of committedness. Are marital commitments rational, or good, for the parties involved? The marriage commitment is good for spouses when it helps them—like tying Ulysses to the mast—protect their best interests against fleeting desires. But as a general defense of marriage, the claim that such commitment is always in spouses' best interests relies on problematic essentialism about the human good. Other defenses of marriage argue that marriage is socially valuable because it teaches spouses the virtue of committedness. But this value must be qualified: Commitment to injustice or vice is no virtue. As John Stuart Mill warned, unequal marriages can be schools of injustice.

Perhaps, however, marriage does essentially involve a commitment to something valuable—to basic human goods, to respect, or to flourishing. In Chapter 3, I examine three of the most influential defenses of marriage; each holds that marriage is the sole permissible context for sexual activity and the unique context for achieving certain related goods. Kant held that marriage morally transforms sexual objectification, permitting otherwise impermissible moral risks, and thereby making procreation morally possible. Natural law accounts argue that basic human goods of procreation and marital friendship can only be attained through marriage. Roger Scruton argues that marriage enables virtuous erotic love, which is an essential contributor to human flourishing. These three accounts, which attribute to marriage a unique transformative role, share a single failing: Entry into a legal institution does not effect, nor is it required for, the psychological transformation that virtues and respect require. Marriage is neither necessary nor sufficient for virtues or respectful attitudes. Basic goods, respect, and virtues can exist outside marriage, as in unmarried relationships. Furthermore, unqualified attributions of value to marriage fail to recognize the variability of real marriages, and they ignore their vices.

But while this calls into question unqualified attributions of value to the institution, some marriages are caring, and interpersonal care might be thought valuable. Chapter 4 takes up the question of whether marriage is valuable because it promotes caring relationships. At a critical distance from care ethics, I argue that care is motivationally and epistemologically valuable, but only in the context of rights and justice. Just and caring relationships have some value, and this value should be recognized wherever it appears. But the special priority accorded marriage and marriage-like relationships marginalizes other forms of caring relationships. To the extent that it sustains "amatonormativity"—the focus on marital and amorous love relationships as special sites of value—marriage undermines other forms of care. For example, the assumption that the most valuable relationships must be marital or amorous devalues friendships. Thus, I argue, marriage and the associated pressures of amatonormativity can threaten care. On the other hand, I argue that contract and bargaining, which are often seen as opposed to care, are not so opposed. In Part Two, I develop a proposal for marriage reform that supports care and allows contractual individualization while avoiding amatonormativity.

Part One is a work in moral philosophy, Part Two in political philosophy. Marriage has significant legal ramifications, which make it a matter of justice. It entitles spouses to benefits, it constructs and protects spousal privacy, it limits exit options, and, in some jurisdictions, it brings exemptions from sexual battery charges. Its legal effects can be life-saving or fatal: entitlement to health insurance—or legal access rights for an abusive spouse. It also carries a rich symbolism of adulthood, full citizenship, and moral respectability. These wide-ranging implications are why access to it is so contentious, whether one thinks that single mothers should be urged in, lesbians, gays, and polygamists kept out, or that the state should cease to recognize marriage entirely.

In Part Two, I develop a liberal feminist marriage law proposal that eschews amatonormativity. Given the weight of critiques of marriage, and the costs of legislating it, the fundamental question is whether there is any good political reason for legal recognition of marriage, and if so, what form of marriage law would respect the many views of the good found in a diverse liberal society. Feminist, queer, and antiracist criticisms of marriage and monogamy support the disestablishment of monogamous amatonormative marriage—a conclusion that, I argue, political liberals must share. My proposal, "minimal marriage," is a legal framework that supports monogamous relationships as well as the rich diversity of adult care networks that do not fit the amatonormative mold.

Chapter 5 begins to build this case by introducing various critiques of marriage law as unjust. Theorists of oppression note that marriage law has historically oppressed women and (in the United States and Canada) people of color and argue that it continues to perpetuate the oppression of women, gays and lesbians, and minority racial and ethnic groups. Social pressures to marry, Simone de Beauvoir argued in her 1949 work *The Second Sex* make women aspire to be wives at the cost of other aspirations. Gender-structured marriage, Susan Moller Okin argued in her 1989 work, *Justice, Gender, and the Family*, makes wives economically vulnerable. Marriage, Claudia Card has more recently argued, distributes benefits such as health care unjustly and can facilitate abuse and violence; in addition, far from serving gay and lesbian liberation, same-sex marriage would encourage assimilation to a heteronormative ideal of monogamy. And as Patricia Hill Collins has argued, marriage law has served racist ends and functioned as an important symbol of racial hierarchy; U.S. marriage promotion continues to be racially inflected in ways that devalue practices found in African American communities. Such critiques are crucial to my politically liberal argument for marriage reform because they demonstrate that the amatonormative marriage ideal conflicts with many other ideals. But they also draw attention to grave injustices that such reform must address. I argue, though, that marriage is not essentially unjust; it can be restructured in ways that address such injustices rather than perpetuating them.

Politically, theoretical commitments do not predict views on marriage. Liberals are not unanimous on marriage law. Some defend "traditional" marriage as supporting state stability or as a prepolitical institution not subject to liberal principles. Others argue that freedom of contract requires contractualizing marriage, assimilating it completely to the contract paradigm. Still other liberals argue that liberal principles require extending marriage to same-sex marriage or polygamy. Chapter 6 continues the argument for marriage reform by reviewing liberal debates over same-sex marriage to show what they have often missed. Liberal defenses of same-sex marriage have not followed the implications of their own reasoning far enough. Attempts within liberalism to produce a rationale for restricting legal marriage to different-sex partners have failed, but so have attempts to produce a rationale for restricting it to monogamous or amatonormative relationships. While child welfare is sometimes given as a reason for restricting marriage, the empirical evidence needed to sustain heterosexual privilege is lacking, and many children are reared outside marriages altogether. On these and other grounds, I argue for separating legal marriage and parenting frameworks. But this may seem to cede the point to marriage contractualists by depriving marriage of any rationale. In the absence of such a rationale, considerations of fairness and efficiency seem to support the abolition of legal marriage.

Chapter 7 takes up the challenges of the preceding chapters by providing a strong rationale for a reformed marriage law. Political liberalism requires the disestablishment of monogamous amatonormative marriage. Under the constraints of public reason, a liberal state must refrain from basing law, in matters of great import, solely on a comprehensive moral, religious, or philosophical doctrine. But only such doctrine can furnish reason for restricting marriage to male-female couples, or to romantic love dyads. Restrictions on marriage should thus be minimized. But public reason can provide a strong, neutral rationale for minimal marriage: Care is a primary good, in the terminology of Rawlsian liberalism, making legal frameworks for adult care networks not only consistent with neutrality and public reason, but required as a matter of fundamental justice. Thus, my argument opposes the wholesale abolition of marriage. Instead, it gives reason for "minimal marriage," a legal framework that avoids amatonormativity, supporting caring relationships including "traditional," polygamous, and same-sex marriages as well as "Boston marriages," friendships, and urban tribes. This proposal allows individuals to select from a greatly reduced set of the rights and responsibilities currently exchanged in marriage and to assign them to whomever they want, so long as the purpose is to support a caring relationship.

The argument of Chapter 7 is ideal-theoretical: It describes marriage law in an ideal liberal egalitarian society. But we do not inhabit such a society. Implementing minimal marriage in our society could lead to injustice. Chapter 8 takes up the problem of implementing ideal theory in a nonideal world. It addresses concerns that minimal marriage would worsen the lot of the vulnerable, especially women, by eliminating antipoverty marriage promotion, mandatory alimony and property division protecting the economically dependent, and permitting gender-structured polygyny. Liberals could consistently support transitional restrictions on marriage law, but liberalism can, and should, also address such problems through legal vehicles other than marriage, especially through education and default rules of financial fairness. Although implementing ideal theory poses transitional problems, it also gives us a distanced and fairer perspective from which to criticize the current state. Actual marriage law has perpetuated patriarchy, heterosexism, and amatonormative discrimination, in ways which familiarity obscures; ideal theory shows us what would be needed for a truly just law of marriage.

It might be thought that marriage law reform is meritorious but not urgent. But there is a serious impetus to this study. U.S. marriage law is unjust and harmful. This should not be taken lightly by anyone who cares about justice. Lack of access to health care or a basic standard of living because one is excluded from marriage or chooses to boycott it is no light matter, nor is the inability (in certain jurisdictions) to press sexual battery charges against one's spouse. Marriage promotion in the United States, with its abstinence-until-marriage education, also impedes the developing sexual autonomy of young adults. Stigmatizing unmarried sex leads to ignorance and shame, conditions that lead to disease, abortion, and teenage pregnancy, and silence about sexual abuse and rape.

Social pressures surrounding marriage can also harm. Marriage is big business—the wedding industry claims to be worth well over $100 billion annually—and marriage marketers peddle dangerous illusions. The promotion of gendered marriage norms reinforces the patriarchal family and encourages women to make themselves economically dependent. It also marginalizes the unpartnered, the polyamorous, the celibate, urban tribes and care networks, lovers who cannot marry or choose not to, and those who are "just good friends." Marriage is not private; it is an exclusionary social institution, a signpost in the social world. A wedding ring announces a person's self-description. It signals how to approach the wearer and demands a certain respect. Like race, class, and sex, marital status is a fundamental category in social interaction. Like race, class, and sex, it can be the basis of unjustified discrimination. And, at least insofar as the state reinforces such discrimination, it is a matter of justice calling for reform and rectification.

Marriage is so widespread as to be invisible. Many of us accept it as we find it, including the central role it plays in our lives and imaginations, the way it shapes our understandings of licit and illicit sex, public and private spheres, and the desirability of dependency. These understandings feed into female and child poverty, domestic violence, rape culture, and threats to reproductive rights. Rethinking marriage is an urgent matter of justice. Marriage reform may be a matter of life and death—for victims of intimate violence, of homophobic hate crimes, of death by lack of health care.

The matter has a personal urgency, too. The topics of this book are something almost every thinking person must consider—at least, every thinking person who is married, contemplating marriage, or needs to RSVP to a wedding invitation. What does marriage entail morally? What obligations does it impose? What are its goods? Can spouses by their own volition guard against the injustices of marriage? Are calls to boycott marriage and wedding ceremonies merited? Should one marry?

Before proceeding, a note on terminology. I avoid the terms *heterosexual* and *homosexual* because they can mislead. There is no guarantee as to the sexual orientation of married individuals; men and women of same-sex or bisexual orientation can enter different-sex marriages. Applying the term *heterosexual* to different-sex marriages, while it correctly describes the marriages, misleadingly implies that the participants are oriented to, and only to, the other sex. The terminology thereby tends to make bisexuals, and those in the closet, invisible. The term *different-sex*, while awkward, reminds us by its unfamiliarity that it is the biological sex, not the sexual orientation, of spouses that is at issue. As applied to persons, the terms *homosexual* and *heterosexual* lend themselves to stereotyping, conflating certain activities or patterns of desire with types of persons; activities and desires do not exhaust identities. And persons can engage in same-sex activities or even seek same-sex marriage without being exclusively oriented toward their own sex.[1]

MULTIPLE MARRIAGES: MARRIAGE IN HISTORY, CULTURE, LAW

Marriage is many-faceted. It comprises legal, social, cultural, and religious institutions that vary by jurisdiction, culture, and theological doctrine. Its meaning, purpose, and scope are disputed. There is debate as to whether it is a natural biological unit (the two-parent reproductive family); divinely ordained; merely a conventional legal status designation or economic unit; or a tool of sexism, heterosexism, and capitalism; whether, in short, it is about children, religion, money, oppression—or, of course, love.

In considering whether marriage has a fixed essence or definition, the historical and cross-cultural diversity of marital practices cannot be overstated. Structurally, it includes polygamy (both polyandry and polygyny) and polygynandry (multiple men with multiple women) as well as monogamy. Nomadic tribal bride exchange and arranged dynastic marriages must be set beside 1950s male-breadwinner unions and 1960s group marriages. In many cultures, extramarital sex has been the norm—including communal sex, spouse-swapping, and sexual double standards. Standards for divorce have ranged from a simple announcement (saying "I divorce you" three times) to a papal annulment or a British Act of Parliament. Some cultures have seen the ideal marital relationship as reserved, others as intimate and amorous; some have seen it as hierarchical, others as an equal partnership. Marriage includes passionate elopements as well as proxy marriages, in which Japanese or Korean picture brides, chosen by photograph, would marry proxies of their husbands in the home country, before immigrating to join their husbands. While most marriage institutions have been different-sex, marital or marriage-like same-sex relationships have been recognized. John Boswell documents same-sex unions in the Greco-Roman era and (controversially) in medieval Europe, Chinese historians report similar practices, and some Native American tribes, with fluid concepts of gender, allowed males to marry each other. Some rare societies have not been organized around sexual partners at all. In "husband-visitor societies" mother and child lived apart from the father or "husband." For instance, the Na, in China, had no marriage practice. Na women lived with their brothers; their male sexual partners were not integrated into the family.[2]

The features usually associated with marriage today are historically contingent. While contemporary "traditionalists" promote monogamous marriage, in the longer historical view, polygyny, not monogamy, has been dominant—and has existed within the Judeo-Christian tradition, a fact for which both Augustine and Aquinas apologize.[3] Nor has marriage always been a matter of legal or religious regulation. In Europe, prior to the sixteenth century, people "considered mutual intent or the blessing of a parent sufficient to solemnize a marriage." Within Christianity, the Church did not call for priestly officiation until 1215, when, to prevent clandestine marriages, it decided to require a dowry, banns, and a church ceremony; governments did not require legal registration of marriages until much later (1753, in England).[4] In the pre–Civil War United States, although laws concerning marriage existed, informal or "self-marriage" and self-divorce (without official authorization), sometimes followed by remarriage, were widespread, as states lacked the resources to oversee domestic life, and many communities tolerated informal alliances and partings.[5]

Strangest, perhaps, to contemporary sensibilities, marriage has historically been more in the service of domestic economies than domesticated love, facilitating property transmission, resource and labor sharing, and kinship bonds. For rich and poor alike, its rationale was money and survival, not love. Arranged marriage practices reflect this economic rationale: Guardians of minors in medieval England could arrange their infant wards' marriages and even sell such marriages for profit. Indeed, some ancient Greeks and Romans, Christians, and Muslims discouraged "excessive" love in marriage. The "love revolution" in marriage dates to the eighteenth century, as economic conditions made young people more independent. From the beginning, the idea of marrying for personal happiness met with resistance as thinkers foresaw that expectations of marital fulfillment would undermine marital stability. Thus, Hegel wrote that arranged marriage is the most ethical form of marriage, because it subordinates spouses' desires to the institution, rather than predicating marriage on the instability of passionate love.[6]

Like love-based marriage, the male-breadwinner marriage, in which the wife makes no economic contribution, is relatively recent. In Europe, before the Industrial Revolution, wives' participation in most domestic economies was vital. The ideal of the unemployed middle-class wife, whose domestic efforts contributed to her family's comfort and pleasure, not survival, became widespread only with post-Industrial prosperity. But this ideal did not and does not reflect the experience of the many married women who worked outside the home. The ideal is not only classist, it is also ethnocentric: Among Native Americans, for instance, women were generally responsible for farming. The disparity between the reality of female physical labor and the angel-in-the-house ideology is illustrated by former slave Sojourner Truth's famous response to the claim that women were too weak to vote: "I have ploughed, and planted, and gathered into barns and no man could head me! And ain't I a woman?"[7] The ideal of the homemaking wife, which emerged along with love-based marriage, was accompanied by an increased emphasis on sexual difference—especially the idea that women were naturally domestic.[8]

Law and custom enforced women's restriction to the domestic sphere that was supposedly natural for them. John Stuart Mill noted the incongruity of this, asking why, if domesticity was natural to women, they should have to be compelled into it. Barring women from education, government, and the professions would "force women into marriage by closing all other doors against them.... It is not a sign of one's thinking the boon one offers very attractive, when one allows only Hobson's choice, 'that or none'."[9] Yet the persistent belief in gender difference underwrote married women's exclusion from civil equality—not to mention workplaces. Well into the twentieth century, marriage deprived wives of full human rights, first in coverture (in which a wife's legal personality was "covered" by that of her husband) and later in spousal rape exemptions and professional bars for married women. Legislatures also imposed gendered standards—"head and master laws." Not until the 1970s, in the United States, did consistent gender neutrality in legal rights and responsibilities take hold.[10]

The changing law of coverture exemplifies how, far from recognizing one unvarying form of marriage, the modern state has constructed and reconstructed the institution. Divorce is another example. The state not only regulates obligations within marriage, it also regulates exit from it. In the United States, for much of the period of state regulation of marriage, exit was difficult: In the mid-nineteenth century, divorce was prohibited in some states, and in others only permitted on fault-based grounds such as adultery, cruelty, drunkenness, or desertion (often with gendered double standards, as in the United Kingdom). Connecticut, following Maine, liberalized its divorce law in 1849, permitting divorce due to "any such misconduct as permanently destroys the happiness of the petitioner and defeats the purpose of the marriage relation."[11] But these laws were overturned by the 1880s, and divorce law continued to be restrictive until the "no-fault revolution" of the 1970s, since which all fifty states have adopted no-fault divorce.

The United States has also rewritten marriage law in ways that reflect changing phases of racial oppression. Enslaved African Americans could not legally marry, and informally married slave couples were torn apart—a salient fact in African American experience. Toni Morrison writes of "the different history of black women in this country—a history in which marriage was discouraged, impossible, or illegal; in which birthing children was required, but 'having' them, being responsible for them—being, in other words, their parent—was as out of the question as freedom."[12] After the Civil War, formerly enslaved African Americans gained the right to marry, and the Freedmen's Bureau began to promote—and enforce—monogamous marriage, fining and arresting the bigamous or unmarried cohabitants. At the same time, now that formerly enslaved African Americans had the right to marry, antimiscegenation laws, banning marriage between whites and African Americans (and, in some states, between whites and Asians) proliferated. Interracial marriage bans did not prevent actual miscegenation so much as they prevented women of color and their children from gaining the entitlements of marriage. In 1967, the U.S. Supreme Court struck down interracial marriage bans as unconstitutional in *Loving v. Virginia*. Some states ignored the Court. Alabama, for example, retained a (mostly unenforced) interracial marriage ban in its state constitution until 2000.[13]

In the United States as elsewhere, the state has restricted the number and sex of spouses, as well as restricting entry by race. Christian monogamy was written into U.S. law and enforced, in the face of the perceived Mormon threat, through an extended nineteenth-century campaign against polygamy, which included removing voting rights from polygamous men. As of 2004, polygamy was criminalized in forty-nine states, and laws against bigamy still included *extramarital* bigamous cohabitation in five U.S. states.[14] More recently, the sex of spouses has preoccupied judges and legislators: Some U.S. states and Canada have recognized same-sex marriage, but many states have passed legislation explicitly barring it. And in 1996, the U.S. federal legislature passed the Defense of Marriage Act, defining marriage, for federal purposes, as different-sex, and exempting states from recognizing same-sex marriages performed in other states. Despite the controversy over same-sex marriage, it has, according to Andrew Sullivan, provoked less opposition than interracial marriage in its time: "In 1968...a Gallup poll found that some 72 percent of Americans still disapproved of [interracial] marriages....It wasn't until 1991 that a majority existed to approve them—by a narrow margin....The polls show that hostility to same-sex marriage in 2004 is markedly less profound than hostility to interracial marriage was in 1968."[15] In considering controversial marriage reforms, it is worth remembering how controversial past reforms, which now seem familiar, were at the time.

At the same time as the state has narrowly restricted entry to marriage, marriage law has simultaneously been used to mark several invidious distinctions, penalizing those excluded from entry and compelling sexually active people into legitimized monogamy. Illegitimate children, defined as children born outside marriage, suffered legal inheritance bars, separation from their mothers, and ostracism. This legal distinction formed the basis for social exclusion: Women who gave birth illegitimately were disowned by respectable families and employers. In the United States, legal discrimination against "illegitimate" children continued until the 1970s. Law has also enforced marital monogamy by criminalizing sex outside of it. Fornication, defined as sex outside marriage, and unmarried cohabitation were at one time criminal in all fifty states; in 2004, at least 10 states still penalized fornication and twenty-three states criminalized adultery.[16]

While marital nonconformity has been penalized in criminal law, with the scope of prohibitions and enforcement varying historically, marriage itself offers significant financial incentives and other tangible benefits. This brings us to the current state of marriage law, and the guiding questions of this book. Marriage now triggers over 1100 "benefits, rights, and privileges" in U.S. federal law.[17] According to legal scholar Mary Anne Case, its "principal legal function" is to designate spouses for third-party benefit claims.[18] Spouses have rights "to be on each others' health, disability, life insurance, and pension plans," to special tax and immigration status, and to survivor, Social Security, and veterans' benefits, and they are designated next-of-kin "in case of death, medical emergency, or mental incapacity."[19] One question of this book is on what grounds, if any, such entitlements can be politically justified.

Marriage can also bring disadvantages. Financially, a high-earning spouse can disqualify the other from federal loan programs, housing assistance, or Medicaid, and spouses are liable for each other's debts. Spouses cannot be considered one another's employees, exempting them from labor law protections in jointly run small businesses. Divorce burdens exit, especially in covenant marriage and in the case of active military personnel, who can defer divorce proceedings. Most gravely, spouses have legal rights of access to each other's person and home and in some jurisdictions are exempt from sexual battery charges.[20] Thus, marriage may legally facilitate abuse. In addition, the social practice of gender-structured marriage causes economic vulnerability for women. A further question of this book is how far restructuring marriage can eliminate unjust burdens and protect the vulnerable.

Ironically, in light of the sexism, racism, and heterosexism of marriage law, there is a long, and continuing, legal tradition of associating marriage with morality. The U.S. Supreme Court opined in 1888 that marriage is "an institution, in the maintenance of which in its purity the public is deeply interested, for it is the foundation of the family and of society, without which there would be neither civilization or progress."[21] In recent years, the United States has pursued marriage promotion with moralistic overtones. The 1996 U.S. Personal Responsibility and Work Opportunity Reconciliation Act (PRWORA), a welfare reform bill, found that "marriage is the foundation of a successful society" and that "marriage is an essential institution of a successful society which promotes the interests of children."[22] The act authorized $300 million annually for marriage promotion through state commissions and proclamations, tax policies and cash assistance, Medicaid, media campaigns, social work, and marriage education. Riding this wave, legislation to abolish no-fault divorce has recently been introduced in several state legislatures, and three states (Arizona, Arkansas, and Louisiana) have introduced the option of covenant marriage, which constrains divorce. Perhaps the most significant marriage promotion tool is federally funded abstinence-until-marriage education, by the terms of which schools "cannot teach anything that contradicts an abstinence-until-marriage message." This message is "that a mutually faithful, monogamous relationship in the context of marriage is *the expected standard of sexual activity*" and that "sexual activity outside the context of marriage is likely to have harmful psychological and physical effects."[23]

U.S. public discourse on marriage is embroiled in claims about morality, the good for society—and the good life for the private individual. Marriage has been upheld, as in *Loving v. Virginia*, as "essential to the orderly pursuit of happiness by free men. Marriage is one of the 'basic civil rights of man,' fundamental to our very existence and survival."[24] The persistent attraction of marriage as the threshold to adulthood and happiness is exploited—and fostered—by the "wedding-industrial complex."[25] It is because marriage is seen as a private and public transformation, a gateway to unique fulfillment, that it is an occasion for elaborate celebration. Such a view of marriage is sometimes, but not always, based in religious views, so it cannot be explained as a religious belief. Nor can it be explained simply as a celebration of love, or of particular lovers, because it is the translation of love into a specific institutional form that gives the ceremony its meaning. Marriage retains, in a secular age, sacramental connotations, and, in an individualistic age, it retains the aspect of communal sanction. This book sets out to determine whether there is any justification for this special status accorded marriage, either as a significant moral transformation or as a gateway to virtue and happiness.

With its predefined terms, marriage is awkwardly positioned between legal contract—which is paradigmatically self-determined—and legal status—a communally defined category standardized and imposed impersonally, as in feudal and caste societies. Marriage law is shaped by, and engages, an accretion of social expectations; it establishes socially defined roles. A relationship without this legal and social recognition is not marriage, although it may resemble marriage in every other respect and even be granted the other legal entitlements of marriage. But it lacks the public standing and social recognition, the status, of marriage. Does this make any important difference? I expect some readers will immediately think "of course not." But not only social conservatives disagree: Arguments for same-sex marriage often depend on the point that "civil union" is not marriage.[26] This book attempts to articulate philosophically what that difference does—and does not—entail.

MARRIAGE IN THE HISTORY OF PHILOSOPHY

Historical discussions of marriage set the agenda for contemporary debate, raising themes that resonate in law and philosophy today: the role of marriage as the bedrock of society and the appropriate context for sex and child-rearing, the nature of gendered spousal roles and their compatibility with equality and freedom, and the place of love in—or outside—marriage. These themes persist through historical works that reflect changing understandings of marriage as primarily an economic or procreative unit, a religious sacrament, a contractual association, or a love-based or companionate relationship.[27]

Contemporary views that marriage is the basis for a stable society originate with Aristotle's response to his teacher Plato's marriage reform proposal (384–322 BCE). In *The Republic*, Plato (427–347 BCE) proposed that "all the women [and children] should be common to all the men." Plato argued that because private affections would detract from the unity of the state, sex and reproduction must be organized so that each Guardian would regard any other citizen "as related to him, as brother or sister, father or mother, son or daughter, grandparent or grandchild."[28] To this end,

Guardians were to engage in temporary, state-arranged marriages; these would allow Guardians to satisfy their sex drives and the state to pursue a eugenic policy through the selection of mating couples. After each marriage festival, mated pairs would separate, and resulting children would be reared in state-run nurseries, so that biological ties between parents and children, or between siblings, would be unknown. Plato reasoned that private families, like private property, produced partiality and undermined attachment to the state; by abolishing the family, he thought, the state could redirect the Guardians' familial love to the state as a whole. Aristotle, however, rejected Plato's family state for a state of families. He argued that abolishing the family would also abolish familial affection, which necessarily attaches to particular others, not to the greater community. According to Aristotle, marriage and the family were of crucial importance to the state: As "the state is made up of households, before speaking of the state we must speak of the management of the household." Not only did families constitute the state, the family was productive in ways that sustained it: It produced future citizens, and virtuous wives enabled their husbands to participate in public life through skilful domestic management.[29] The view, inherited from Aristotle *via* Hegel, that marriage supports the state by producing virtuous citizens is among the defenses of marriage interrogated below (Chapter 2.iv).

The Greek philosophers focused on marriage as a political and economic unit; indeed, Plato's *Symposium* addressed sex and erotic love as a topic completely independent of marriage. But early Christian philosophers of marriage introduced a stern sexual morality that understood marriage as the only legitimate context for sex. In St. Augustine (354–430), we find a condemnation of sex outside marriage and lust within it; in *The City of God*, he explains that lust is a reminder of original sin, which originated with Adam and Eve's disobedience—as evidenced by the failure of the sexual organs to comply with the commands of the will. Without original sin in paradise, the sexual organs might have obeyed the will as the hands and feet do. Within this moral theology, the purpose for which the marital sexual act is done determines whether it is virtuous or vicious. Using marital sex solely to satisfy lust is sinful; sex performed for the goods of marriage—procreation and spousal companionship in chastity and fidelity—is not. St. Thomas Aquinas (ca. 1225–1274) reached similar conclusions, emphasizing the good of mutual fidelity as a relationship between spouses, including "the partnership of a common life" and payment of the "marriage debt" (the obligation to engage in sex).[30] In the natural law tradition of Aquinas, contemporary natural lawyers such as John Finnis and Rolf George defend marriage as the unique context for basic human goods related to sex (see Chapter 4.ii below).

The emerging medieval courtly love tradition, in counterpoint, suggested (perhaps ironically) that if marriage was marked by duty and chastity, then erotic love must be pursued outside marriage, in adulterous affairs such as the celebrated legend of Guinevere and Lancelot. In *On Love* (ca. 1185), the twelfth-century chaplain Andreas Capellanus presented the rules of courtship and dispensed advice for the lovelorn. The first of his "Rules of Love" is "Marriage does not constitute a proper excuse for not loving"—for not loving someone other than one's spouse, that is. In one of the fictional dialogues embedded in the text, an attempted seducer, twisting the logic of Christian sexual morality, tries to persuade a married woman that erotic love cannot exist within marriage because a married couple who enjoy one another "beyond affection for their offspring or discharge of obligations" commit a sin, "for as we are taught by apostolic law a lover who shows eagerness toward his own wife is accounted an adulterer." The judge to whom they appeal settles the dispute in the seducer's favor: "love cannot extend its sway over a married couple. Lovers bestow all they have on each other freely, and without the compulsion of any consideration of necessity, whereas married partners are forced to comply with each other's desires as an obligation." Love's spontaneity, freedom, and uncertainty, as well as its secrecy (Rule 13: "Love does not usually survive being noised abroad"), are contrasted with the stability and duteousness of marriage.[31]

Related juxtapositions of love and marriage, still located within a Christian tradition, emerge in the letters between the medieval nun Héloïse (ca. 1100–1163) and her former lover and husband, the philosopher and monk Peter Abelard (1079–1142). Héloïse exalted their love above marriage, suggesting that, for women, marriage cheapened love with pecuniary motivations. She wrote: "I never sought anything in you except yourself; I wanted simply you, nothing of yours. I looked for no marriage bond, no marriage portion, as it was not my own pleasures and wishes I sought to gratify, as you well know, but yours. The name of wife may seem more sacred or more binding, but sweeter for me will always be the word friend (*amica*), or, if you will permit me, that of concubine or whore." She adds that a woman marrying for money or position would "prostitute herself to a richer man, if she could," impugning the dominant understanding of marriage as an economic venture.[32] For Héloïse, marriage as an economic necessity was incompatible with love. These medievals sound another recurrent theme in the philosophy of marriage, the alleged conflict between passionate or erotic love and duty. We will pick this thread up again with the nineteenth-century free lovers.

For the ancients and medievals, marriage was unproblematically structured hierarchically by gender; the perceived natural order was a model for institutional arrangements, and unchosen characteristics such as sex were seen as a fitting basis for the assignment of social roles. The authority of the father within the family was as well-founded as that of the hereditary monarch within the sovereign realm. But as doctrines of the equal rights of man and of contract, or free consent, as the basis of political authority emerged, the unequal and involuntary content of the marriage contract posed theoretical problems, even if contract theorists tried to sweep the inconsistencies under the metaphorical rug. Social contract theorist Thomas Hobbes (1588–1679) had the intellectual honesty to acknowledge that his argument for the rough equality of human beings applied to women as well as to men. He wrote in *Leviathan* (1651): "[W]hereas some have attributed the dominion to the man only, as being of the more excellent sex, they misreckon in it. For there is not always that difference of strength or prudence between the man and the woman as that the right can be determined without war." Such equality—that of every person's posing a threat to every other—underlies the social contract that is the basis of political authority, in which men empower a sovereign to protect their rights. Although their equality, in this sense, would seem to imply that women would enter the contract as equals, Hobbes complacently explained that law tends to favor husbands in marriage, ceding them authority, "because for the most part Commonwealths have been erected by the fathers, not by the mothers of families." But in light of their equality, this explanation is inadequate—if women posed an equal threat to men, they should have entered the social contract on equal terms.[33] The same reasoning that implied all men were roughly equal also implied that women were roughly equal, and marital hierarchy became difficult to justify.

The problem arose in a different form for another social contract theorist, John Locke (1632–1704). Locke explicitly argued that consent, not natural hierarchy, was the basis of authority in the state as in the family, yet he cited men's natural ability as grounds for their authority in marriage. While he described marriage as a "voluntary compact," he also held that within it, "the rule ... naturally falls to the man's share as the abler and the stronger." But Locke had argued that all men had equal rights, despite differences in intelligence, strength, and ability; thus, natural differences between men and women, like those between men, should not, in his view, license subjugation.[34] As Locke's contemporary critic the protofeminist Mary Astell (1666–1731) asked, "If *all Men are born free*, how is it that all women are born slaves? as they must be if the being subjected to the *inconstant, uncertain, unknown, arbitrary Will* of Men, be the *perfect Condition of Slavery*?"[35] Locke's and Hobbes's difficulties prefigure those of later liberals, who would relegate the family to the private sphere, excluding it from justice, at the risk of inconsistency. The main argument of Part Two, in this vein, charges that liberals have failed to apply principles of justice consistently to marriage, and that this has resulted in injustice.

In the defense of marriage offered by Immanuel Kant (1724–1804), Augustinian sexual morality and social contract theory converge. Kant saw sex as inherently objectifying and so in conflict with the respect demanded by morality. Marriage, in his view, morally ameliorated sex through an equal contractual exchange of rights of possession, which permitted otherwise impermissible treatment. Even in marriage, only procreative sex was virtuous.[36] Kant's account is notable for attempting to explain how marriage morally transforms the relation between spouses, altering the moral structure of the relationship. While it has been derided as reducing marriage to an exchange of rights for sexual use, it is important for its conjecture that juridical rights can establish conditions for mutual respect and morally structure intimate relationships.[37] It makes a distinctive philosophical contribution in attempting to explain how entry into the legal institution is morally significant; however, in Chapter 3.i, I use Kant's own distinction between justice and virtue to argue that any such attempt faces insuperable problems.

In his 1821 *Philosophy of Right*, G.W.F. Hegel (1770–1831) dismissed as "disgraceful" Kant's view that the moral nature of marriage is essentially contractual. Unlike Kant, whose account of the moral role of marriage focused on the external institutional structure of rights, Hegel focused on the internal psychology of the marriage relation. According to Hegel, spouses enter the marriage contract only to transcend it in a relationship of ethical union, which is opposed to the individualistic bargaining of contract. Spouses think of themselves as part of a unit, not as individuals: "[T]he substantial basis of family relationships is…the surrender of personality." The ethical content of marriage "consists in the consciousness of this union as a substantial end, and hence in love, trust, and the sharing of the whole of individual existence."[38] While it might be thought that this account obviates the need for legal marriage, Hegel rejected his contemporary Friedrich von Schlegel's free love arguments that marriage inhibited passionate love. Hegel called this the argument of a scoundrel (it does resemble Capellanus's seducer!) and, like Kant, defended the necessity of marriage: Ethical love could exist only through the public assumption of spousal roles. Ethical love, Hegel held, was superior to mere passionate love: "Marriage should not be disrupted by passion, for the latter is subordinate to it."[39] Like Aristotle, Hegel integrates his account of marriage with his theory of the state: Ethical union prepares citizens for membership in the state while simultaneously providing a way for individuals to satisfy their sexual drives. In this way, marriage reconciles desire and duty, and contributes to a harmonious social whole (the function of ethical life, on Hegel's view). Hegel's idea that marriage and the state transcend individual self-interest, and preclude contractual bargaining, has inspired modern communitarian critiques of liberalism—and of contractual bargaining within the family—to which I respond in Chapter 4.iv.

Part One of this book investigates issues raised by Hegel: the moral significance of the social recognition of marriage, and how—or whether—marriage incorporates passionate love. It also takes up feminist and free love criticisms of marriage. Five years before the publication of Kant's account of marriage in *The Metaphysics of Morals*, Mary Wollstonecraft (1759–1798), in her 1792 *Vindication of the Rights of Women*, criticized marriage as commonly no more than "legal prostitution."[40] As John Stuart Mill (1806–1873) and Harriet Taylor (1807–1858) argued, society, by denying women independent ways to make a living, constrained their choice to marry, and once married, wives lost their legal rights under coverture. Mill compared women's legal status within marriage to slavery, noting that two factors made women's subordination more entrenched: Slavery only served the interests of a few, but women's subordination served "the whole male sex." Moreover, women lived in intimacy with their "masters" and had powerful incentives to please them.[41] Feminist criticisms of marriage, discussed in Chapter 5.i, continue to focus on the contribution of gender-structured domestic relations to women's inequality.

One question such critiques pose is how far marriage, with its deeply patriarchal history, can be reformed. Mary Wollstonecraft, John Stuart Mill, and Harriet Taylor argued that women's equality would improve marriage. They advocated an ideal of marital friendship based on the model of classical friendship, in which spouses know each other intimately and "care about the good in and for one another."[42] Women's subordination impeded this ideal. Wollstonecraft pointed out that a relationship with a subordinate could not be truly satisfying, and Mill argued that women's emancipation would lead to equality of minds and tastes in marriage, enabling a mutually enriching friendship. However, more than a hundred years after the publication of Mill's *Subjection of Women*, feminists were still comparing the legal institution of marriage to slavery. Despite intervening reforms, we might ask if these advocates of marital friendship were overly optimistic: How far can marriage outgrow its patriarchal past?

For free lovers, the impediments to equality posed by women's economic dependence and unequal legal status in marriage were reasons to reject the institution. Free lovers also rejected marriage on the grounds that legal compulsion was incompatible with love, which must be given freely, and not out of economic or legal necessity. The American free love and women's rights advocate, Stephen Pearl Andrews (1812–1886), argued that sexual relations were debased by the husband's legal power: "Let the idea be completely repudiated from the man's mind that woman...could, by possibility, belong to him, or was to be true to him, or owed him anything, farther than as she might choose to bestow herself."[43] Emma Goldman (1869–1940) wrote that "[e]very love relation should by its very nature remain an absolutely private affair. Neither the State, the Church, morality, or people should meddle with it." Goldman's critique of marriage extended to its exclusivity, suggesting that marriage, as a form of private property, leads to possessiveness and jealousy. Voltairine de Cleyre (1866–1912) went further by arguing that monogamous "free unions" as well as marriage limit individual growth and self-sufficiency by encouraging mutual dependency.[44]

Feminist critique of marriage also formed part of the "Communist Manifesto," in which Karl Marx (1818–1883) promised that the abolition of the private, bourgeois family would liberate women from male ownership, ending their status "as mere instruments of production."[45] Friedrich Engels (1820–1895) argued in his 1891 *Origin of the Family, Private Property, and the State* that, historically, marriage had created the conditions for private property, including property in women. The ancient transition from matriarchy to marking descent through paternal bloodlines was the "*world historical defeat of the female sex.*" The shift to monogamy followed closely: "[T]he origin of monogamy...was not in any way the fruit of individual sex love, with which it had nothing whatever to do...[but was the effect of] economic conditions—on the victory of private property over primitive, natural communal property." Monogamous marriage allowed men to control reproduction and facilitated private property arrangements, "the express purpose being to produce children of undisputed paternity...[who are] to come into their father's property as his natural heirs."[46] These charges illuminate the free lovers's complaint that marriage is not a good vehicle for passionate love: In their view, the institution is about property, including property in one's spouse, not love.

In light of such critiques, suspicion arises that the belief in the moral value of marriage is merely ideological, a tool of patriarchal capitalism. How, indeed, could the exclusive, possessive, legal institution of marriage foster the goods of love and care associated with it? To what extent does its subordination of individual desire to duty and the perceived common good threaten the good of individuals? And in light of its origins in force and the legal subordination of women, can any marriage law be just? We can now embark on answering these questions.

PART ONE
De-Moralizing Marriage

1

THE MARRIAGE PROMISE
IS DIVORCE PROMISE-BREAKING?

Can you break an engagement off slowly?...What's an engagement made of, do you suppose? I think it's made of some hard stuff, that may snap, but can't break. It is different to the other ties of life. They stretch or bend. They admit of degree. They're different.[1]

The speaker of this passage, the heroine of *Howard's End*, muses that being engaged, or *a fortiori*, married, is like being pregnant: One either is or one isn't—there are no shades of grey. This is true of legal marriage; one either has the legal status or one doesn't. But does marriage bring a moral transformation analogous to this legal change? The sacramental understanding and its secular inheritors suggest it does, that marriage effects an instantaneous moral change, sometimes understood as an unbreakable unity: "Have you not read that the Creator from the beginning made them male and female and that He said: This is why a man must leave father and mother, and cling to his wife, and the two become one body? They are no longer two, therefore, but one body. So then, what God has united, man must not divide."[2]

One of the most pervasive and defining social expectations regarding marriage (despite statistics) is its bindingness: It would be odd to say about one's impending wedding, "and if it doesn't work, we can divorce." Marriage has the permanence of (unchosen) family relationships; it is seen as ineradicable, like a biographical tattoo. One can leave any number of partners yet have always been single; but if one leaves a marriage, one is still marked by it, as a divorcé(e). It is life-defining, identity-conferring; it forever affects which box one checks on tax returns or passport applications. This aspiration to immutability is behind Hegel's thought that arranged marriage is the most ethical form of marriage—it completely removes marriage from the vagaries of the spouses' choice. But is there a convincing secular philosophical account of what creates such an engulfing and permanent moral transformation?

One approach to answering this question is suggested by the fact that marriage, unlike equally permanent kin relations, is entered voluntarily. In Christianity and recent Western legal tradition, marriage requires consent; intuitively and legally, a forced marriage would not be a "real" marriage. The moral transformation, then, seems likely to be effected through a voluntary undertaking—and moral obligations undertaken voluntarily are most often promises. A second appealing alternative, given that marriage involves spousal roles, is that spouses voluntarily agree to take on spousal roles and related obligations. Such role obligations might be thought to begin in a promise, or simple consent, to take on the role, but once established, their content may be defined by the role in a context-sensitive way. Thus, a doctor, for instance, may take on role obligations such as helping the ill, but the specific way in which she does this will depend on the specific ailments presented, and this obligation may sometimes be weighed with other role obligations, such as respecting patient autonomy.

Before assessing these candidates for the marital moral transformation, we should examine the moral significance of the legal rights exchanged in marriage. If one is morally obligated to fulfill legal obligations, then the legal obligations of marriage generate supervening moral obligations. And if promissory obligations supervene on legal contractual obligations, then the legal contract is also a moral promise. The legal marriage contract is unusual in that spouses may not know their legal obligations because there is no formal document stating its terms. But it seems reasonable to assume that spouses promise to take on the legal obligations of marriage, whatever those may be.[3] If so, legal marriage does effect a moral transformation. But these legal obligations do not account for the significance that many people attribute to marriage. Presumably marriage brings a deeper moral transformation than a promise to abide by marital property laws and terms of dissolution. Of course, it might be thought that the undertaking of legal support obligations is a significant obligation, but these are not distinctive of marriage—one can take on support obligations without marrying. Furthermore, in jurisdictions that allow divorce, the promise supervening on the legal contract is not "forever"; it is a promise to maintain these legal obligations and status unless and until the burdens of exit (filing for divorce, paying alimony, etc.) are met.

Wedding vows are a better candidate for enacting the significant moral change thought to be involved in marriage (this approach also has the virtue of explaining what couples who get married, "but not legally," think they are doing). Such vows typically involve promises: "I promise to love, honor, and cherish." A relationship can be morally transformed through the creation of promissory obligation. Some philosophers, understanding marriage as the institutional form appropriate to love, have argued that marriage necessarily involves a promise to love. Can we understand marriage as involving such a distinctive and transformative promise? Of course, it seems that people can promise to love one another without marrying, so, to distinguish marriage, we may understand its distinctive (nonlegal) promise as the promise to love and to accept spousal roles vis-à-vis one another.

One way to illuminate the content of marital promises is to ask what would be involved in breaking them. I'll therefore begin by addressing the morality of divorce (setting aside for now other morally significant elements of divorce, such as effects on children or society, as the focus here is how the relationship between spouses is changed by marriage). Although many people see marriage as a serious undertaking, divorce—when "irreconcilable differences" threaten one or both spouses' happiness—is not widely seen as a serious moral wrong. However, breaking a promise *is* widely seen as a serious moral wrong. This suggests an inconsistent triad:

1. Wedding vows are promises.[4]
2. Promise-breaking is morally impermissible in the absence of morally overriding circumstances or release by the promisee.
3. Unilateral divorce (an unreciprocated decision by one spouse to leave a marriage) is generally morally permissible.

If wedding vows are promises (1), then unilaterally willed divorces are acts of promise-breaking, which, according to (2), are *prima facie* morally impermissible. But as divorce is generally permissible (3), it cannot be an impermissible act of promise-breaking. How shall we resolve this?

Before reviewing the options for resolution, let me say more to motivate (3)—that unilateral divorce is generally morally permissible. Granted, many people simply do view divorce as a serious moral wrong. But in defense of (3), I offer two cases of unilateral divorce that I suspect most readers will deem permissible. Frank and Ann marry young; years later, their young son dies.[5] As they diverge in the grieving process, Ann begins to see Frank in a new light—he is distant, unreliable, unsupportive—and discovers that divorce is her only chance at happiness. After a waiting period and much counseling, she leaves, against his will. Or imagine that Jane Austen married young (and that divorce was an option for her!). Her spouse—call him "Mr. Austen"— wants children, but Jane discovers her novel-writing vocation and believes children would preclude it. Each feels the other is demanding a terrible sacrifice. After many attempts to change his own priorities, Mr. Austen leaves in the hopes of being able to remarry and reproduce.

My own intuition is that Ann and Mr. Austen are justified in refusing to sacrifice their own happiness, and that, far from doing wrong, they did more than was strictly required in trying to save the marriage. But an intuition may be wrong, and in this case there is an argument against mine: If wedding vows are promises, then *prima facie* Ann and Mr. Austen have each broken a promise and done wrong. (Notice that, so long as each abided by the legal terms of divorce, they have not failed in their legal, and supervening moral, obligations.)

I will consider four options to resolve the triad. The first is to reject (3) and hold that unilateral divorce is in most cases impermissible promise-breaking. I call this the "hard-line" response. It sets a high standard for morally overriding conditions for promises. The second option is that the morally overriding conditions referred to in (2) are present in most divorces, so that even if unilateral divorce is *prima facie* impermissible, it will rarely be impermissible all things considered: I call this the "hardship" response because it holds that the hardship of a failed marriage overrides the promissory obligation. Another possibility is that marital promises are contingent; they are tacitly conditioned on continuing love—or, they are invalidated by a crucial mistake made at the time of promising, the mistaken belief that love would continue. I argue that this does not fit with our understanding of marriage or of promises. I will defend a fourth option: Wedding vows, in large part, are not promises at all. I will make my case focusing first on love, then on spousal roles.

I. THE HARD-LINE VIEW

On the "hard-line view," my intuitions concerning Ann and Mr. Austen should be rejected; unilaterally willed divorce is generally impermissible promise-breaking. Spouses promise to love one another forever, or take on spousal roles, and thereby create an obligation that neither can unilaterally dissolve.

Even the hard-line view allows some unilateral divorces. Certain circumstances permit a promisor not to do what she has promised, as (2) acknowledges. For one, the promisee can release the promisor. For another, a *prima facie* obligation to keep a promise can be overridden by a more stringent moral duty. To take a classic example, imagine that I have promised to meet a friend for lunch, but on the way to the restaurant I see a small boy drowning. I may permissibly save the boy, although doing so will cause me to fail to meet my friend. The duty to rescue overrides the promissory obligation.

These promissory escape clauses suggest two cases where divorce is not promise-breaking, even if marriage does involve a promise that divorce would otherwise break. The spouses might release one another from the promise.[6] Such bilateral divorces do not involve promise-breaking, which is why I am focusing on unilateral divorce. Alternatively, a more stringent duty might morally override the promise. For instance, a duty to protect oneself or one's children in an abusive marriage would override the promissory obligation. Assuming for the sake of argument that such clear overriding conditions are not the norm (although as we will see in Chapter 5.i, rates of spousal violence are high), such conditions do not hold in most of the cases generally deemed permissible.

Other circumstances may invalidate a promise. If default by one party to a reciprocal promise releases the other party, then a spouse would be released if the other defaulted—for example, by engaging in extramarital sex. Finally, were a marriage conducted under false pretences, the marriage promise would be nullified, like a fraudulent contract. (But how far does this exemption extend? Would sporting dyed hair, or pretending to be more amiable than one really is, or feigning an interest in the other party's stamp collection, count as a false pretence? These sorts of premarital deceptions may be legion. Here I mean to pick out intentional lies or deception designed to lure the other party into marriage, in the knowledge that it would not take place otherwise, though I will revisit the issue below.) The problematic—and interesting—cases are those in which none of these conditions obtains: unilateral divorces with no duties morally overriding the promise, no fundamental deception, no default by the other party. The hard-line approach deems these problematic cases impermissible, for it is relatively parsimonious regarding conditions under which promises may be broken. Unhappiness and discontent do not excuse promisors from their obligations.

The hard-line view is entailed by (1) and (2), given a high bar for morally overriding conditions for promises. Also in its favor is the intuition that some unilaterally willed divorces are wrong. Someone who leaves his home-making wife penniless, or who absconds a week after the wedding, or who walks away after the first tiff, likely does wrong. However, the wrongness of some divorces does not establish that divorce is generally wrong. The wrongs done in these examples need not be wrongs of promise-breaking. They might instead be, for example, failures to honor legal support obligations or duties of care or virtue.

One preliminary objection to the hard-line response must be set aside. This is that public policy considerations and basic liberties require that divorce be legally permitted, and so any views prohibiting divorce must be rejected.[7] But the hard-line view does not entail the legal prohibition of divorce. Many acts of impermissible promise-breaking are legally permitted. This objection confuses morality and the law, which should not enforce all moral obligations. The state's role is to enforce the contractual obligations assumed in marriage, not all aspects of the supposed promise.

The legal dissolubility of the marriage contract is not anomalous. Many contracts specify the conditions for their own dissolution. As a contract, marriage is odd: Contractors often don't know the terms of the contract, some of its terms are defined unalterably, and the state restricts the sex and number of parties to it. But it is not odd in being dissoluble. One cannot usually compel performance of contracted services. When individuals are unwilling to perform contracted services, the contract itself, or contract law, supplies terms of dissolution. For example, if you make a six-month contract with a massage therapist and she decides to go into philosophy instead, the state cannot compel her to massage you, although she may owe you financial compensation. *A fortiori*, even if legal marriage were to institute (bizarrely) an obligation to love or take on spousal roles permanently, performance could not be compelled. Compulsion would be unjust (as well as, in the case of love, impossible). Thus, divorce is perfectly in line with the standards of legal contract. The hard-line view at most entails that it is *morally* wrong to break wedding vows, not that one should be *legally* compelled to keep them.

II. THE HARDSHIP VIEW

The "hardship view" permits divorce by allowing a more extensive set of overriding circumstances. The thought is that the promisor's unhappiness, not only exceedingly stringent duties to protect herself or others, and the like, can morally override her promissory obligation. But is such a view of overriding conditions justifiable? One might suggest that promissory obligations are not so very weighty after all. But (excluding simple act-utilitarian views) a promise is not outweighed simply because a greater value may be obtained by breaking it. The hardship view needs to show that personal unhappiness can override promissory obligation.

One approach would be to show that a more stringent moral duty typically overrides the promissory obligation in unhappy marriages. But what would this duty be? One candidate is a duty to prevent the other spouse's unhappiness. Given that spousal unhappiness is likely to come in pairs, one spouse might say to the other, "It will be better for us both if I go." He might claim that the duty to prevent the other's unhappiness overrides the promise. In addition, it is sometimes given as a necessary condition for promissory obligation that the recipient should want the promised object, and presumably the other spouse does not want to be unhappy.[8]

But this excuse sounds disingenuous. To echo Hegel's criticism of Schlegel (who was arguing for sex outside marriage), this sounds like the argument made by a scoundrel![9] Unilateral divorce might well cause the abandoned spouse greater unhappiness than staying married, and she might want the object of the promise— her spouse's continued presence and affection—even if it brings unhappiness as a side effect. Moreover, this is an uncomfortably paternalistic justification of unilateral promise-breaking. Compare these excuses: "I know I promised to buy you some cake, or support your application, or pay you, but I no longer think that the cake, or position, or money will make you happy." If the excuse doesn't hold in these other cases, it should not here. The problem is that the promisor is predicting consequences and imputing a preference ordering which only the promisee has the right to judge.

A second candidate for a morally overriding duty is a duty to *oneself* to prevent one's own unhappiness. Kant, for instance, posited such an indirect duty on the grounds that unhappiness leads to vice.[10] Indeed, when one thinks of how nastily unhappily married people can behave toward one another, the possibility of marital misery leading to vice doesn't seem so far-fetched. If there is such a duty, perhaps it can override a promissory obligation.

But this doesn't seem right either. In Kantian terms, if promissory obligations are perfect duties, allowing for no latitude in their execution, they constrain the ways in which one can fulfill the imperfect duty of self-perfection. In other words, one can't permissibly seek to strengthen one's virtue by doing something immoral such as breaking a promise. More generally, while one might think that personal fulfillment or achievement can provide broadly ethical justification for leaving one's spouse—as did the painter Gauguin—this is not a moral justification.[11] Within the moral realm, promises have a certain weight. There may be a serious moral duty to prevent one's own misery, but it is unlikely to be stronger than a promissory obligation, because promissory obligations correlate to promisee's rights, which are morally weighty. An agent's misery might override such obligations if it were severe enough to lead to mental illness, incapacity, or self-destruction. But the average unhappy marriage does not produce such effects.

The view that promises can be overridden by the unhappiness their performance will bring the promisor makes promises too light. Morality requires promise-keeping even at the cost of personal unhappiness. Consider a final example: Marcel has promised Albertine a yacht. But having priced them, he reconsiders: Sacrificing so many resources will prevent him from seeing Venice or impressing his aristocratic neighbors (two of his life goals), and besides, he now thinks the yacht is a frivolous, even dangerous, toy, possession of which is not in Albertine's best interests. Albertine disagrees. If Marcel, having promised, still morally owes Albertine a yacht, by analogy, Ann and Mr. Austen morally owe it to their spouses to stay.[12] In the problematic cases, the hardship response fails.

III. PROMISES, MISTAKES, AND CONTINGENCY

Another solution is to posit special release conditions for marital promises: They are contingent upon love's continuance.[13] *Prima facie*, this view is unpromising (no pun intended): After all, standard vows include the phrase "until death do us part"—not "until I cease to love you." Typical vows simply do not state conditions under which the promise dissolves.

Perhaps unilateral divorce falls under a more general account of promissory contingency. One might subscribe to the Parfitian view that "all promises must be conditional; all promises must be short-term"; this would de-moralize marriage in a different way, by making unconditional promises impossible, so it is compatible with my main thesis.[14] I set it aside here. Giving a more specific account of promissory contingency, Dan Moller has speculated that promises can permissibly be broken, or are simply dissolved, if the promisor was mistaken in some crucial respect—if "some fundamental assumption made [by the promisor] at the time of the promise has turned out to be false."[15] In the case of marriage, the mistaken assumption would be the durability of love.

Moller gives two supporting examples: An uncle promises to rear an apparently orphaned nephew but is released from the promise when the boy's mother turns up alive, and a professor promises to teach but is released when the university cancels the class. But Moller's "mistake" view of promissory dissolution is not needed to explain these cases. Surely the uncle is released because the mother's parental rights cancel the promissory obligation—as his continuing guardianship would violate her rights, it cannot be obligatory. So too with the teacher: Performance of the promise has become impossible and so is not obligatory.

More importantly, the "mistake" solution strains our understanding of promising. Consider analogous cases: I promise to sell you a picture from my attic for $100 and then discover it is a Picasso, or I promise to drive you home and then discover it is further than I thought. If mistakes released us in such cases, promising would not have much point.

If these examples do not convince, there is a reason to think that wedding vows, in particular, are not contingent or dissolved by mistake. Wedding vows are intended to indemnify the relationship against various contingencies, especially threats to love. Many vows state an intention to hold fast *however things turn out*—"for richer, for poorer, in sickness, in health, for better, for worse." Illness, infertility, changing interests, lack of interest in sex, annoying but nonvicious habits—things which might jeopardize love—are not good reasons to break these vows, in particular. Even if it fit with our understanding of promises, which it doesn't, it would belie their explicit content if these vows were contingent on love's continuation.

Promises, marital or not, obligate, even when they are premised on risky assumptions. Say I promise to sell you a painting for $100, knowing there is a 40 percent chance it is a Picasso. If it turns out to be a Picasso, my reneging on grounds of mistake is unconscionable. Promising under such circumstances is reckless; surely a promisor is not released if she knew the odds when she promised. In the contemporary United States, these are roughly the chances of divorce. People getting married know there is some chance of "irreconcilable differences." This makes it difficult to see this eventuality as an inadvertent and excusing mistake (as perhaps one might be tempted to think in the Picasso case if the would-be seller had no inklings whatsoever of the painting's value at the time of his rash promise).

Some erroneous assumptions do undermine promises—for instance, if one's spouse is a fraud. Henry James' character Isabel Archer believed her fiancé Gilbert Osmond to be honorable and misunderstood; he turned out to be a deceitful fortune hunter with a long-term mistress whose child he was passing off as that of his dead wife. But this is just a standard case of fraudulent contract; we don't need the mistake view to explain why Isabel is morally released from her promise.

The limits on our ability to assess character make some mistakes of mate selection inevitable—one might say "You're not the man I thought I married," without implying any deception. James' character Lambert Strether thought of his fiancée, Mrs. Newsome, as upright and respectable until, broadening his horizons in Paris, he realized those same attributes made her intolerant and insusceptible to pleasure. But, had he promised marriage to her before this discovery, it's not obvious that his mistake would dissolve it; as Forster's heroine suggested, an engagement does not admit of degree.[16] In another kind of significant undeceived mistake, one's spouse could turn out to be a different sex or gender than originally supposed, if his or her intersexed condition or "gender identity disorder" were discovered after marriage. But just as this eventuality does not undermine legal contracts, it does not undermine promises. What these difficult cases point to, I think, is the strangeness and imprudence of promises concerning love, sex, and lifelong companionship. As George Bernard Shaw wrote: "When two people are under the influence of the most violent, most insane, most delusive, and most transient of passions, they are required to swear that they will remain in that excited, abnormal and exhausting condition until death do them part."[17]

Until now, I have assumed that the content of wedding vows is such that, if they *were* promises, divorce would break them. But their content needs clarification. If the marriage promise is a promise to "love, honor, and cherish," it is presumably often broken well before divorce—at the moment when one spouse stops loving.[18] On the other hand, divorce need not break a promise to love; one could divorce but continue to love. This suggests two points at which the marriage promise may be broken: first, the cessation of love, and second, the end of the marriage and casting off of spousal roles. I will consider these in turn.

IV. PROMISES TO LOVE

I hope to have raised doubt about whether it is permissible to break the marriage promise in the problematic cases. I have argued that neither mistake nor hardship override promissory obligations. But I do not think that Ann or Mr. Austen deserve moral blame. This is because the emotional content of wedding vows—as distinct from their legal contractual aspect—cannot be the subject of promise. Wedding vows—insofar as they concern love—are not promises. When marrying parties recite, "I promise to love, honor, and cherish," they may *intend* to promise, but they do not succeed. My view has two key premises: (a) we cannot promise to do what we cannot do, and (b) we cannot command our love. The basic problem was stated by Jane Austen: "[W]e can command our actions, but not our affections."[19]

a. One Can't Promise to Do What One Can't Do

If you visit me in Calgary, I might say, "I promise to show you Calgary's historic downtown blues bar, the King Eddy, where some of my colleagues once took Elizabeth Anscombe," only to find that developers have torn it down; in that case, I never promised you anything. I tried to promise, but didn't succeed: I didn't obligate myself to show you the bar because the act is impossible. My failure to perform is not wrong, nor is it promise-breaking. (Of course, as I believe I have a duty, I should try to fulfill it.) Someone who makes a "promise" while knowing its execution is impossible is making a false or lying promise, which she does not intend to fulfill; but someone who truly intends to carry out a promise whose performance is impossible simply fails to promise. One can't promise the impossible, because a promise creates an obligation and ought implies can. If one *can't* do some act, one can't *promise* to do it.

Promising obligates. This is not controversial, whether promising is understood as an instrumentally valuable convention or derived from a more general principle of fidelity.[20] Whichever one thinks the underlying rationale of promising is, specific promises must be taken as obligatory; otherwise, the institution would be pointless, and so cease to be instrumentally valuable. Obligation is central to promising. Not too much depends here on which account of its obligatoriness one prefers.

Someone might object that we constantly promise to do things whose performance is outside our control. Our actions depend on the world's cooperation, so that even an ordinary promise such as meeting for lunch depends on traffic, good health, and the nonoccurrence of cataclysmic disasters. If we couldn't promise actions whose performance is partially outside our control, we couldn't make promises at all. But this quotidian way in which events are outside our control differs from love's uncontrollability. Meeting someone for lunch is something I can bring about under normal circumstances, although it may be occasionally impossible (I fall ill; the city floods). But love is not the kind of thing I can control, under any circumstances; controlling love is at least a general, and perhaps a conceptual, impossibility.

Promised acts that are temporarily impossible may leave residual obligations.[21] The promisor is excused from the specific performance, but may be obligated to "make it up." But general and conceptual impossibilities cannot be the subject of obligation at all. A general impossibility is something which, as a contingent matter, no one can do. No one can promise blue skies. If a blue-sky machine were invented tomorrow, then one could. The accuracy of one's meteorological claims is not what makes the difference. A weather-machine is a control mechanism. Without such a mechanism no one can control the weather. To be obligated to do something, there must be some reliable procedure by which one can do that thing. It must be within one's power. While a general impossibility could become possible as circumstances change (scientists invent a weather machine or a love pill), a conceptual impossibility, which involves a contradiction, can never be the subject of obligation.

My argument so far employs the premises that *ought* implies *can* and that promising obligates. That *ought* implies *can* is not uncontroversial, especially when *can* is understood in the sense of "general impossibility" or "within the agent's power."[22] But, for those who reject "*ought* implies *can*," there is a theoretical reason specific to promising to think we cannot promise in these cases. One function of promising is to enable interpersonal reliance. Promises to bring about generally impossible outcomes would undermine this function of the convention of promising, making promissory assurances unreliable. The convention should not allow promises that, by their nature, would undermine the convention itself.

The point can also be supported with an argument by analogy. Consider examples analogous to a promise to love, in which performance is known to be unpredictable. Can one promise not to shoot oneself when playing Russian roulette? Sometimes performance is uncertain due to external contingencies: surviving a bungee jump with a frayed cord, finding a rare wild orchid, or succeeding in a surgical operation. Imagine that one knows one has a 50 percent chance of failure, whatever one does, and that the outcome will not be determined by one's efforts but by something external—the strength of the strands, the patient's resilience. In such cases, one cannot promise to survive, find the flower, or save the patient. The agent who fails in these tasks is not blameworthy for promise-breaking; if one is disappointed by him, it is more natural to say "he shouldn't have promised—he knew that he might fail." The same applies to actions depending on the contingencies of one's own body and mind: running a four-minute mile, not getting cancer, conceiving a child, memorizing a poem. If one knows the probability is 50 percent and the deciding factor is beyond one's control, it would be foolhardy and misleading to attempt to promise these things.

It would undermine the point of promising. Were one to say, "I promise not to get cancer," one would fail in promising, for the words don't establish the obligation that is promise's hallmark. The lack of control makes promising impossible. It make no difference whether the risk factor is outside oneself—a frayed cord—or within—a cancer-causing gene. If one cannot promise in such risky cases, it must be shown that they differ from continuing to love to show that continuing to love can be promised. Indeed, specifying a precise demarcation of possible promises will be difficult—can one promise if there is a 10 percent chance of failure?—but if it is granted that a 40–50 percent failure rate is high enough to invalidate promising, then the divorce rate is good evidence that promises to love are invalid.

b. One Can't Control Love

The next step is to show that controlling love is a general impossibility. In this respect, love is akin to other mental phenomena: Sometimes normal persons cannot banish undesired thoughts or feelings (anger, worries, desires), and sometimes we cannot conjure desired thoughts or feelings into existence (warmth, interest, a belief or desire). Commands to feel a certain way have an air of paradox, as in John Wilson's examples: "'Fear not!,' 'Don't be angry!,' 'Keep calm!'"[23] One can try not to be afraid, angry, or anxious—but one does not always succeed. Emotions have an uncontrollable phenomenological and physiological element.

Perhaps some rare individuals—Zen masters—can perfectly control their emotions. But their rarity is telling. Not only is such ability rare, but most of us in a position to make wedding vows don't have much evidence about our own abilities in that regard. Neither the inexperienced nor the divorced have good evidence of their ability to control love! It may indeed be possible to love another person "forever"—my point is that it is generally impossible to control whether one does. (Analogously, it is possible not to get cancer, but impossible to control whether one does.) Even if some rare individuals do have such control, most of us are not in a very good position to know what will be the case with us.

Perhaps, indeed, no one can control love. Perhaps controlling love is not merely a general impossibility but a conceptual impossibility. The very concept of love may include—as the medieval courtly lovers and nineteenth-century free lovers suggested—uncontrollability or spontaneity, because it involves desire or attitudes of respect or admiration or care which, by their nature, cannot be forced. One can be guided to admiration or desire, but one cannot be compelled to it, even by oneself.

Moreover, my love for another person does not depend only on me. People change, and "time simply brings out latent differences. People slowly grow apart in innumerable subtle and less subtle ways."[24] I may learn things about my beloved which destroy my love: Perhaps I discover that what seemed like a strong moral sense is mere conformity, or that apparent adventurousness is really self-destructive recklessness. Or he may have changed—become morally corrupt, or lost his sense of fun. The point is that if love responds to qualities in the other, then it depends on the (uncontrollable) other. One cannot control what properties the other has, so—conceptually—one cannot control love.

My argument thus has two threads. The *"can"* in *"ought* implies *can"* can be interpreted either as general or conceptual possibility. If *can* is interpreted as conceptual possibility, the dictum is uncontroversial; if the conceptual impossibility of controlling love is granted (a full argument for this would require a detailed account of love), the conclusion that one cannot promise to love follows easily. If *can* is interpreted as general impossibility, however, my case for *ought* implies *can* depends on the argument by analogy and the point that promising requires predictability, so that promissory obligations in particular imply possibility. Moreover, I must show that controlling love is generally impossible. What considerations might I add to those already given? I might marshal some platitudes: Affections change, the human heart is fickle, the strongest passions can quickly cool. I encourage readers to consider their own experience. Of course, for some, this may immediately suggest an objection.

V. OBJECTION: WHAT ARE WE TALKING ABOUT WHEN WE TALK ABOUT LOVE?

This view of love, the objector may say, is adolescent.[25] Thudding hearts and passionate embraces are very nice, and indeed not subject to an act of will, but they are not the essence of married love. This consists in steady affection, reciprocal kindness and sympathy, and, even, a patient effort to quell annoyance and get along.

However, such settled love is also subject to involuntary dissipation. True, romantic and sexual love is especially notorious for its short shelf-life. But more stable affections also sour and dissolve. A good comparison is family or friendship. To the skeptical question, "Can you really love someone forever?," someone might respond, "Certainly; I will love my parents, siblings, children, friends, forever. Why not my spouse?"

But this is an idealized view of family and friendship. At some level even this love is conditional (they do not turn out to be sadists) and certainly has been known to decay. The question, again, is not whether we *can* love someone unchangingly, but whether we can *control* doing so. Any affection is liable to diminution, and if it begins to fail, we may not be able to save it through an act of will.

Moreover, we need to consider what people marrying intend to promise and be promised, for this "mature" understanding of married love seems untrue to the vows themselves. Indeed, in contrast to the claim that married love is a matter of settled affection, many people hold marital love to a higher standard of intensity, intimacy, and exclusivity than love for family and friends (an expectation that may account for marital instability!). And, presumably, many spouses do not want to be offered a settled affection out of a sense of duty—which is what the purported obligation to love would entail once spontaneous love fades. Sartre's point is persuasive: "Who would be satisfied with the words, 'I love you because I have freely engaged myself to you and because I do not wish to go back on my word'."[26]

Above I suggested that if love is conceived as love for the beloved's properties, it may be conceptually uncontrollable. But another view of love holds that love bestows value on the beloved object, rather than simply appraising her valuable properties affirmatively. When we love, the properties that initially drew us to the beloved—his wit, her strength—become valuable as his or her particular properties; "[L]ove creates a new value, one that is not reducible to the individual or objective value that something may have." The beloved becomes valuable "for her own sake." Even her faults become valuable, because they are hers; if she changes, she is still herself, the beloved, and so valuable as such.[27] This understanding of love would theoretically indemnify it against change, or the discovery of faults, in the beloved. But bestowal is still not subject to the will; it is a transformative perception or imaginative state that we cannot turn on or off as desired. Although bestowed value may originate in the lover, as a perceptual condition or way of seeing the other, it is not directly under volitional control.

Another objector might respond that while emotions like love are changeable, they are not uncontrollable. Emotions are not merely urges or physical feelings like hunger or pain. There is an interesting literature criticizing the "dumb view" of emotions, which understands them as noncognitive, instinctual feelings.[28] Emotions are complex, trainable, shot through with reason and belief. To some extent, they are under rational control; we can train our dispositions through virtuous action or cognitive therapy. You can't think yourself out of pain, but you might be able to think yourself into love (Sartre quotes André Gide: "A mock feeling and a true feeling are almost indistinguishable").[29] If emotions respond to beliefs, perhaps one can nurture love by nursing positive beliefs about the would-be beloved; perhaps one can train one's perceptual faculty of bestowal.

While correcting the "dumb view" of the emotions is apt, it is possible to overstate their rationality and susceptibility to control. For example, Iddo Landau writes that "we can, and frequently do, influence our emotions. It is incorrect, then, to describe emotions as uncontrollable, if by that one means that they are completely immune to the influence of deliberate acts."[30] But this sets up a false dilemma. Of course we can influence emotions—by choosing between a comic novel or a horror story, by taking Prozac or eating chocolate, by meditating on our beloved's faults or merits—and patterns of such choices affect our dispositions. But the claim that we cannot command love is compatible with the claim that we can influence it. One can stimulate amorous emotions by reading romance novels, going for moonlit walks, or meditating on the beloved's virtues. But these methods are not certain. All the romantic walks in the world will not lead to love in some cases, or preserve it in others. And one does not know what the outcome will be in one's own case.

In developing a view similar to Landau's, S. Matthew Liao argues that love can be kindled and rekindled through various internal and external controls. While he admits that these methods are not certain, he points out that "[g]uaranteed success is...not necessary for an action to be deemed commandable."[31] An act may be commandable, and hence obligatory, if it has only reasonable chances of success. But as Liao admits, the notion of a reasonable chance of success involves probability. And as I argued above, the high divorce rate suggests a low probability of rekindling marital love—a probability so low that it makes promising reckless. Liao could respond that spouses, like parents, have a duty to try to love.[32] But the sticking point here is that most spouses do not actually promise to *try* to love, but rather, they try to promise to love.

VI. REWRITING THE PROMISE

a. Promising to behave

If the distinctive marriage promise is not best understood as a promise to love, perhaps we can more happily reconstrue it as a promise to behave a certain way. While we can't command our affections, we can command our actions. So wedding vows could be promises to *act* lovingly. Historically, people did understand marriage as undertaking behavioral roles requiring certain actions. But since the "love revolution," the Western understanding of marriage involves a crucial emotional component. Spouses may explicitly promise specific acts like sexual fidelity or cohabitation. But surely most do not intend to promise, or be promised, mere behavior.[33]

Landau suggests that the marriage promise is a promise "to invest work in performing certain acts that are likely to sustain the love." But while one can promise to perform love-sustaining acts, this is not a reasonable way to construe the promise people are trying to make when they marry. Landau acknowledges this: "Most [marrying couples], I believe, are not completely clear about the nature of the promise they are making."[34] But this is a very unusual view of promises! Conceptually, promising to perform an action requires an intention to promise to perform that action.[35] I have not promised to undertake "love-sustaining acts" if it has never crossed my mind that this is what I am promising, and if I believe I am promising to love someone forever. The same objection applies to the suggestion that we promise to protect love through efforts to perceive the other lovingly. As Wilson points out, this does not tally with spouses' intent. A bridegroom "is not in fact saying that he will undertake some course of action which will eventually lead to his loving" the bride.[36]

Because promising requires intending to promise, arguments that people getting married intend to promise to love, but really promise something else, are nonstarters. If they intend to promise to love, then they do not promise to try to love, or to act as if they love, or to perform love-sustaining acts; they try—and fail—to promise to love. They succeed in stating an intention to love one another forever—but not to promise. A promise is not merely an expression of intention. It also is the assumption of an obligation.

b. Promising as Prediction

This discussion leads us to consider the nature of promising. There may be a type of promise that does not concern the promisor's future agency but instead issues warrants. In practice, promises are sometimes used to "*take responsibility* for something [outside our control] being the case." For instance, we might reassure a child by saying "I promise it won't hurt,"[37] or reassure an anxious date by saying, "I promise the party will be fun." The obligation established in such a promise is not to bring about the relevant state of affairs but to be answerable if it does not turn out as promised. The wedding promise can be seen as such a predictive promise or epistemic commitment regarding our own future behavior. Just as we might promise a child that an injection won't hurt, we assure our spouse that our love will continue. The promise to love is like a manufacturer's guarantee, indemnifying the spouse in case of the world's failing to turn out as promised. For the sake of argument, I'll assume that this analysis holds for some promises, that one function of promises is to vouch for states of affairs outside our power, thereby making ourselves accountable.

But, arguably, such promises are unsuccessful if either promisee or promisor is unaware of their nature. Consider the statement: "I promise that if you work hard, you'll get an A in the course." A parent might make such a promise predictively. But if uttered by a corrupt professor who has just accepted a bribe, it could be a promise to perform. Now imagine that the words are spoken encouragingly by an unbribed professor. She could simply be making a prediction: "If you work hard, I predict your work will be of A quality." Or she could be promising a performance: "If you work hard, I will give you an A as a reward." In cases where it is not obvious that the promised state of affairs is outside the promisor's control, the promisor should state that the promise is merely predictive. Imagine that the professor's course is entirely computer-graded, and she has no control over the grading process. Even though a predictive promise is the only kind she can make, if the student does not know this, the professor must make the nature of the promise explicit. Otherwise she has misled him, and if promises require uptake, it is doubtful whether a promise has indeed been made.

Wedding vows are exactly such an ambiguous case. The promisee cannot be assumed to know that controlling love is outside the promisor's power. The idea that we can promise to love appears to be a widespread philosophical confusion. If wedding vows do not explicitly state that they are predictive promises, the promisors mislead the promisees, and the promises fail due to lack of uptake. And if the promisor herself is not aware that she cannot control love, and hence does not believe she is making a predictive promise, a second problem arises. Surely one necessary condition of making a predictive promise is awareness that one is making a predictive promise. If the promisor is not attempting to make a predictive promise, she does not succeed in promising.

There is another oddity of the predictive interpretation of wedding vows. In a predictive promise, the promisor takes responsibility for a state of the world outside her control. But treating wedding vows as a predictive promise makes spouses seem oddly alienated from their own emotions. Indeed, wedding vows are typically phrased in terms of what the parties intend to do. "Love," "honor," and "cherish" are active verbs. In contrast, warranty-type promises typically take the form "I promise that it (not 'I') will...." Surely wedding vows concern spouses' intentions as agents—not predictions about their future emotional life.

Finally, epistemic commitments require good evidence. But high rates of divorce mean spouses are not in a good position to guarantee enduring love. Nietzsche writes, in *On the Genealogy of Morality*, of the "human being who is *permitted to promise*," the "*sovereign individual*," as the finest achievement of morality. Such a being "promises like a sovereign, weightily, seldom, slowly... [he] gives his word as something on which one can rely because he knows himself to be strong enough to uphold it even against accidents, even 'against fate'."[38] It may be only a few who are certain enough of themselves to promise love (either predictively or as performance). Ironically, one implication of my challenge to the promissory status of wedding vows to love is that they are often not taken seriously enough: The attempts at promising are recklessly made and misleading, often to the detriment of both parties.

VII. SPOUSAL ROLES AND MARRIAGE PROMISES

I have argued that we should take promising seriously—so seriously that if wedding vows were promises, divorce in the problematic cases would be morally wrong. I have also argued that much of the customary understanding of marriage—its emotional component—cannot be the subject of promise. But wedding vows involve other promises. Parties promise to adhere to the legal terms of marriage and to take on spousal roles, as they understand them. They may also attempt to promise specific actions or omissions, such as sexual exclusivity or material care taking. Friends of mine vowed to "fight for justice together" in their wedding ceremony.

While the legal content of marriage depends on the jurisdiction, other specific actions promised depend on what the individuals involved actually say. Not all such attempted promises will succeed. Specific acts, such as spending time together, can generally be promised. What Kant calls "practical love," taking the other's ends as one's own and acting to further them, can be promised precisely because it is not an emotion (although this kind of love is presumably not what spouses intend to promise—presumably they intend the love which is *delight*).[39] But some specific acts cannot be promised because doing so would alienate inalienable rights. Arguably, sexual autonomy precludes alienating the choice of whether to have sex on a given occasion; if so, spouses cannot promise sexual access.[40]

Where spouses succeed in promising specific acts, unilateral divorce, separation, or other failures to perform may break that promise. Once again, divorce need not break the promise supervening on legal obligations; because marriage is dissoluble, spouses comply with their legal contractual obligations so long as they fulfill the legal terms of exit. But a third component of wedding vows, the promise to take on the spousal role "until death do us part," raises complications. This involves a voluntary undertaking of a public status and social role. However, given diverse understandings of what the spousal role entails, its content can only be specified by the intentions of the people getting married, which in turn derive from their communities, upbringing, choices, and so on. In a multicultural, multireligious society, not all spouses will understand their roles in the same way; what they intend such a role to involve is fixed by their explicit agreement and, if they are embedded in a homogenous community with a shared understanding of marriage, its understanding of the role. Promising to take on a role requires that spouses understand and intend to take on the relevant obligations, so the communal understanding must be mediated through the promisor's intentions.

However, it may be the case that spousal role obligations are dissolved if a spouse ceases to love. Presumably role obligations are conditional on the continuing ability to carry out the essential elements of the role. If the spousal role involves emotional content—loving, trusting, cherishing—and a spouse becomes unable to fulfill this component, she may be unable to fulfill the role altogether. Analogously, a doctor who becomes unable to treat patients—perhaps he has lost his memory—is released from his role-related obligations. If spousal role obligations are not exhausted by a discrete set of performances, but involve a central emotional feature that cannot be promised, it is unclear whether one can promise to remain in this role forever. The ability to promise depends on how the role is understood: The more the spousal role is understood in behavioral, not emotional, terms, the more fit it is to become an object of promise; and the more it is understood in emotional terms, the less fit it is to be the object of promise.

The social and legal diversity of marriage suggests that there is no single essential marriage promise that all spouses make. (Of course, some views, such as natural law, hold that marriage necessarily involves certain obligations; I examine such arguments for the essential moral nature of marriage in Chapter 3.) This does not mean that just any promise—a business agreement—could count as marriage. What distinguishes modern Western marriage is the idea of an enduring voluntary affection-based association. But the specific elements of this association vary greatly. Different spouses, communities, and religions bring different understandings to marriage. In this age of individualized vows, there is no single promise every couple tries to make.

Indeed, while I have assumed that wedding vows aim at enduring love, even this is an idealization. People do not always marry believing that they will love each other forever. They may love each other but be open to the possibility that love will not last. They may marry for a host of legal or practical reasons, such as economic benefits, work visas, health insurance, or pensions. They may marry for social and psychological reasons such as respectability, recognition, emotional security, or parental or peer pressure. These may not all be good reasons for marrying; but the social meaning of marriage is composed of this vast array of understandings of marriage and its purpose. What is promised depends in the end on what the promisors say. And this suggests a mundane piece of advice—be careful what you promise!

The (attempted) promise to love is a case of widespread philosophical confusion. Does such a mistake matter? To the extent that it interferes with rational planning by inducing a belief that love can be controlled and secured, yes. In a culture that takes marriage very seriously, the promissory content of marriage may not be taken seriously enough. Searching for sample wedding vows, I surveyed several wedding magazines: *Brides*, *Modern Bride*, and *Elegant Bride*. What struck me about them was their narrow focus on the wedding day—dress, cake, decor, and so on. The topics of marital promises and obligations, long-term planning, and legal ramifications were absent.

Here is some advice from *Brides* magazine on wedding vows:

Write your vows separately and keep them secret from each other until your wedding day, which will up the emotional factor....

Set a 30-second time limit—this will force you to really think about what you're saying and make each word count.[41]

This secrecy and brevity seem like bad policy. There are good reasons to consider marital obligations carefully, articulate them precisely, and agree on them explicitly. In the worst case, one's happiness may depend on breaking them. Realism in framing the promise may obviate such promise-breaking. The wise spouse will promise only what she knows she is able to perform.

2

HOW TO COMMIT MARRIAGE
A CONCEPTUAL GUIDE

Marriage is often said to involve another sort of voluntary undertaking: commitment.[1] People freely choose to enter it yet cannot freely leave; they mean thereby to give up some freedom. The bindingness of marriage has few secular analogies: an oath of loyalty, a deathbed pledge, the lifelong tie to someone whose life one has saved, parental and filial duties. Marriage attempts to create an identity-defining, immutable tie, to safeguard a fragile emotional connection. This attempt to bind oneself against the hazards of an unforeseeable future can be understood as commitment.

The aspirations voiced in wedding vows are better understood as commitment than as promise; but the concept of commitment needs considerable clarification. Delineating commitment will help to define the moral significance of marriage and raise questions about the rationality of entering it. Paradigmatic commitments are distinct from promises: They do not necessarily establish interpersonal obligations, and they typically attach to complex, temporally extended goals. "Commitment" itself is ambiguous between a psychological state and a self-binding action (such as a promise). Disambiguating "commitment" allows us to articulate the crucial point that making a commitment does not amount to having a commitment.

This disambiguation also helps to illuminate the moral complexities of commitment. Some, but not all, commitments generate interpersonal obligations, but one cannot be obligated to have a commitment. Nor need commitments be exclusive or unconditional. These simple points have implications for the moral status of marriage. Marriage is a way of making a commitment, but it does not obligate spouses to be committed, nor does its nature as a commitment entail that marriage must be monogamous, permanent, or that it is a good.

Indeed, binding oneself to ensure that one's trajectory continues according to one's current preferences, as by making a marital commitment, is subject to rational choice analysis as a strategy for preference satisfaction. Understanding marriage as a commitment allows us to ask whether the marital commitment is rational, in the sense of *instrumental* rationality: Is it likely to serve one's self-interest, to maximize one's preference fulfillment, over the long run? I ended Chapter 1 by suggesting that specific marital promises are weighty; it might be asked whether it is prudent to take on such weighty moral obligations as well as the legal constraints of marriage. Making commitments is instrumentally rational when foreclosing some options allows one to satisfy stronger preferences. Only given certain preference structures is marriage a rational enterprise—and even then, I will argue, it is a flawed precommitment strategy. I will also consider here the argument that marriage is socially valuable because it teaches citizens to be committed, to carry through reliably on commitments they have made.

I. COMMITMENTS VERSUS PROMISES

Commitments and promises are often conflated. Susan Mendus, for example, argues that wedding vows express an unconditional commitment, which she equates with a "promise to love and honour."[2] Similarly, Iddo Landau, using "commitment" and "promise" interchangeably, argues that the marriage promise has a point because commitment to a relationship strengthens it.[3] Both are perfectly correct in this usage; promising is one way in which to make a commitment. But conflating commitment and promise obscures important differences, and such arguments can subtly draw upon connotations of a sense of "commitment" that differs from promising. Paradigmatic cases of commitment present a moral phenomenon distinct from promising.

The term *commitment* is ambiguous between an internal psychological disposition that manifests in action (as in "she showed her commitment through her hard work") and an act of voluntarily undertaking responsibility (as in "she made a commitment to her work").[4] These two senses can be verbally distinguished as "*having* a commitment" (dispositional commitment) and "*making* a commitment" (an act). The approbative adjectival form "being committed" and the noun "committedness" usually refer to having a commitment. Having a commitment consists in the internal psychological disposition to accord an object deliberative priority (an "internal commitment").[5] A disposition is a stable propensity consistently to feel or deliberate in a certain way, and as a stable pattern of thought and feeling it necessarily exists over time. If I have a commitment to the environment, the environment will figure in my deliberation whenever I decide what to do. Having a commitment to some object requires that the object itself figure as important in deliberation, that it is perceived as valuable in itself: Working just to receive a paycheck is not commitment to one's job. Internal dispositional commitment requires that one value, or care about, the object.

Paradigmatic cases of having commitments are enduring, complex, attitudinal, and not wholly voluntary. Such commitment persists over time through changing, often unforeseeable, circumstances. The objects of such commitments are typically complex—causes, long-term goals, relationships. Paradigmatic cases of having commitments differ from promising in five key features: duration, dispositional aspect, relation to obligation, voluntariness, and the complexity of their objects. In the remainder of this section, I will trace the differences between making commitments, having commitments, and promising.

Making a commitment, in contrast to having one, is undertaking, privately or publicly, to give deliberative priority to a person, group, or state of affairs. It can be either a mental or external act. One can make a commitment in many ways: solemnly stating a firm intention, assuring, guaranteeing. Making commitments overlaps with promising, as in "she made a commitment to me to hand in her essay tomorrow."[6] Such public makings of commitment, even if they do not invoke promising specifically, induce reliance and invoke commissive conventions, which, in some theories, are hallmarks of promising. But commitments can also be made privately with oneself. Furthermore, although one can make a commitment to perform a discrete action (such as handing in the paper tomorrow), making commitments, in paradigmatic cases, characteristically differs from promising in involving a more open-ended, extended self-dedication to complex goals, the sort of goals that typically require having internal dispositional commitment for their successful completion. Of course, there is conceptual and vernacular overlap between "commitment" and "promise." But the point is that there is a contrast between self-bindings establishing interpersonal obligations to perform some discrete action (typically, promises) and self-bindings orientating one's priorities to long-term goals whose completion typically requires psychological committedness (typically, commitments); between, for example, promising to wash the dishes half the time and committing to give the relationship priority, whatever that may take.

Making a commitment and having a commitment are related: Making a commitment (at least in paradigmatic cases) expresses internal dispositional commitment or tries to reinforce it, and the kinds of goals involved generally require internal dispositional commitment. Still, making and having commitments differ. One essential difference is that having a commitment involves a psychological disposition, while making a commitment does not. Thus one can say, "She made a commitment to the cause, but is she really committed?" A second difference is that making a commitment involves a conscious decision, whereas this element may be much less salient in having a commitment. One can have a commitment without having consciously decided on it; one can recognize, after the fact, that one's pattern of conscious intentions and choices has forged a dispositional commitment to continue in the same vein. This is why one can suddenly discover one has a commitment (this is distinct from a mere habit, as the commitment involves intentionally according continuing deliberative priority).

Making a commitment expresses an intention to have a commitment but is not sufficient for doing so. Making a commitment can fall prey to the Prufrockian vacillation of "a hundred visions and revisions" before teatime.[7] Having a commitment requires more than a single expression of intention: It requires a series of deliberative acts. Making a commitment fails to develop into having a commitment if the committer does not acquire appropriate dispositions. Thus when Marcel toys with the idea of commitment, one day declaring he is committed to Andrée, the next to Gilberte, the next to Albertine, he does not have a commitment. Sincerely stating, "I commit to Albertine" is not sufficient for Marcel to have a commitment to Albertine. Marcel must remain committed over time to have a commitment. This temporal requirement follows from the fact that having a commitment is dispositional. But it is also a matter of human psychology: Having commitments typically requires rearranging priorities, retraining preferences, and habitually subordinating some desires to others. Sudden conversions, perhaps, can achieve similar results, but it usually takes time and effort to order one's preferences stably in the service of a long-term goal.

The temporal difference also distinguishes promising and having commitments. A promise is made through a speech act at a point in time. Having a commitment extends over time because it involves a stable psychological disposition, a series of psychological states, which requires temporal duration. The differing temporal requirement supervenes on the dispositional difference between having commitments and promising.

One might ask how much time is required for a disposition to emerge. An hour or day is probably insufficient, but precise durations are elusive, because they depend upon the object of the commitment. Thus, a commitment to rear a child, or write a book, differs in length from a commitment to grow gladioli this year. Depending on the time to maturity of gladioli, one might exhibit a commitment to this goal after only a few weeks. But in embarking on a longer-term or more challenging endeavor, like quitting smoking or writing a novel, two weeks of enthusiasm could turn out to be a flash in the pan. Having a commitment does not require achieving one's goals or persisting irrationally in the face of overwhelming difficulty, but it does require outlasting early distractions and frustrations.

Having a commitment is essentially psychological, but it normally issues in action. Yearning for something impossible or which one is powerless to bring about is wishing, not commitment. Commitment implies that the agent can act, somehow, in pursuit of the goal, although success is not guaranteed. Because commitment requires relatively high deliberative priority, it would be odd if an agent claimed to be committed but never acted accordingly. However, it is possible that a highly prioritized object could be continually trumped by an even higher object: We might say that Ilsa, in the film *Casablanca*, had a commitment to loving Rick, but fighting the Nazis had an even higher priority, and so she does not act on her love. Having a commitment normally will, but need not always, lead to action; the disposition, not action, is essential. For the same reason, committedness may falter on occasion without dissolving. Breaking one's diet once in a while is consistent with being committed to it. Commitment is temporally demanding, but it is also a forgiving notion.

Promising differs temporally and dispositionally from having a commitment, and it has a different moral structure. If I make a commitment to conserve the environment, but I continue to drive an SUV, patronize big agribusiness, and so on, I simply do not have a commitment; it failed to take hold. We might say I have let myself down or compromised my integrity, because I have failed to develop a commitment. Promises are different: If I promise to protect the environment, but fail to do so, I did not fail to make a promise—I broke it. A promise creates an obligation, which the promisor cannot unilaterally dissolve. In contrast, being committed, having a disposition to deliberate a certain way, is not inherently obligating. Having a commitment does not directly obligate the agent to another person (unless, contingently, its expression induces reliance). One can be committed to a cause or state of affairs—entities which cannot be owed obligations. Pace certain views in environmental ethics, one cannot owe an obligation to the wilderness as one does to a person; yet one can be committed to protecting it. Commitments obligate their makers to themselves, if anyone, as a matter of integrity.[8] (This does not entail that one can renege on public commitments without blame, given the possibility of having induced reliance in others.)

There is a further difference between commitments and promises: Having commitments involves a significant involuntary element. This point can be overstated. Stan van Hooft, for example, writes that in romantic love, an agent discovers, rather than chooses, commitment, "an alteration of the will which differs from a conscious decision."[9] He takes the following kind of case as exemplary: Marcel has known Albertine for several years. Suddenly, he realizes that it is Albertine and no other without whom he cannot live. This discovery strikes him like a thunderbolt when Albertine becomes unobtainable. Marcel's commitment is discovered rather than chosen. But this overstates the uncontrollable, unchosen aspect of commitment. Commitment involves more choice and work than being struck by lightning.

Having a commitment involves a series of deliberative acts in which one exercises choice. While it may feel as if one suddenly discovers a commitment, having a commitment emerges from a series of choices (forcing oneself to go to the gym, deciding not to date people other than one's beloved). One may indeed suddenly discover that one does feel strongly for something or someone. But this discovery does not constitute a commitment, but a reason to make one. On van Hooft's account, Marcel is committed to Albertine when the thunderbolt strikes. But this is not enough: Marcel is not committed to Albertine, because the next day another thunderbolt might strike. Just as having a commitment is not forged through a single speech-act, it is not forged through a single emotional experience. To have a commitment, Marcel must renounce possibilities excluding a relationship with Albertine, choose to maintain the affair with her, and so on: He must prioritize the relationship and deliberate accordingly over time. Discovering that one has a commitment does not consist only in an emotional experience, but in realizing that one has been according an object deliberative priority, noticing, for example, that this year one's resolution to go to the gym did not fade. Only over time does it emerge that a given intention is one we won't revise.

However, van Hooft is correct that having a commitment does involve an involuntary and uncontrollable element. Unlike promises, commitments are not made through acts of will alone. We have commitments because we care about their objects or about some ends to which these objects are necessary. Commitment is not solely a matter of forcing oneself to go through the motions (although much of it may be just that!). While one can influence, through habit or therapy, what one cares about, one cannot simply choose it. Caring cannot be forced. Of course, one may stop caring but still continue to give deliberative priority to an uncared-for object. What one cannot control is whether one cares about it. It may be thought that such inability shows lack of willpower.[10] But what we care about changes as we change. What we care about—in life, in art, in love—structures many of our deepest commitments, and these are less a matter of choice than of being struck by a certain kind of beauty or grace or value, which one cannot force oneself to see, or not to see.[11]

One other feature distinguishes commitments from promises. Paradigmatic commitments are complex in execution in a way that promises need not be. Carrying out a commitment involves negotiating with the changing world over time and with other commitments. It involves continual weighing of priorities and continual deliberation about the best means to the chosen end. Whether the commitment is to eating healthily or getting fit, producing a novel or a body of artwork, caring for one's friends or children, or to causes such as feminism or environmentalism, the objects of paradigmatic commitments are achievable only over long periods of time and with much planning, deliberation, and exclusion of other options. Cheshire Calhoun takes readiness to refuse alternatives as a hallmark of commitment: The committed person turns down competing goals or ways of life that would lead away from the commitment, even if such options would otherwise be attractive. Commitment involves a "resistance to reconsideration" of the commitment itself.[12]

Causes such as environmentalism or goals such as health involve unavoidable complexity. One must continually give the object decision-making priority and subordinate or exclude other attractive options. But there is no definite rule to follow: There are too many contingencies and choices forced upon us by the world. One simply holds the object of commitment as important and adjusts accordingly as the world changes. This complexity piggybacks on the complexity of some worthwhile endeavors, success in which would be impossible without long-term dispositional commitment. In pursuing complex goals one faces difficult choices, limited information, and occasional failure. Committedness brings the requisite persistence, flexibility, and readiness to shrug off failure and start again. For example, a commitment to the environment may be challenged in numerous ways: My housing budget might run to only one of solar power or sustainable building materials, my only way of getting to an environmental forum might be a gas-guzzling rental car, I might be able to patronize the local farmers' market only by driving, and so on. In making the environment a priority, I must adjust to new situations, challenges, and conflicts, and accept compromise. I must choose between different courses of action under conditions of uncertainty, and keep choosing appropriately. The complexity of pursuing such goals is further exacerbated by the fact that people rarely have one commitment as absolutely top priority. Commitment to acting morally may be a trump, but otherwise we strive to balance different commitments. Without a stable disposition to prioritize complex goals in the face of challenges and distractions, we could not succeed in achieving them: It is the complexity of such goals that necessitates commitment. Such goals may be of no more inherent value than short-term goals that do not require commitment; my point is simply that commitment facilitates achieving long-term and complex goals—such as the aspiration, with which people typically enter marriage, of maintaining an intimate interpersonal relationship over time.

II. COMMITMENT, OBLIGATION, LOVE, AND MARRIAGE

Commitment captures the emotional content of wedding vows, which is so poorly understood in promissory terms. Intimate relationships are paradigmatic objects of commitment—enduring, complex, evolving. In marriage, spouses make a commitment because they have, or want to have, a commitment: a stable disposition to give the relationship deliberative priority. They will exclude other alternatives, and take on obligations burdening exit, to protect and sustain their mutual caring about one another, even their love. This recalls Landau's analysis of the marriage promise as undertaking to perform love-sustaining acts: While this failed as an understanding of the marriage promise, it is a reasonable description of the commitment spouses might make to one another.

But understanding marriage in terms of commitment reduces the extent of its obligations, as compared with the (rejected) promissory account. Commitments, including marital commitments, function differently, morally, than promising. Making a marriage commitment can, indeed, establish moral obligations and bring social and legal pressures to bear in favor of keeping those obligations. But no one can be obligated to be committed, to sustain the state of caring about the object. And there is no decisive moral or prudential reason to be committed—not even in love relationships. While some have argued that love entails commitment and that marital commitment entails unconditionality and exclusivity, neither commitment itself nor love requires this. I will discuss each of these points in turn.

Having a commitment does not in itself entail interpersonal obligation. In Dickens' *Great Expectations*, Pip's benefactor labored anonymously on Pip's behalf, but his commitment to benefitting Pip did not obligate him to do so. However, in the normal course of things, having commitments entangles us with others in ways that create obligations. Simply saying, "I am committed to you" creates certain expectations in the hearer, who could then be hurt if those expectations go unfulfilled. Among other costs, the hearer might forgo other opportunities in the expectation that the relationship will continue. At the very least, the general duty to refrain from gratuitously harming others requires us not to express commitments recklessly. Publicly making a commitment can create interpersonal obligations by inducing reliance; making marriage commitments typically creates expectations such as material support, a continuing relationship, and sexual exclusivity, which spouses may be morally blamed for disappointing. A spouse will make plans and forgo opportunities in the expectation that the other will perform; a spouse who fails to perform is thus morally responsible for the costs of forgone opportunities as well as whatever specific obligations he has left undone.

Insofar as being committed has an involuntary component of caring about or valuing, one cannot be obligated to be committed. Spouses cannot be obligated to continue caring about their relationship. But they can have moral or prudential reason to continue to give it deliberative priority and to work to maintain their internal dispositional commitment. However, having a commitment in itself does not give one decisive reason, moral or otherwise, to continue having the commitment. One can be committed to record-collecting or baking, and when one finds oneself ceasing to care or developing a new interest, one may abandon the old commitment. Indeed, one can be committed to morally abhorrent causes, in which case one ought to abandon them. Having a commitment is simply a disposition to prioritize an object, an object not necessarily valuable in itself. The disposition to prioritize it is a fact about the agent that does not generate obligations to continue prioritizing it. At best it generates defeasible reasons to try to maintain the commitment, as pursuing commitments will typically increase the rewards (one will become a better baker, for instance).

There is one apparent moral reason for nurturing one's internal commitments: Doing so may help develop qualities of stability and consistency in commitment that can reliably sustain moral action. Simply put, if one can consistently prioritize nonmoral objectives, then one has a strength of character that will help in consistently prioritizing moral ends. We may think of willpower of this sort as a muscle, strengthened through exercise. Overcoming recalcitrant desires and developing strength in positively willing ends required by morality may have moral worth, as Kant would have it. But this moral reason for nurturing committedness is a prima facie reason only, because such strength of character can be put to immoral purposes as well as moral ones. For this reason, morality requires that we reflectively evaluate our commitments: Blind commitment, which risks having evil objects, is a vice. There is, then, moral reason not to be unquestioning or inflexible in one's commitments. Morality thus gives only a defeasible reason for persistence. Moreover, the image of willpower as a muscle may be misleading: Perhaps it is more like a scarce resource, in which case devoting too much to nonmoral ends may diminish internal moral commitment.

From a broader ethical perspective, stability in commitment is related to personal integrity.[13] But this is not a decisive reason to maintain commitments either. Any account of integrity must allow change over time; integrity does not require that our commitments be unvarying. Indeed, failure to develop may be a symptom of inauthenticity. Constantly changing commitments, it is true, may suggest instability or a lack of integrity. But as people learn and mature, they typically develop new interests that alter their priorities. Intellectual and emotional growth and consequent change are consistent with integrity and stability, as is abandoning some old commitments for new. Of course, if someone's central commitment were a commitment to never changing his commitments, then change would threaten integrity. But integrity does not require that we commit to invariability, and indeed, prudence and morality counsel against it.

From a prudential perspective, persistence in commitment is valuable for completing long-term projects. But prudential reason, the objective of which is the reasoner's own good, also allows abandoning commitments as one's preferences change over time. Indeed, it is not clear that long-term projects always provide more satisfaction than a series of short-term projects. Henry David Thoreau's many changes of employment, for instance, may have sustained a vitality and focus that commitment to a single job would have drained from him. Calhoun has argued compellingly "that shaping one's life around some set of commitments is not obviously a better strategy for making one's life go well than not doing so."[14] One reason commitment might be thought conducive to a good life is the long-term nature of some goals and the pressure to choose among different objectives in order to accomplish any. But Calhoun argues that mere intending, without commitment's "strong barrier to reconsideration," may suffice to establish and complete long-term projects. For example, a couple may stay together for many years without ever having committed by deciding to give the relationship priority and excluding other alternatives. Presumably many friendships evolve in this way. Further, Calhoun adds, in cases where agents change goals frequently rather than sticking to one, "it's unclear why changing course, even changing course frequently, should be regarded as a waste of time, energy, and resources to be avoided rather than as a wise seizure of the opportunity for trading up."[15] Nor does a meaningful life require commitment to an overriding long-term goal: Someone "who has many varied and easily pursued objects of lesser care may end her life having spent more of its days and hours in meaningful activities than her more single-minded, passionate counterpart."[16] Commitment does not universally make lives go better, but is of most value to those with particular normative and temporal styles: prizing, as opposed to appreciating widely, and a preference for familiarity over the unknown.[17]

There is no decisive moral or prudential reason to develop or maintain commitments. Nor need commitments, when we have them, be unconditional or permanent. Commitments to projects, goals, or persons may be full and whole-hearted without being permanent or unconditional. They may have built-in temporal limits, such as a role-based mentoring relationship like doctoral supervision. The commitment is only for the duration of study. Not only is such a commitment temporary, it is conditional. The commitment will end if the student drops out of the program or fails to meet its standards. This also applies to causes: I may commit to environmentalism only until certain goals are met. While "commitments" which shift like weathervanes, lacking reliability and constancy, are not real commitments, this does not show that commitments must be lifelong or unconditional.

Indeed, excepting the commitment to morality, commitments should not be unconditional. They should be conditional on the moral permissibility of their objects and the necessary means thereto. Committed agents typically set other conditions, such as personal safety and compatibility with other commitments. Were an agent suddenly to discover that a commitment were life-threatening or precluded some other important commitment, we would not conclude that she had not been committed if she gave it up. Rather, she was less committed to extreme sports, say, than to survival. Moreover, reasonable people realize that their interests may change, or that the discovery of new facts may undermine existing commitments. For these reasons, unconditional commitments or commitment to invariability are morally risky and potentially imprudent.

It is sometimes argued that love-based and marital commitments—unlike other commitments—must be unconditional. In general, interpersonal commitments can take many forms, with differing conditions and durations: One can be committed to helping a needy individual, supervising a student, or mentoring a colleague. But Susan Mendus argues that commitment in love has inherent requirements; just as commitment to a friendship might be thought conceptually to entail prioritizing the friend's welfare, being loyal, spending time together, and so on, commitment to love and marriage, she argues, must be unconditional. She claims that someone truly making a marriage commitment "cannot now envisage anything happening such as would make me give up that commitment." (Here marriage is construed as the institutional context for love, a view I accept now for the sake of argument, but will revisit in the following chapters.) The reason she gives for this is that love is experienced as unconditional: While love may alter, "love is not love which allows in advance that it will so alter."[18] In other words, a true lover cannot contemplate the possibility of love's demise. However, this seems false, unless love is question beggingly defined as excluding any apprehension of its possible ending. A rational person can surely contemplate the possibility that love will end, although she may hope it will not. If love necessarily involves a denial of this possibility, then it is intrinsically delusional, raising the question of whether persons in such a state of mind are competent to make commitments at all.

Mendus argues, in favor of the unconditionality condition, that it is unconditionality that distinguishes love from sentimentality, on one side, or respect, on the other. But this is not so. Love can be distinguished from sentimentality by concern for the beloved as a particular person, and not an idealized object, as in sentimentality, and from respect by delight and affection. Mendus also argues that love is unconditional because it attaches to a particular person, not a set of properties (such as being blond, intelligent, funny, and so on). She assumes that love-for-properties could admit the possibility of change if the properties were to change, but love-for-persons, because it attaches to the person independent of her properties, will predict its own continuance no matter how the person changes. But love is a two-part relation: A lover may recognize that her own feelings may fade independent of changes in the beloved. Of course, love's intensity may cloud this, as may the Proustian intuition that one's identity depends on what one loves, so that the death of love is the death of the self. But a lover can still stand aside from such fears to anticipate the death of love—just as one can anticipate one's own death. Nothing in the nature of love commitments requires permanence or unconditionality.

Not only does love not require unconditional commitment, love does not require commitment at all. In contrast, van Hooft understands love as an "alteration of the will" that lovers discover only retroactively; on his view, by the time the lover discovers that she is in love, her relationship with the other is part of her identity and is already a commitment.[19] But this overlooks the voluntary element of commitment— commitments do not just happen to us. I may find a certain desire or propensity as part of my psychological make-up and choose to reject it; I may discover that I am in love dangerously or inappropriately, and turn away from that love. The alleged commitment does not reflect a stable and voluntary prioritization, but a possibly episodic psychological fact about the lover. On van Hooft's analysis of how a lover is committed, a reformed alcoholic might be said to be committed to drinking. Moreover, van Hooft's view would not allow that there are cases of love (for someone inappropriate, dangerous, or immoral) in which the lover rejects commitment, yet still loves.

Parenting might be thought to present a strong case for unconditional interpersonal commitment, but even this commitment must be qualified. No commitment should continually trump all others. Commitment to a child must coexist with other commitments—to other children, one's own health, friends, morality. Nor should such commitment lead to sacrificing public goods for private, for example, prioritizing the child's slightest whim over contributing to a stable polity and healthy environment. An unconditional commitment is generally not an overriding priority, but requires balance. Moreover, an ideal of unconditional parental love may be harmful. Parents should not forgive to the point of self-harm, or be committed to parenting when it threatens the health or life of parent or child. But with these qualifications in mind, commitment to parenting should usually be only minimally conditioned because children are vulnerable and need continuity of care. Temporary or highly conditional parental commitments risk harm (although in constrained circumstances, as when the parent cannot continue to care for the child, they may be the best available option). But marriages, taking place between adults, lack the feature that grounds the exceptionally strong commitment of parenting: Spouses do not have infants' developmental needs for long-term continuity. Love between adults does not by its nature require commitment—and a fortiori does not require marriage.

It is also sometimes argued that commitment in love, and hence marital commitments, must be exclusive. Commitments in general, of course, do not exclude other commitments. Most people have many simultaneous commitments, even loving interpersonal commitments—to friends, family, work, hobbies, self-improvement, causes, and ideals. van Hooft argues for the exclusivity of the love commitment on the grounds that "[c]ommitments of differing types can coexist, but commitments of the same type will tend to be exclusive" due to the potential for conflict.[20] But one can have coexisting commitments of the same type: to teaching as well as writing, to painting as well as dance, to antiracism as well as environmentalism, to a number of friends and family members. The exclusivity thesis rules out being committed to more than one child or friend at a time! One forestalls conflict through time management and prudent planning, not by making commitments exclusive. Although human finitude limits the total number of commitments we can make, there is no reason to think they must be limited by category. There is, after all, potential for conflict between different categories—between career and family, between love and art. If potential conflict between commitments is a reason for exclusivity, then we should have only one commitment!

Potential conflict may seem more problematic in the case of romantic love due to its intensity and the threat of jealousy. But these conditions are not unique to romantic love—nor do they obtain in all romantic love relationships! Not all jealousy is sexual. Jealousy can arise within friendships, too, or between fellow employees or competitors; in these cases, agents may choose to endure or control it rather than make friendships exclusive or withdraw from competition. Further, spouses might be jealous not only of potential romantic interlopers, but of their spouses' commitments to their careers or other callings. Although some spouses may seek an exclusive interpersonal commitment trumping all others, this aspiration is probably imprudent. Commitments to careers, religion, family, friends, and avocations reflect spouses' independent needs and interests. Interpersonal commitments, even in marriage, coexist with competing commitments that may provoke jealousy.

It is often claimed that competing sexual interests are different in kind, that external romantic love interests or extramarital sex are incompatible with a love-based commitment. For some individuals, the strength of sexual jealousy and the threat to romantic love posed by extramarital sex may be strong reasons for exclusivity. A number of contemporary philosophers have argued for the exclusivity of marriage on precisely these grounds.[21] But this depends on the psychological propensities of particular individuals. These arguments for exclusivity in love and sex must confront the testimony of people for whom jealousy is not as strong, or who sustain polyamorous loving and sexual relationships, or who prefer to endure some jealousy to obtain greater variety and interest.[22] Overwhelming sexual jealousy and the need to be most important for one other person—as opposed to being important to a number of people, within a group or a constellation of overlapping relationships—are not universal. The structure of prudent love commitments is not defined by the nature of romantic love, but depends on the preferences and propensities of each individual good. This brings us to the question of when, and whether, it is rational to bind one-self in a marital commitment.

III. IS MARRIAGE RATIONAL?

Humans can be fickle and easily distracted and confused. We make commitments (in part) to safeguard commitments we have (or want to have). We cannot always control our internal states, and so we seek to bind our future actions. Rational choice theory has analyzed these self-bindings as precommitment strategies, strategies designed to protect our current commitments against changing preferences or disruptive passions and their distorting cognitive effects. By using precommitment strategies, one can improve one's situation by excluding certain options. Where passion or change of preference threaten long-term goals, eliminating distracting options can be a rational strategy. These self-binding methods tie us to a course of action to prevent us from giving into intense or cognitively distorting short-term preferences, just as Ulysses tied himself to the mast of his ship to hear the Sirens sing without succumbing to their call.[23]

"Ulysses contracts" attempt to circumvent our own imperfect rationality. Aware that we are liable to weakness of will or preference change, we use self-binding or precommitment strategies to restrict our future actions to promote our long-term best interests. For example, an advancing army might burn bridges behind it to preclude retreat, an addict might disable her access to her money to prevent herself from buying drugs, a smoker might tell friends that she plans to quit smoking so that social embarrassment will prevent a relapse, a spendthrift might authorize the bank to place a percentage of her salary in savings to prevent her spending it, and a lover might marry to erect legal and social barriers against leaving the relationship for passing fancies or after trivial quarrels. There are many different kinds of precommitment strategies, and marriage can be seen as employing several. It imposes a delay before spouses can exit the marriage (in some legal jurisdictions), it creates economic costs (the cost of divorce itself and, possibly, alimony) and costs of social disapproval on exit, and it creates incentives to remain (whatever benefits law and third parties provide as well as social approval).[24]

Marriage is a way of publicly making a commitment that binds the self and offers incentives to the spouse to do the same; it protects spouses against the Sirens of temporary lapses in love or affection. It reduces exit options by making exit burdensome, thus discouraging spouses from leaving without a reason strong enough to outweigh the burdens. Such incentives could be set up without marriage. For example, a legal contract requiring payment on default would serve a similar purpose. But marriage is distinguished by the scope of its penalties—legal, economic, social, and moral.

Legally and economically, spouses must go to the trouble and expense of obtaining a divorce and fulfilling property and support requirements. Socially, people leaving their spouses risk disapproval. Morally, spouses incur obligations and create expectations that they may be blamed for disappointing.

Marriage is also distinctive in effecting these disparate incentives and penalties through a single act. Again, precommitment is not unique to marriage; barriers to exit may be erected outside of it. Unmarried partners can make promises, announce their partnerhood, cohabit, mingle their finances, and make legal contracts. Marriage is simply a one-stop solution, invoking moral, social, legal, and economic costs and incentives. In addition, in some jurisdictions marriage does invoke unique legal pressures, such as the waiting periods to divorce in covenant marriage, and social and religious pressures, such as ostracism of divorced persons. Its publicity is essential to these functions. While marriage can be secret, it cannot be private. It is a social form, and its recognition as such is one of the pressures it summons.

Agreeing to marital obligations is a means of exacting the other spouse's reciprocation as well as of self-binding. The classic analysis of precommitment strategy comes from Thomas Schelling's work in deterrence theory, which focuses on how precommitment influences other parties in a bargaining situation. Burning bridges will not only motivate the advancing soldiers, it will make their threat more credible to the enemy. While marriage influences many third parties—gift-giving wedding invitees, deterred rivals, proud parents—its most significant effect is (presumably) on the spouse's willingness to reciprocate. Marriage secures reciprocity; spouses assume obligations such as sexual exclusivity to receive the same in return. Taking on binding legal obligations assures spouses of their mutual seriousness. A common theme in romance and tragedy is how one can trust professions of love.[25] While marriage does not necessitate love or trust, its public and legal status offers evidence of trustworthiness greater than a private promise can because it invokes legal, moral, social, and economic pressures.

Understanding marriage as a precommitment strategy articulates a more complex relation between its public social and legal aspects and its internal emotional content than did the idea of a promise to love.[26] The wedding ceremony does not create the internal commitment; the commitment made in marriage is only indirectly related to having one, for it only emerges over time that spouses have a commitment, that this is a decision they won't revise. But while marriage does not guarantee that spouses will be committed, it creates a strong incentive structure of social pressures, financial benefits, and legal barriers to be committed, to work on maintaining the commitment (as through Landau's "love-sustaining acts"), and to exclude tempting alternatives. The burdens on exit mean that—unless the costs of staying are even greater—spouses are better off prioritizing the relationship and continuing to care about it. Indeed, even if spouses marry for reasons other than love, as in an arranged marriage, marriage still gives them incentive to become committed to the relationship.

While marriage has been used as a standard example of a precommitment strategy, Jon Elster, a precommitment theorist, has rejected his earlier analysis of marriage as a precommitment strategy as "a mistake, or at least misleading." The reason is that (except in the case of optional covenant marriages) "the delay [on exit] is always imposed by the state rather than chosen by the spouses themselves.... The legal rights and duties of marriage come as a package." Only if there were an option to marry without burdening exit would it be clear that marriage is a precommitment strategy "because only in that case could restrictions on the freedom to divorce be the motive for marrying."[27] Spouses might marry for immediate benefits—health insurance, immigration eligibility, social recognition—not in order to make leaving the relationship more difficult. This seems to allow, at least, that some spouses may use marriage as a precommitment strategy, whereas others have other intentions.

In either case, given that marriage creates burdens on exit and incentives to stay, we can ask whether it is rational to set such an incentive structure into place. Ulysses's strategy of tying himself to the mast was rational because he preferred survival to death by drowning; similarly, precommitment strategies that help one to stop smoking, save money, and so on, are rational when one's preference to achieve the long-term goal outweighs the preferences to pursue fleeting temptations. Through the lens of instrumental rationality, the rationality of our courses of action is determined by how well they will fulfill our competing preferences over time. Marrying might be rational, then, if the goods it provides, including the reciprocal cooperation of the spouse, outweigh the opportunity costs.

However, we inevitably choose under conditions of uncertainty, and Dan Moller's "Bachelor's Argument" against marriage holds that, under these conditions, marriage is always irrational because it runs too great a risk of a strongly dispreferred outcome: Divorce rates suggest there is a 40 percent chance (roughly) that a marriage will end unhappily, and most people have a strong preference to avoid unhappy marriages. Marriage thus exposes the agent to a significant risk of an outcome she would strongly prefer to avoid.[28] We might compare this to forging professional credentials or driving recklessly—if the risk of exposure or a crash is high enough, and the consequences sufficiently unpleasant, then it is irrational to so act, even for the chance of a good job or the short-term thrills of speeding. However, the reasoning of the Bachelor's Argument would also militate against entering any long-term committed relationship, because it might end unhappily; passionately supporting a team or cause, because one's side might lose; or undertaking any projects that might fail and risk disappointment—applying to law school, running for office, publishing a novel, sending a paper to an academic journal. By parity of reasoning, embarking on any valued enterprise, where failure is strongly dispreferred, with a high chance of failure is irrational. But this applies to many competitive or ambitious activities! The Bachelor's Argument would have us avoiding any life plans with high risks of failure—no matter what the possible rewards.

The Bachelor's Argument holds for the extremely risk-averse; but in most cases, it weighs the preference to avoid marital failure too heavily. It discounts the value people place on the good years of marriage, even if it ultimately ends, and it ignores the fact that an unhappy marriage is not a permanent condition but a phase that may lead to an amicable divorce. Finally, while most people probably do strongly prefer to avoid an unhappy marriage, many also have strong preferences to share their lives with another person, or persons. The argument underestimates the value many people place on being in relationships—even if they risk unhappy endings.

Still, we can supplement the Bachelor's Argument with a generic Feminist's Argument against marriage. Statistically, marriage has significant costs for women: economic vulnerability caused by a cycle of dependence and risks of abuse facilitated by legal access rights and burdens on exit. According to Susan Maushart, married women suffer more health and psychological problems than do unmarried women, they face an unequal division of domestic labor, and they benefit less from marriage than do men. "Wifework," the extra work married women typically do, has economic and emotional penalties for women, and economic vulnerability makes it difficult for women to exit abusive marriages.[29] But marriage also protects economically dependent wives through divorce law; ironically, it enacts measures to protect against the vulnerabilities and dependencies that gender-structured marriage creates.

The question of how law can protect the vulnerable without encouraging dependency is pursued in Part Two. For now, recall that marriage can serve as a bargaining tool. By assuming obligations, spouses can secure reciprocity. But marriage also offers an opportunity for negotiating individualized and self-protective terms—not only through legally binding prenuptial agreements, but also through informal agreements. Thus, women could negotiate shared housework, for instance, at the outset.[30] Or they could follow the model of Aristophanes's *Lysistrata*, in which women refuse to engage in sex until their husbands end the Peloponnesian War. Of course, the social context of economic and power inequality between men and women affects women's bargaining power, but some women may be able to leverage their marital commitment against the gendered division of domestic labor. Finally, the bonds of marriage may prove burdensome to men as well as women: Husbands face social pressure to undertake an impersonally defined male provider role, and entry into marriage could be a point for defying these gender role expectations rather than simply internalizing them.

However, not only do some theorists argue that contractual negotiation is inappropriate in loving relationships (a point I will dispute in Chapter 4.iv), some philosophers, and the free love tradition, have argued that obligation is anathema to love, which by its nature is spontaneous. This suggests a Bachelor's (and Bachelorette's) Argument Redux. Obligation may threaten love; as Eric Cave has argued, marriage may disproportionately burden the "contract-intolerant," those who strongly prefer to avoid relationships characterized by obligation.[31] And individuals who flourish in multiple sexual or intimate relationships may be emotionally or sexually starved by the obligations of monogamous marriage. Marriage may be irrational for the contract-intolerant, the polyamorous, the bisexual, the asexual and solitudinous, and those who are happier among networks of friends than in one exclusive relationship.

But for those with strong preferences for long-term exclusive intimate companionship and with relatively weak competing preferences, marriage appears to be a rational strategy for preference satisfaction. However, even for such people, marriage is an imperfect strategy. The higher the exit penalty, the more effective the strategy, but the higher the chance of being trapped in an undesirable situation. As Robert Frank writes, a "contract lenient enough to allow termination of hopeless marriages cannot at the same time be strict enough to prevent opportunistic switching."[32] The obstacles to exit are not insuperable; nor should they be, due to the substantial dangers of precluding exit. In structuring the exit penalties of marriage, the harm to victims of abuse must be weighed against the relationships protected.[33] Moreover, precommitment strategies (when marriage functions as such) allowing no revision, when the goal is to satisfy one's own preferences (and not to deter an enemy), appear defective. In the case of marriage, self-binding surely assumes that the relationship will be in one's long-term best interests despite temptations to stray; but if the original preferences permanently alter, the original strategy is no longer instrumentally rational. For Ulysses, the alternative was death; in the case of marriage, the alternative may be significantly brighter. Indeed, people marrying may be uniquely ill-placed to judge their long-term interests: In "a state of infatuation, young people may overestimate the benefits and underestimate the costs of making themselves unable to yield to an extramarital passion later."[34]

There is another problem with marriage as a commitment strategy—call it "the problem of emotional laziness." Making a commitment does not suffice for having one. At its best, the trust marriage establishes allows spouses to extend themselves and take productive risks. But marriage may be taken as a substitute for the maintenance work that relationships involve, creating complacency. Marriage may be an attempt to stave off loss and try to cheat impermanence—a psychological state the novelist Richard Ford calls the Permanent Period, the illusion that nothing will change. From this angle, marriage can appear to be a self-deceptive denial of existential responsibility. Sartre saw love as prompting an inherently unrealizable attempt to capture permanently the free and spontaneous reciprocation of the beloved.[35] To the extent that marriage creates the illusion that this can be done, it may be a self-defeating, and self-deceiving, strategy. Elster cites Montaigne on the self-defeating point: "We thought we were tying our marriage knots more tightly by removing all means of undoing them; but the tighter we pulled the knot of constraint the looser and slacker became the knot of our will and affection. In Rome, on the contrary, what made marriages honoured and secure for so long a period was freedom to break them at will. Men loved their wives more because they could lose them."[36]

In sum, it may be rational to marry when the incentives are high enough and accord with one's preferences. But the necessity of providing exit options and the emotional laziness problem suggest that marriage is not an ideal precommitment strategy, though it may serve other purposes. I have argued that its rationality simply depends on individual preferences, and that neither prudence nor morality require commitment. But these claims conflict with a number of influential defenses of marriage and commitment, to which I now turn.

IV. THE GOODS OF COMMITMENT

Setting aside instrumental rationality, let us assume there are some goods independent of subjective preferences. Is commitment in general, or in marriage, such a good? I argued above that commitment itself is morally neutral: The value of a commitment depends on its object. There is a long philosophical tradition of arguing that marriage uniquely enables certain human goods, and that its value, in part, consists in motivating commitments that yield such goods. In the previous section, we saw reason to doubt the effectiveness of marriage for motivating commitment, and in Chapter 3, I will critically assess the most influential arguments that marriage uniquely yields basic human goods. Deferring consideration of the value of the object of marital commitment, in this section I focus on the argument that the disposition to commit readily and steadfastly is valuable, and that marriage promotes such a disposition.

Influential arguments for marriage have suggested that it teaches virtues closely related to committedness. Hegel, for instance, argues that marriage creates stable dispositions to trust and identify with others, which men then bring to their roles as citizens.[37] Marriage habituates family members to see themselves as members of a common enterprise. By giving spouses a purpose higher than their individual desires, it teaches them to subordinate their arbitrary desires to a greater good and to think in communal, nonindividualistic ways. As a family member, one learns not to separate one's own interests but to consider the good of the whole. From this perspective, contractual analyses of marriage are destructive, subjecting marriage to the desires of individuals, instead of teaching them to subordinate their desires to the institution. For Hegel, marriage teaches commitment, subordinating the vagaries of the individual will to the common good, leading to social stability and personal self-realization.

More recently, Allan Bloom, castigating the prevalence of divorce, has argued that indissoluble marriage habituates children into socially valuable dispositions of unconditional allegiance to a common good. To be precise, Bloom endorses a readiness to form a Rousseauian "general will." Divorce evidences the failure of spouses to unite their "particular wills" into a "general will": "In the absence of a common good or common object...the disintegration of society into particular wills is inevitable....Children who have gone to the school of conditional relationships should be expected to view the world in the light of what they learned there." For this reason, divorce "is surely America's most urgent social problem."[38] Bloom's view of the good of marriage, like Hegel's, includes commitment to the common good over individual desires.

In a simpler form of this argument, Scott FitzGibbon takes marriage as a school of moral duteousness: "those who do wed form a relationship which embraces obligation as a fundamental component." In marriage, commitment can be instrumental to other goals ("paying off the mortgage"), but it, and associated qualities of character, are also intrinsically valuable: "commitment, steadiness, loyalty, and fidelity to obligation are good in a basic way and a part of the basic good of marriage."[39] Drawing on Aristotle, FitzGibbon argues that commitment within marriage promotes virtues: "[F]irmness, stability, and steadiness of character are a major part of the good for man."[40]

Both Bloom and FitzGibbon link increased divorce rates to a decline in committedness and related virtues. However, commitment is not only expressed through marriage, and marriage is not necessary to develop committedness; institutions other than permanent and exclusive marriage can express or promote dispositions to commit. Unmarried cohabitation or polyamory can also manifest commitment (and, if the emotional laziness argument holds, perhaps encourage stronger dispositional commitment). A commitment is no less a commitment because it coexists with other commitments; a preference (such as FitzGibbon's) for "traditional" marriage arbitrarily privileges monogamy. If teaching children commitment through parental example is the main concern, exclusivity is irrelevant so long as children are reared in a stable environment. What is important is that children are raised by individuals who keep commitments—not the number or sex of their parents. Moreover, Bloom's child-focused argument does not demonstrate the need for permanent marriages, but at most marriages that endure through children's formative stages. Why should the marriage commitment be lifelong, unlike other commitments? Once again, commitments may be full and whole-hearted without being unconditional or permanent.

Committedness can be promoted in multiple ways. It is an error to overlook the role of other institutions in creating committed citizens. Citizens are not only made in marriage, but by schools and single parents, in friendships and larger affiliations. Bloom assumes that permanent commitments within sexual relationships are more fundamental to social cohesiveness than commitments in other settings. This is of course because male-female sex can produce children. But one parent—or three— can be just as committed as two. And a child can learn commitment through his teacher's attitude to her class, his mother's commitment to her career, or his sister's to social justice. Further, a child will only fully learn how to make and have a commitment by doing so, not simply by witnessing her parents' marriage. A child might join the Girl Scouts, pledge a loyalty oath to school or country, pledge "best friends for life" or "blood brothers," undertake a long-term project, join a team, or adopt a pet. Some of these activities might be institutionalized through schools, religions, workplaces, or other groups.

So far I have suggested that marriage is not necessary for the virtue of commitment; but it might be responded that what is important is that it does teach committedness, and that divorce undermines that lesson. But committedness is not unconditionally valuable. One can be committed to evil or harmful objects. It is as important that citizens evaluate their choices as that they persist in the ones they've made. If capriciousness and fickleness are vices, so too are obstinacy and rigidity, or a tendency to apathetic or passive, let alone resentful or bitter, acquiescence. Unconditional marriage commitment might create these vices in citizens who blindly, uncompromisingly, or unhappily stick to prudentially or morally bad choices.[41] The pressures of marriage, its reduced exit options or economic benefits, might keep spouses in bad situations out of apathy or fear. It might predispose them against living and acting independently or striving for better things. Or, the resentments of carrying out unfulfilling, unreciprocated, even detested obligations could provoke moralism, vindictiveness, and self-righteousness. Finally, unconditional commitment to marriage is disastrous if it encourages women to stay in abusive relationships. A sense of obligation cannot be a good if it encourages someone to submit to exploitation and abuse.

Rather than teaching virtue, unconditional commitment, especially in unequal marriages, may teach vice. If marriage incorporates hierarchy between spouses, or if economic dependence produces power inequality within it, it may, as John Stuart Mill wrote, become a "school of despotism," leading to social instability and undermining the virtues of citizenship.[42] Some studies have shown that girls raised within inequitably gender-structured families will be more tolerant of political injustice.[43]

Unconditional commitment to a family run on inequitable principles is no better than unconditional commitment to an unjust government, and learning obedience to unjust authority is a dangerous and deforming lesson. Ironically, the virtues of self-sacrificing altruism, which Hegel thought the family fosters in men, have been developed to their detriment in women lacking a sense of their own entitlements.

Once again, we should note the gap between the formal public commitment of marriage and internal dispositional commitment. Adhering to the formalities need not manifest, or teach, committedness. Conservatives like Bloom assume that the option to exit degrades or lessens the worth of marriage, making it contingent rather than an unconditional priority. But only the free choice to remain in a relationship demonstrates that partners do value it enough to choose it.

Arguments that marriage promotes virtues like committedness have been influential in recent political discourse. Marriage-promotion policies in the United States take commitment as an essential element of marriage and blame female and child poverty on male irresponsibility, which is to be remedied through marriage. Conservatives have blamed feminism, permissive divorce law, and premarital sex for creating irresponsible parents, rudderless children, and selfish citizens. But idealizing unconditional commitment is dangerous. It obscures the costs for women of being trapped in unequal marriages or with abusive husbands. It also focuses on the wrong links in the causal chain: Divorce and male irresponsibility create economic hardship for women only if women's economic status depends on marriage to men. Finally, many men may be prevented from supporting their children by poverty, not irresponsibility.

I have argued that the value of commitment depends on its object. In the next two chapters, I examine various alleged goods within marriage that could make the marital commitment valuable.

3

MARRIAGE, SEX, AND MORALS

[A] mutually faithful, monogamous relationship in the context of marriage is the expected standard of sexual activity.—U.S. Social Security Act[1]

Historically, marriage law has defined licit and illicit sex and reproduction—with harmful results for lesbians, gays, bisexuals, polyamorists, marital nonconformists, illegitimate children, and their mothers. Recent U.S. abstinence-until-marriage education and federal marriage promotion have sought, in public schools, through state governments and social workers, and with economic incentives, to re-entrench the idea that sex is only appropriate within marriage. (And, of course, where people of the same sex cannot marry, this doctrine implies all same-sex activity is unacceptable.) The stated public health goals of these policies could be better served by sex education than by abstinence education, and the stated intent of protecting children's interests could be better served by policies directly targeting children in poverty. This chapter does not assess these goals, but rather the claim that is within the purview of philosophy: Marriage is the precondition for morally permissible or virtuous sex.

I will address three influential arguments for a special moral relationship between sex and marriage. The first, drawn from Kant, takes a dark view of sex as objectifying and therefore a threat to human dignity, which marriage remedies by instituting juridical rights. Second, new natural lawyers, such as John Finnis, combine Kantian concerns about the dehumanizing effects of sex outside marriage with natural law arguments that certain basic human goods can be attained only within marriage. A third approach, taken by Roger Scruton, argues that marriage contributes to human flourishing by enabling the virtue of chastity. Marriage, Scruton argues, is a social practice that shapes sexual dispositions chastely and establishes a private sphere within which chaste erotic love can flourish.

As their historical lineages suggest, these lines of argument have been long-standing subjects of philosophical discussion; they are reviewed here in light of their resilience and influence. A study of marriage in philosophy would be incomplete without attention to them. In criticizing these views, I will develop a topic raised in the previous two chapters, the gap between public institutions and internal psychological states; I argue that the external legal framework of marriage cannot effect the changes in the agent's psychology that constitute respect, virtue, or love. Here I employ, against his own account and the others, Kant's distinction between justice, the external system of juridical rights, and virtue, the agent's inner willings. While marriage, as discussed in Chapter 2, may to some extent serve instrumental purposes of securing reciprocation, negotiating responsibilities, and invoking pressures on commitment, it cannot perform the moral "magic" of transforming spouses into virtuous agents. That requires their effort, not entry into the institutional framework.

The arguments considered here claim that marriage is morally transformative, in that it is the morally appropriate context for sex. To show that marriage is necessary for some moral transformation, an argument must show that either its legal or social recognition (or their conjunction) is necessary for it. Kant focuses on legal rights, while natural law and Scruton focus, to a greater extent, on social practices. But none of these arguments succeeds in showing that marriage is necessary or sufficient for the morally salient effects it is supposed to have. If marriage is not necessary or sufficient for respectful sex, basic human goods, or chastity, then the most influential philosophical attempts to distinguish it morally from unmarried cohabitation fail. Recall that I began with the question of whether marriage makes a moral difference. Here I argue that marriage is not universally and uniquely morally transformative; different marriages, in their specificity, bring different goods and evils, vices and virtues, which can also be found in unmarried relationships.

I. OBJECTIFICATION, SAFETY NETS, AND RESPECT

The dark view of sex focuses on its risks. This view surfaces in various contexts. For one, the U.S. Social Security Act prescribes that abstinence education teach that "sexual activity outside of the context of marriage is likely to have harmful psychological and physical effects."[2] Radical feminists have argued that sex is degrading or harmful to women in particular: "The social relation between the sexes is organized so that men may dominate and women must submit and this relation is sexual—in fact, is sex."[3] On this view, society defines women in terms of their sexuality and defines this sexuality as inherently submissive and passive; society objectifies women as sexual beings. In MacKinnon's epigrammatic statement: "Man fucks woman. Subject verb object."[4] The idea that women are treated in sex as less than fully human, in a way inconsistent with their moral personhood, links these contemporary feminists to Kant. Indeed, Kant's account of sexuality influenced Jean-Paul Sartre and Simone de Beauvoir, and through them, modern feminists.

For Kant, sex outside legal marriage is morally impermissible because both parties wrongly allow themselves to be used as mere means, whereas humanity should always be treated as an end. Unmarried sex violates the dignity of the human person by treating him or her as a mere object for use. The legal rights of marriage morally transform this use, making it permissible, but only, in Kant's own explanation, by permitting use; the marriage right is a "right to a person akin to a right to a thing," which simply allows a person to be treated as a thing without violating her humanity.[5]

Leaving aside the details of Kant's notorious account, the question is why marriage should be required, or how it could suffice, for respectful sex. I will consider two Kant-inspired arguments that marriage is the only permissible context for sex. The first, like Kant and the Social Security Act, focuses on the idea that marriage is a moral precondition for a risky activity. Sex risks unintended physical and psychological harm and vicious treatment, but the juridical rights and responsibilities of marriage create a "safety net." Marriage protects against the risks of sex, risks which—the argument must go—it would be impermissible to inflict without such a safety net. Marriage doesn't do away with the risks of sex—it simply provides a guarantee morally required in order to place someone in a position of vulnerability and risk. It enacts legal rights and responsibilities morally required for parties consenting to the sort of risks people run in sex: unintentional pregnancy, disease, heartbreak. Marriage, at least, provides financial protections against abandonment. The claim that marriage is required in order to run such risks suggests a strong principle that prohibits imposing risks such as pregnancy or disease without a promise of support.[6]

But this principle faces numerous counterexamples. We run physical risks comparable in gravity to pregnancy and sexually transmitted disease in other contexts (sports, workplaces, driving) without elaborate contracts. Surgery might seem to be a counterexample, since law provides for damages if someone is hurt. But this just goes to prove the point: Even if someone is permanently disabled, the most he can require is compensation, not a personal relationship, and the surgeon is only obligated if she is somehow at fault and if a harm actually occurs. Child support, not marriage, is analogous to such compensation; it only applies after the fact, if a child is conceived. These examples suggest that an institution like marriage is not necessary to permit risks of harm.

However, pregnancy does not merely involve costs and health risks to the pregnant woman, but the vulnerability of a third party—the child. Where reliable contraception is available, this risk is small. Rather than supporting abstinence, this rationale could suggest at most that biological parents would be morally required to marry if conception occurs and the woman chooses to bear the child. But children might be protected in a number of ways other than marriage; they might be reared by single parents or nonbiological parents. The question is what framework needs to be in place for child protection, and the answer, as I argue in Chapter 6.iii, is not obviously their biological parents' marriage.

But Kant's focus was not primarily on harmful consequences of sex, but on how sexual desire, as an appetite for a person, can obliterate moral regard. He writes that "carnal enjoyment is *cannibalistic* in principle.... [E]ach is actually a *consumable* thing...to the other," as, he adds, each can actually be harmed, in childbirth or through male sexual exhaustion.[7] Appetites such as hunger and thirst threaten to overwhelm reason, but sexual desire, unlike hunger (except for cannibals!), is an appetite for a person, and so affects moral judgment precisely where the treatment of a person is at stake. Sexual desire thus intrinsically involves, according to Kant, a failure of respect. Moreover, the strength of this desire might lead to further violations of rights. One might think that the marriage contract addresses these moral risks by creating legal rights and imposing obligations that require recognition of the other's moral status.

The intimacy of sex indeed poses special moral risks. It typically involves seclusion, exposure, and vulnerability. In some situations, such as (nonsexual) interactions with the postman or taxi driver, one can show respect simply by observing common courtesies: refraining from swearing, spitting, and so on, and saying "please" and "thank you." More intimate interactions require more effort and judgment to maintain respect: In friendship, one must delicately negotiate the limits of privacy, support, and closeness. As intimacy deepens, the possibility of certain vices—interferingness, cruelty, insensitivity—grows, and so the requirements of respect grow accordingly. For example, a lover may know her partner's secrets, so she must be careful not to betray them. The emotions associated with sex can be intense, requiring—as with reading a shy friend's poetry—sensitivity and honesty. Yet, one might think, with a lover as with a friend, one could negotiate these territories without a pledge of lifelong commitment or juridical rights. No formal rights are required—only, perhaps, solicitousness mingled with discreet reserve. A sexual relationship, however, is not, for Kant, like friendship; it involves an overpowering appetite for another person. Thus, there is moral need for a safety net. The normal measures one takes within friendship—tact, considerateness, and so on—simply aren't enough. The sexual drive is too powerful; the risks are too great.

However, marriage is not necessary to deter rape and abuse: Laws against these are already in place. Not only is it not necessary to deter, it is not sufficient, and in a gender-structured society may make abuse more likely by creating economic dependency and exempting spouses from sexual battery charges. The safety net argument fails. Better safety nets against unintentional pregnancy and disease are sex education and public health promotion; better protection against rape and abuse can be provided through the criminal law, social work, and shelters.

But it might be thought that marriage, by instituting juridical rights and responsibilities, morally transforms sexual objectification by creating the conditions necessary for respect.[8] Kant suggests that unmarried sex treats another as a mere means because sexual desire takes a person as an object to satisfy an appetite (Kant writes of discarding a sexual partner "as one throws away a lemon after sucking the juice from it").[9] Desire is thus intrinsically objectifying. We might question this dark view of sex: A good account of objectification is hard to find. What differentiates sex morally from massage or wrestling, for instance?[10] But let us set this issue aside.

One might think that sexual use—like other uses of a person as an object—would be permitted so long as the agent at the same time treats the other person as an end. After all, one uses the postman or the massage therapist as an object or a means to an end, but so long as one accords him respect, this is permissible. But Kant's view is that sexual use extends to possessing the entire person, and so the only way to treat one's sexual object as an end is to exchange equal rights of possession with him—that is, on Kant's analysis, to marry him. According to Kant, these rights make sex compatible with respect.

How might they do so? Marriage might ameliorate morally problematic objectification by instituting respect, that is, recognition of the other as an end, a source of legitimate claims. Pledging to take on another's welfare as one's own demonstrates concern for him as a being with his own needs, and not simply as a sexual object to be used and discarded. In a one-night stand, a lover can ignore her partner's welfare, but cannot do so quite so easily in a typical marriage. Nor can a sane person be unaware that his freely, legally contracted spouse is an independent person, an autonomous agent. This evokes Barbara Herman's charitable reconstruction of Kant: Marriage right establishes the juridical equality of spouses and so creates conditions necessary for respect. It "block[s] the transformation of regard that comes with sexual appetite" by "secur[ing] regard for one's partner as a person with a life, which is what the sexual appetite by itself causes one to disregard."[11]

Clearly, modern marriage is not necessary to see another as a juridical equal: This is already established by equal citizenship. Moreover, marriage isn't sufficient for treating another with respect or consideration. Spouses can and do commit grossly immoral acts against persons whom they recognize as juridical equals or as having needs. (Indeed, barring insanity, objectifiers must know that those whom objectify are not mere objects!)

But one might think that marriage transforms sex in a different way, by placing it into a context of legally secured shared goals, shared "happiness or misfortune, joy or displeasure."[12] One might think that in sex outside marriage, one can intend to use the other person for pleasure only; but if marriage has a purpose other than sex—child-rearing, home improvement—the maxim (the morally assessable principle under which we act, in Kant's theory) is relevantly altered. Sex becomes part of a larger project of a shared life. But why think that sexual maxims can only change through sharing ends? If maxims involving sex can be changed, they can be changed simply by viewing the other with respect. This can conceivably occur in a one-night stand as well as in a marriage. Sharing goals may or may not help. A can share a goal with B yet use B as a means only (for example, an army general and a private). Even if A's goal is B's good, this is still compatible with lack of respect, as in paternalism.[13]

In any case, not all spouses have their spouses' good as their end. The more general problem with this account is that juridical change, such as possessing a legal right or status, does not automatically change the internal content of maxims (as Kant puts it, a law cannot bring about a subject's having an end).[14] In one sense, of course, law can change the content of maxims: If I gain a property right over an object, my description of a course of action might change from "drive that car" to "drive my car"—making the difference between theft and permitted use. But the intention we are concerned with here, of treating a person as an object for mere use, does not automatically change when the other is redescribed as spouse. Respect for the other must be internal to the agent. Objectification is a psychological state, and hence not directly remediable through external structures of formal legal rights. Legal marriage does not create the psychological state constitutive of respect. Nor does the risk of sexual objectification entail that a special legal framework for sexual relationships is morally necessary. On a Kantian account, all that is required is respect. Marriage is neither morally required, nor sufficient, to transform objectification.

Kant's own distinction between justice and virtue clarifies a common problem for arguments for the transformative value of marriage, including his. Justice concerns coercively enforceable legal rights governing actions that affect others. Legal marriage is an institution of justice: It creates legal rights enforceable by the state. Virtue concerns psychological states internal to the agent, which cannot be brought about by external legislation—including marriage.

> Duties of virtue cannot be subject to external lawgiving simply because they have to do with an end which (or the having of which) is also a duty. No external lawgiving can bring about someone's setting an end for himself (because this is an internal act of the mind), although it may prescribe external actions that lead to an end without the subject making it his end.[15]

Institutions can shape our attitudes over time or nudge us toward certain choices and away from others, but they cannot transform agents' internal psychological states simply by entry into them. Law cannot institute virtue. This gap is problematic for Kant's as well as the following accounts of marriage as morally transformative.

II. NEW NATURAL LAW AND THE GOODS OF MARRIAGE

One of the most prominent arguments for the special value of marriage emerges from the natural law tradition associated with Aquinas, which holds that reason reveals basic human goods associated with our animal and human nature. Practical reason requires us to seek the good. Right action is action in accordance with reason, and wrong action frustrates or makes impossible the ends that reason gives us. Among the many basic human goods, there are special goods associated with sex, which, according to one natural law account, can only be obtained within marriage. This view holds that marriage is a necessary condition for permissible sex, because non-marital sex is not conducive to the goods of marriage and it habituates the agent in ways that impede his pursuit of the marital good.

A simplified natural law argument for marriage might run as follows: Sex is associated with the good of procreation, which encompasses child-rearing, and children need both parents; thus, sex can only properly achieve its good (and is thus only permissible) within a relation that commits both parents to child-rearing together. This relation is marriage, uniquely apt for conceiving and rearing children, and this purpose dictates its features—monogamous, different-sex, lifelong. Sex outside marriage or any nonprocreative sex frustrates this purpose, because it cannot lead to the marital good of procreation, and so is wrong. Sex is not just a tool for pleasure—which would involve objectifying, dehumanizing use of oneself and one's partner (the Kantian inheritance of new natural law)—but it must be open to the purpose that reason tells us is it has. And, since procreation defines marriage, same-sex marriage, which cannot naturally lead to procreation, is an impossibility.

This simplified argument provokes many objections. There are general problems with natural law's essentialism about the human good: Not everyone's reason discerns the same goods, and it is implausible that there is one set of basic goods for all humans, in their individual and cultural diversity. Historically, child-rearing has taken many forms, and has been done most often in extended or polygamous families. And even if reason were to reveal certain basic human goods, it's difficult to see why choosing otherwise (in self-regarding action) is morally wrong, rather than simply imprudent. Beyond these general problems, the simplified account above raises other questions. Does this natural law view entail that taking pleasure in sex is wrong? Doesn't the argument deployed against same-sex marriage imply that marriages between infertile men and women are similarly defective? If so, doesn't the view hold a double standard for infertile same-sex and different-sex partners?

New natural law defenses of marriage address these questions. John Finnis, taking a cue from Aquinas, argues that different-sex, monogamous marriage is the unique context not only for the good of procreation, but also for the good of "the mutual support and *amicitia* [friendship] of spouses who, at all levels of their being, are sexually complementary." Their "exclusive and permanent cooperative relationship" is characterized by "mutual self-giving" and shared domestic life as well as sexual difference.[16] This marital union—two people merging into one—is a basic human good that the biological unity of sexual intercourse expresses and that procreation "actualizes" (i.e., it makes the union actual in a child). So long as sex expresses marital union and is open to procreation (i.e., not contracepted), it is a reasonable use of the sexual capacities, taking pleasure in which is part of the marital good.

On this view, sex is good when it is part of the good of marriage. Sex oriented toward the goods of marriage—procreation and marital friendship—is not only permissible, it is valuable in itself because it instantiates and makes possible the goods of marriage. Taking pleasure in sex of this kind is apt. Natural law does not object to pleasurable sex, or even to sex performed for pleasure as part of the marital good; it objects to sex performed merely for pleasure, without aiming at the marital good. This kind of sex treats the sexual attributes instrumentally, as means to the end of pleasure, and violates the basic good of marriage.

This rules out any acts that cannot be open to procreation or express a sexually complementary union. Same-sex relationships—mere "imitations" of marriage—are unable to instantiate the marital goods of procreation or sexually complementary union.[17] (Artificial reproductive technology employing gamete donors would also fail to actualize the union of the spouses.) However, as infertile male-female couples cannot procreate, it would appear that their intercourse likewise fails to be open to procreation, and thus that such infertile "marriages" are also mere imitations of marriage. Finnis acknowledges that, by his reasoning, childless marriages are defective marriages ("a secondary...instantiation of the good of marriage"), but he argues that unlike same-sex partners, infertile different-sex spouses can still achieve a sexually complementary union. More opaquely, he claims that their sexual acts can still be open to procreation.[18] Intercourse between a man and woman, even when one or both is infertile, is, he says, reproductive in type, in that it is of the kind that issues in conception, even if it is not reproductive in effect. It is the same sort of action someone intending to procreate would do, although many such actions, even between fertile couples, do not result in pregnancy.[19] In contrast, same-sex activity is not reproductive in type, and thus same-sex relationships, even when loving and caring, lack the basic human goods associated with sex and so are as morally worthless as prostitution or masturbation.[20]

Not only are such nonmarital acts not conducive to the goods of marriage, they violate these goods by threatening their attainment for the agent and for others. Same-sex, unmarried, masturbatory, contracepted, and nonreproductive sexual acts psychologically damage the agent, diminishing his ability to attain the marital goods. Sex that cannot attain the marital goods uses the sexual capacities merely for pleasure and so treats them as instruments, not as part of an intrinsic good. Such acts also harm married couples who are merely innocent bystanders, if the prevalence of such acts leads spouses to condone them in theory. Merely condoning nonmarital sex damages spouses' capacity for marital commitment because, Finnis argues, it expresses a kind of hypothetical willingness to have sex for instrumental reasons: "[T]he thought 'It's OK for them' will convey the judgment that the conduct in question has some value." Completely excluding nonmarital sex "from the range of acceptable and valuable human options" is thus a precondition for true marital commitment.[21] In my view, this account of how extramarital sex threatens the married is unconvincing. One can promise to do some action while believing that one is not obligated to make the promise; the important belief is that the promise obligates. Similarly, one can commit oneself to a spouse, exclusively and permanently, while believing that it would be permissible not to do so. And one can judge that someone else's action is permissible, even that it has value for her (watching the Eurovision Song Contest, eating snails), without judging that it has any value for oneself.

There is a wide literature attacking new natural law accounts of sex and marriage; here I will present only a few points I find most telling. First of all, the view is draconian in its moral strictures. Moreover, because Finnis denies that there are basic human goods in nonmarital sex, his view implausibly consigns all nonmarital sex (including all contracepted sex) to the same value as anonymous sex, prostitution, or masturbation. As Macedo writes, it is "simplistic and implausible to portray the essential nature of *every form* of nonprocreative sexuality as no better than the least valuable form."[22] While I would not follow Macedo in judging certain forms of sex "least valuable"—different interactions might have different merits, and each should be judged on its own—the point is that even relatively conservative sexual moralities draw distinctions not purely based on procreation and sex difference. Goods— including basic human goods recognized by new natural law—such as "pleasure, communication, emotional growth, personal stability, long-term fulfillment" can be found in same-sex or unmarried relationships.[23]

Furthermore, new natural law does not consistently apply such exacting prescriptions regarding basic human goods and their frustration in other areas of life—it does not attack sedentary lifestyles and sugar consumption as violating the basic good of health, for example. This suggests a disproportionate focus on one set of basic goods—those involving sex.[24] New natural law accounts are also sometimes inconsistent in the application of their principles to same-sex activity, particularly regarding legal implications. Such accounts hold that marriage, as a legal and social institution, encourages us to make choices that will lead to basic human goods, and so law should exclude same-sex marriage, which cannot lead to those goods. But to the extent that natural law reasoning is taken to have legal implications regarding same-sex marriage, parity of reasoning implies that the law should also preclude divorce, contraception, nonmarital sex, extramarital sex, and nonprocreative sex acts between spouses. At the very least, the failure for opponents of same-sex marriage to pursue this agenda suggests an arbitrary focus on gays, lesbians, and bisexuals.[25] This double standard, like that regarding infertile couples, betrays an arbitrary bias against same-sex activity. Although new natural lawyers have tried to address the latter double standard by arguing that infertile different-sex spouses can have sex for the same reasons as the fertile, they simply cannot have sex for the motive of procreation if they know they cannot procreate.[26] When a woman has had a cancerous uterus or ovaries removed, or is already pregnant, for instance, there is no possibility of procreation; in what significant respect can she have "reproductive-type" sex or be open to procreation? Her only option is to hope for a miracle, an option equally available to same-sex partners. If a woman intends to get pregnant, she will not seek out a man who has had his testicles removed due to cancer; and if a man wants to conceive a child, he will not go about this by seeking out a woman who has had a hysterectomy. These are not reproductive-type acts.

Finally, the idea that only male-female sexual "union" can express the good of marital friendship raises more problems. As Macedo points out, procreative sex does not unite bodies but a sperm and an egg.[27] Moreover, the understanding of marital friendship relies on essentialist views regarding male and female sexual complementarity. Invoking such a complementarity between all men, on the one hand, and all women, on the other, inaccurately portrays sex difference. Sex differences are statistical generalizations; in reality, individuals—including intersexed individuals—fall along a continuum; the supposed complementarity is a caricature. Furthermore, as John Stuart Mill argued in *The Subjection of Women*, many such differences are social in origin, and we cannot infer natural differences so long as the influence of social conditioning cannot be excluded

in the case of women, a hot-house and stove cultivation has always been carried on of some of the capabilities of their nature, for the benefit and pleasure of their masters. Then, because certain products of the general vital force sprout luxuriantly and reach a great development in this heated atmosphere and under this active nurture and watering, while other shoots from the same root, which are left outside in the wintry air, with ice purposely heaped all round them, have a stunted growth, and some are burnt off with fire and disappear; men, with that inability to recognise their own work which distinguishes the unanalytic mind, indolently believe that the tree grows of itself in the way they have made it grow, and that it would die if one half of it were not kept in a vapour bath and the other half in the snow.[28]

Most importantly, friendship, love, and faithfulness are psychological and emotional states, and their characteristic attitudes do not depend on the biology of the parties. Nor do they depend on legal frameworks or external institutions. To reassert Kant's distinction between justice and virtue, friendship, trust, loyalty, identification, and mutual care and concern can exist outside marriage. The institution of marriage is not necessary for them, nor is it sufficient for them.

III. THE ALLEGED VIRTUE OF CHASTITY

Like the new natural lawyers, Roger Scruton argues that marriage makes possible distinctive sexual goods, but his account focuses on chaste erotic love, not procreative sexuality. On his view, marriage shapes individual dispositions so as to contribute to individual flourishing, and it enables virtuous flourishing by protecting chaste erotic love. My response to this account will once again turn on the gaps between the psychological states of virtue and flourishing, and the external framework of marriage.

Institutions play an important role in virtue ethics. They can shape our preferences and expectations, promoting virtuous or vicious dispositions. They also create the social world, carving it up so as to mark off areas of life, such as public and private spheres, appropriate for the exercise of certain dispositions. In *After Virtue*, Alasdair MacIntyre writes that institutions, by providing incentives of external goods, such as wealth and power, sustain practices which incorporate internal goods or excellences; participating in these practices, in turn, fosters virtue.[29] Scruton's argument that marriage enables *eudaimonia* or flourishing suggests that marriage sustains, through external goods such as economic benefits, a practice of sexual exclusivity that makes possible the virtue of chastity.[30]

Scruton's account begins with his analysis of sexual desire as a desire for interaction with an individualized object. Sexual desire seeks "interpersonal intentionality," a responsiveness from a particular other. Its end or *telos* is erotic love, a component of human flourishing: To "receive and give this love is to achieve something of incomparable value in the process of self-fulfillment." Erotic love provides an identity-confirming recognition: "[I]n erotic love the subject becomes conscious of the full reality of his personal existence, not only in his own eyes, but in the eyes of another."[31]

The capacity for erotic love is, according to Scruton, fragile. He argues that "misuses" of our sexual attributes can destroy it, and hence our ability to flourish. These "misuses" are vicious because they impede flourishing; they include (he argues) sexual fantasy, "obscenity," pornography, prostitution, "homosexuality," masturbation, promiscuity, and "perversion." Flourishing requires that we habituate ourselves to desire as reason requires—chastely. This is where marriage comes in. By offering an expected standard for sexual activity, it provides a social endorsement of virtuous sexuality. It also creates the privacy that, on Scruton's view, is needed for erotic love.

Scruton sees marriage as providing a social shield for erotic love, carving out the private realm love needs and prompting respect from third parties. Love "demand[s] recognition…from the surrounding world, which might otherwise threaten [its] exclusiveness, or rebel against the unfair privilege which every love contains." Scruton says that those who think that "if the obligations of love are private, they need no public institution to protect them" are making "a serious mistake about the character of civil society." Society puts a "public pressure" on individuals, judging them, but marriage socially excludes others, removing their judging gaze; it "brings inquisition to a close, and fills the resulting silence with an unspoken answer."[32] The idea seems to be that society is nosy, envious, interfering, and hypercritical, and that the harpies who make it up will destroy loving relationships (put them under "inquisition," treat the lovers as "fair game") unless they are recognized as marriages, in which case the gossip, attempts at home-wrecking, and so on, will immediately stop.

Now it might seem that even if marriage is effective at stopping the gossip and seduction attempts, this argument would only show the need for a social, not a legal, institution of marriage.[33] But Scruton presses the point that "it is…necessary for the state to join in the institution.… Only an institution which imposes a single, invariable obligation on all who elect to join it can create this public recognition, by making clear that the meaning of the individual action is to be found, not in the private desire which prompted it, but in the public custom which gives it form."[34] Indeed, to impose a "single, invariable obligation" state involvement is required; otherwise, religious and secular marriage providers might spring up everywhere, offering a smorgasbord of marriages. The state is in a position to legitimate a single form of marriage. But the question is whether such uniformity is indeed beneficial.

Scruton's thought is that by getting people to recognize marriage, the state "*creates* the private…the space from which others are excluded," and that erotic love requires this privacy. Flourishing is in jeopardy outside legal marriage, thanks to society's judging gaze. But even if society's gaze is harmful, marriage alone does not avert it. Scruton's metaphors of watching mislead: What kind of space is the private?

Property rights and rights against trespassing and voyeurism, a heated room of one's own, are the preconditions for privacy—and they don't come with marriage! The most important kind of privacy depends on material conditions, not marriage.

Scruton ignores the material conditions for intimacy to argue that marriage is a psychological condition for intimacy, creating "legitimate exclusion."[35] The idea, again, is that busybodies will not censor, or nose about, the married, as they will the unmarried, that *femmes* or *hommes fatales* will not seek to horn in, and that spouses will feel entitled to keep others out. But this seems, for one thing, optimistic (marriage is not going to stop all those trouble-makers). Moreover, the judging gaze of society will differ considerably depending on the context: In small-town Alabama people may fuss about an unmarried couple, but not in New York City. In many contexts, marriage is not necessary for privacy.

Nor is it clear that erotic love and flourishing need such privacy. Lovers more robust in the face of public opinion might be more virtuous, more apt to flourish and stable in their dispositions, than those whose relationships are so fragile that they need a social barrier against curiosity, jealousy, and encroachment. And recall Plato's worries about the potential for division in separating the married couple from society. Desperate housewives stranded without community in suburban single-family dwellings might flourish more with less privacy.

Most importantly, Scruton, like the new natural lawyers, ignores the abuse that occurs within marriages. Scruton says that society's judging gaze, which marriage excludes, is, when turned inward, the root of the moral sense. He thinks it a desirable effect of marital privacy that people avert their moral gaze from the married. But the idea that marriage is removed from society's judging gaze is chilling from a feminist perspective sensitive to the historical exclusion of the private sphere from justice. That it removes the public gaze, if it does, is a reason against marriage; some aspects of some erotic love relationships—violence, abuse, subordination—need judging.

The privacy argument attempts to show that a married relationship can flourish as an unmarried one cannot, and so that marriage is transformative. This fails. But Scruton has a second argument that makes marriage instrumental to, not required for, flourishing. This is that marriage is a shared practice whose value as a form of social life consists in shaping dispositions virtuously, and, by reducing exit options, seconding virtue by constraining spouses to remain. It is "a tradition—a smooth handle on experience...worn...into the shape required by human nature," and also "a story" which informs our expectations and creates recognition of familiar forms of life.[36] The idea (shared with some new natural lawyers) is that the familiarity of marriage guides us to seek it; the institution disposes people to seek the kind of relationship that will allow them to flourish.

But does marriage really promote erotic love? Will a society with an institution of different-sex, monogamous marriage have more erotic love relationships than one without? Not only received wisdom but biological and social science support the view that, whatever marriage is good for, it is not particularly good at sustaining sexual desire across a lifetime.[37] Nor does Scruton's ideal relationship justify only current marriage law: Presumably erotic love could flourish in a variety of institutions, such as limited-term marriages, marriages without property arrangements, same-sex marriage, and polygamy. Michael Bayles, who gives an account similar to Scruton's, admits that neither of his arguments "supports monogamous [as opposed to polygamous] marriage per se. Logically, the objection is quite correct. But it is a misunderstanding of social philosophy to expect arguments showing that a certain arrangement is always best under all circumstances."[38] However, the viability of alternate institutions is at issue because people *do* seek the recognition of, and claim to flourish only in, such alternative forms.

The fundamental question is whether humans flourish in only one kind of relationship. Where erotic love is concerned, it is more plausible to think that a thousand different kinds of flower may bloom—that is, people flourish in many different ways. Problems arise with Scruton's essentialist claims about sex and the human good, as they did with new natural law. Scruton is slippery on the grounds for these claims: Sexual desire, he writes, is "a social artefact," yet one "natural to human beings."[39] Moreover, the case for the connection between chastity and flourishing is weak. Philosophically, understanding sexual desire as desire for "interpersonal intentionality" rather than simply for sexual stimulation is controversial.[40] Empirically, anthropology and observation suggest that humans can be happy in a wide range of love relationships. A Don Juan or Savonarola might flourish without erotic love. If so, we have an argument—explored in the next chapter—against current marriage law modeled on Mill's *On Liberty*: By prescribing one form of relationship for all, current marriage law inhibits experiments in living and thereby limits the flourishing of some individuals.

On Scruton's view, flourishing is limited to chaste different-sex erotic love relationships. Thus someone with strong desires for members of the same sex cannot fully experience erotic love in a same-sex relationship; but if this is her only route to sexual satisfaction, it's difficult to see why she should care about erotic love, as Scruton defines it. Scruton defends Aristotelian virtue ethics because it can explain why agents should be motivated to be virtuous—because their flourishing is at stake. But he cannot explain why those with strong same-sex or polyamorous desires should be motivated by his account.

Scruton's arguments that erotic love must be exclusive and between different-sex partners are particularly weak. His argument against same-sex activity is that "interpersonal intentionality" requires an object different from oneself. But members of the same sex differ in many ways, just as men and women can be similar. Scruton's reasoning might also seem to suggest that erotic love requires a partner of a different race or ethnicity, class, intellectual background, and so on. His argument for exclusivity depends on the perishability of the capacity for erotic love: Scruton suggests that too many sexual encounters or fantasies will numb the agent, making her unfit for love.[41] But it seems possible for a promiscuous agent to preserve her capacities for love; much depends on how it is done, as a virtue account should realize. Humans have different capacities, and needs, for love, variety, and exclusivity. Once again, this suggests the psychological and emotional costs, for those not fitting the model, of a one-size-fits-all practice of marriage. Add to these the costs of reduced exit options if one spouse is abusive—or if the parties are simply ill-matched and becoming vicious (deceptive, irascible, controlling) as a result. Even happy marriages might promote vices: partiality, emotional dependence, possessiveness. If the goal of marriage law is to nudge people toward flourishing, current law does not seem the best way to achieve this.

Arguments for the transformative power of marriage fail because they fail to respect the distinction between justice and virtue. No external law or social pressure can compel agents to adopt virtuous ends, or any ends, as their own. Thus, the institution of marriage can serve as a model only. Entering it will not necessarily transform one's attitudes, nor is it needed for agents to adopt virtuous attitudes.

The value of marriage can be, at most, only to guide agents to choose as a virtuous person would and to reinforce virtue by constraining spouses to remain. Marriage certainly does put certain external incentives in place. But it is odd to see these as supporting virtues: On this model, a spouse is kept from vice like Ulysses tied to the mast—the costs of exiting marriage may not diminish his nonvirtuous desires, but only impede his acting on them. The virtuous agent should choose the act as valuable in itself, and not for its external benefits.

Virtue-ethical defenses of institutions must be grounded in claims about their long-term effects, not immediate transformations. They thus cannot distinguish unmarried and married relationships. But it is true that institutions over time shape dispositions and carve the social world. My response to these less direct defenses of marriage is twofold. Individuals flourish in many different kinds of relationships, and their sexual activity is permissible so long as they treat their (consenting, adult) partners with care and respect. Guiding everyone into one relationship model is a recipe for misery, not flourishing. There are reasons to promote self-control in sexual matters: preventing disease and unwanted pregnancy, and guarding against objectification, sex addiction, or victimizing behavior. But these goals do not require monogamous marriage. They are better served by sex education, which allows citizens to make informed choices, than by abstinence education, which is more likely to lead to unhealthy shame, fear, and reluctance to talk to doctors, counselors, or police. Virtue accounts also tend to ignore the costs of marriage—the harms it may protect and the vices it may create.

Second, as I explain in Part Two, while I have engaged with new natural law and virtue accounts on their own terms here, political liberalism precludes framing legal institutions on the basis of claims about virtue and flourishing. We will have to look elsewhere for a political justification of marriage.

4

SPECIAL TREATMENT FOR LOVERS
MARRIAGE, CARE, AND AMATONORMATIVITY

I have argued that marriage does not produce a unique moral transformation or promote civic or sexual virtues, and that the institution has costs for individual members—burdens on exit, inegalitarian gender roles, spousal violence, a restrictive one-size-fits-all relationship model. But it might be thought that marriage promotes something else of value and that a reformed institution could minimize its costs. Marriage might be thought valuable in promoting an idealized caring relationship. Hegel, for instance, thought it created altruistic attitudes transcending self-interest. Are such caring relationships valuable, and does marriage promote them?

In this chapter, I will focus on caring relationships characterized by intimacy— close particular knowledge between parties. I will begin with a brief review of care ethics; distancing myself from that view, I offer reasons to think that care within relationships is an important, sometimes necessary, constituent of right action therein. I offer an account of care's value that can be accepted by a range of moral theorists. At the same time, I emphasize that this value is contingent: Care is valuable only in the context of justice.

I then turn to assessing the question of whether marriage is a valuable institution in that it promotes such caring relationships. However, current marriage does a poor job of such promotion. Not all marriages are caring. Even where an ideal of mutual care prevails, many actual marriages involve abuse and unidirectional caring. In addition, current marriage undermines caring relationships with others, outside the nuclear family. On this basis, I criticize marriage and the associated romantic dyad ideal as "amatonormative." Current marriage is not valuable because it promotes care—rather, it jeopardizes caring relations that do not fit the norm. However, an institution that promoted all caring relationships, in conjunction with justice, would be valuable. Finally, I address some long-standing worries about the compatibility of care with contractual negotiation.

I. CARE ETHICS

Contemporary care ethics offers rich resources for theorizing care. Care ethics is one branch of feminist moral theory, controversial among feminists, in part because it emphasizes traditionally feminine qualities used to exploit women's labor. In this section, I briefly survey its development in order to set the stage for my own account of the value of care, which is intended to be compatible with a range of moral theories.

Following Virginia Held, I understand care as involving emotion and action: It commingles caring about, taking a benign interest in someone, and caring for, acting to meet her needs and promote her well-being.[1] While some material "care" could be carried out impersonally by robots or bureaucrats, care, in this discussion, is personal; personal engagement gives the carer particular knowledge of the other needed to meet her needs and promote her well-being. The affective component of care, while not necessary for all caregiving work, influences how such work is done: consistently and enthusiastically or sporadically and resentfully, solicitously or indifferently. The activity of caring involves caregiving labor; it is a practice, or set of learned skills, not simply instinct.[2] While care takes many forms, including that of parents, lovers, friends, or aid workers, "all care involves attentiveness, sensitivity, and responding to needs."[3]

Care ethics originated as revaluation of (supposedly) female qualities in response to moral theories that took a (supposedly) male perspective as the norm. Psychological research done by Carol Gilligan purported to show that in considering moral dilemmas women attend to narrative context, particularities, and relationships, whereas men judge from generalized principles. Gilligan and subsequent care ethicists argued that women's perspectives had been excluded from moral theory, which utilized typically male abstract, generalized, principled reasoning. Early care ethics stressed oppositions between care and justice, the particular and the general, relatedness and independence, emotion and reason.[4]

Whether gendered distribution of the qualities attributed to men and women is innate or socially conditioned, and whether these attributions are even accurate, has occasioned much debate. But the claim that moral theory should pay more attention to care and relationships need not presuppose anything about sex difference. The key point is that moral philosophy has undervalued human interdependence, emotions such as empathy, and an epistemic stance marked by attention to particularity, and that it should correct this exclusion.

The earliest sustained philosophical articulation of care ethics, Nel Noddings's *Caring*, rejected moral principles entirely and made caring motivation the sole criterion of moral action: Action "is right or wrong according to how faithfully it was rooted in caring...in a genuine response."[5] Noddings focused on the affective aspect of care, defined as an emotional response, occurring spontaneously in natural caring relationships, and characterized by perception of particular others in the context of their lives. This perception of the other prompts the carer to act "as though in my own behalf, but in behalf of the other."[6]

This emphasis on emotional responsiveness to a particular other prompted Noddings to reject universal moral principles on the grounds that they obscure the particular needs of particular individuals. Another early statement of care ethics, Sara Ruddick's *Maternal Thinking*—which takes mothering as the moral paradigm—similarly argued that abstract principles deflect attention from concrete individuals and can thereby "justify" harm, for example, by reducing persons to military units.[7] Within care ethics, an emphasis on the particular, or concrete, other emerged from attacks on the "generalized" other of moral theory.[8] Moral theory centered on the particular other sees individuals as valuable by virtue of their particularity—their concrete histories, situations, and attributes—and focuses on meeting their specific needs. In contrast, moral theory centered on the generalized other sees persons as valuable on account of their shared features, such as rationality, autonomy, or sentience. To critics, such generalizations obscure what is truly valuable and impede moral action by obscuring, not revealing, the other. To such critics, the veil of ignorance in Rawls's contract, for instance, does not truly universalize, because it excludes individual differences.

These early contributions illuminate the potential dangers in an ethic solely of care. General rules for treating generalized others provide guidelines for treating others as certain sorts of beings—respecting them because they are autonomous, refraining from causing them pain because they are sentient. Noddings's understanding of care as the sole, unprincipled criterion of morality results in a dangerous subjectivism: A carer may provide alcohol to an alcoholic to save him from short-term suffering. Someone might object that a caring person would consider the alcoholic's best interests. However, this assumes an objective measure of well-being. Because Noddings's caring directs the carer to take on the other's ends, moral action is determined by whatever the cared-for happens to value. If right action is defined in terms of care, and care is defined as response to another person's ends, then right action becomes subjective, dependent on individual perceptions of value. Ruddick corrected this by defining care in terms of objective maternal goals such as preservation and growth. Other care ethicists, such as Held, focus on objective outcomes such as well-being.

However, even with an objective account of well-being, principles are still required to guide moral action. Harm can be done by caring but ignorant or impulsive or presumptuous or overly imaginative agents as well as by uncaring principled ones. Individuals have interests in making certain decisions themselves. Care may prompt paternalistic (or maternalistic) infringement on autonomy. For instance, a carer might disclose information about her friend's state of health to his co-workers thinking it is in his best interests, or she might decide not to tell her father that he is terminally ill. Someone might object that a caring person would consider her father's interest in knowing the truth and respect her friend's interest in making her own decisions. But this response suggests that care presupposes respecting autonomy, building a principled constraint into care.

While care ethics critiques the ideal of autonomy understood as atomistic independence, feminist accounts of relational autonomy allow that competent adults have an interest in having significant options and making certain choices for themselves.[9] This interest implies that care should motivate respect for competent adults in making certain decisions themselves. But the account of which decisions deserve such respect comes from outside care—from theories of relational autonomy.

There are other reasons to supplement care with principles drawn from outside care. Moral principles stave off some possibilities of self-deception. Care may be mingled with conflicting, intense emotions that can prompt self-deceived action not truly in the cared-for's best interests. Also, care contains no guidelines for fairness. Noddings suggests that agents should offer care to everyone they encounter, but not that they should actively seek to encounter people who might need it. Care rooted in response to particular others cannot respond to injustice so long as the injustice remains distant. Some degree of abstract concern is necessary to bring a privileged individual to act on behalf of the worse-off in different parts of the country or globe. Caring only for those whom one encounters creates lacunae in moral consciousness. To address social inequalities and the distant effects of our actions, care must be supplemented with an account of fairness and universal equal worth.

The importance of justice can be seen when we consider the injustices wrought by excluding justice from the family. Certain interests—freedom from abuse, civil rights—demand protection. And care without reciprocity-requiring fairness can exploit the carer. But a carer can acknowledge the need for justice: A morally educated desire for the good of another will entail a desire to respect her rights and treat her fairly, though one may have to look outside care to learn what that involves. The dichotomy between care and justice is misguided.[10]

II. CARE'S VALUE

Care is not sufficient for right action, but it may be important, even necessary, for it. In this section I offer an account of the moral value of care in intimate relationships.

Care helps agents, motivationally and epistemically, to fulfill general moral duties and special obligations of relationship.

Most moral theories recognize general duties to meet the needs and promote the good of others. There are also special obligations in close relationships, explained by moral principles such as reliance, gratitude, and fidelity. If Sally tacitly and knowingly leads her friend to rely on her through repeated interaction, she gains obligations to fulfill his expectations unless she explicitly repudiates them and he makes other arrangements. Caring relationships typically lead parties to expect that the other will promote their well-being. Thus, promoting the well-being of the other is typically an obligation within relationships. Further, when parties lead each other to believe that they are committed to the relationship, inducing reliance, they must give it deliberative priority. For example, a partner considering whether to accept a job offer in a far-off city should consider the effect on the relationship.

Obligations of relationship depend on context and history. One does not owe special consideration to just anyone who cares about one—care may be unwanted or boundary-violating. On the other hand, a jaded spouse, who no longer cares, will continue to be obligated. Some obligations created in relationships depend on intimacy or shared projects and dissolve when the relationship ends. But obligations of gratitude, reciprocity, and reliance may trail off rather than stopping cold.

Care motivates agents to fulfill such obligations and to respond to the needs of others and promote their well-being. It prompts agents to care about the good of others as if it were their own. In times of stress and pressure, it may provide a powerful countervailing motive to temptations to neglect. Care also helps agents avoid moral risks specific to intimate relationships, prompting parties to weigh each other's interests when shared daily existence constantly brings their interests into conflict.

As a motivation to promote another person's well-being, within the bounds of fairness, care can be recognized as valuable by consequentialists and some deontologists. Kant raises a troubling challenge to the claim that care is a source of moral motivation.[11] On his view, only acting from duty will unerringly result in right action; emotions are unreliable, and moral agents are prone to self-deception. But morally educated care contains a desire to do one's duty by the cared-for, so that morally educated care can include the motivation of duty. The sympathetic philanthropist in Kant's famous example could have been acting from duty all along, if his philanthropy expressed what he thought was the right thing to do when sympathy prompted him to help. But this internal connection between care and morality can fail if it is not fully grasped or if duty and the cared-for's well-being conflict. Once again, this points to the need for care to be complemented by principles of justice and fairness.

Care has epistemic as well as motivational value. Caring relationships involve intimate knowledge of the other. As moral agents, we are constantly limited by our inability to perceive others' particularities. The best one can do, often, is to conjecture. This inability diminishes as intimacy increases. Intimate knowledge is not just recognition of the other as a particular self with her own interests, but knowledge of the details of her body, history, psychology, and so on. Intimacy familiarizes parties with each other's hidden desires and needs and the complex bases of their well-being. Such knowledge enables carers to carry out duties to meet others' needs and promote their well-being. Some such duties may only be carried out with intimate knowledge. Relationships provide knowledge that is ordinarily inaccessible, and shared experience over time deepens it. Caring relationships with others enable unusual fine-tuning of right action to particular circumstances.

Moral judgments in particular cases require full apprehension of the context, of all the features that are morally relevant. Seeing another in her particularity is essential to understanding how to treat her. Intimate relationships are the best case for the moderate moral particularist view that right action involves fine-tuned judgments in particular circumstances. As intimacy deepens, promoting another's well-being and meeting her needs becomes more complex as one appreciates her complexity. As well, shared history and ongoing interdependence contribute additional considerations, so that interactions bristle with morally salient details. This is not to reject universal principles. In cases involving very fine judgment, so that principles cannot guide action, universalism expresses that one should act likewise in relevantly like circumstances. But within relationships laden with history and knowledge of the other, there might, indeed, never be circumstances that are relevantly similar, and this suggests a pressing need for detail-oriented attentiveness and judgment. These points are drawn from Martha Nussbaum's discussion of particularism, especially in the novels of Henry James. For James, she writes, the "highest and hardest task is to make ourselves people 'on whom nothing is lost'" that is, people of unbiased and full awareness.[12]

In concrete situations with complex shared histories and mutual intimate knowledge, it may require a good deal of investigation and deliberation to work out how universal moral principles apply. In such situations, the methodology of applying a universal rule is likely to be inadequate. If the universal principle proscribes harm, what counts as harm? What if harm is mingled with good, or if all alternatives harm, or there are different kinds of harm at stake? And how can applying a principle show us how to promote the well-being of another when that involves fostering a complex individuality and is more an act of creativity than rule-following? Given such complexities, David McNaughton writes that the "only method of arriving at correct moral conclusions in new cases will be to develop a sensitivity in moral matters which allows one to see each particular case aright. Moral principles appear to drop out as, at best, redundant and at worst, as a hindrance to moral vision."[13]

The particularist emphasis on attentive judgment as opposed to rule-following is most apt in close relationships with subtle, nuanced decisions. Once again, such judgment must be constrained by justice; respecting rights, ideally, becomes part of the background of such relations. But care is valuable within such relationships motivationally and epistemically, and, as responsiveness to the particular other, it may even be necessary in cases requiring particularist judgment. Caring relationships, then, are valuable as generators of morally supportive motives and opportunities for uniquely fine-grained moral action. Moreover, because they allow such fine-grained meeting of needs and promoting of happiness, they may create great well-being. At the same time, they can also become sites of uncommon cruelty, and the resources contributed to the relationships may tax other duties, such as helping strangers; their value must be weighed against these costs.

This analysis of care's value would allow us to attribute a conditional value to marriage insofar as it promotes caring relationships—conditioned on those relationships being just—but current marriage does not efficiently promote caring relationships. Many actual marriages are care-deficient. They involve abuse or unidirectional caring. Care is gendered; between men and women care may characteristically be asymmetric. Care within gender-structured marriage may result in exploitation of the female caregiver, whose care is unreciprocated. Moreover, caregiving may emerge from oppression: When women depend on men economically, they may have little choice but to act caringly. When care is exploited, the relationship does not meet the justice condition.

Moreover, marriage and the associated ideal of a dyadic love relationship undermine caring relationships with outsiders. Legally and conceptually, dyadic marriage and amorous partnerships create the conditions for a separation of individuals from the community. Care ethicists and communitarians criticize liberal individualism as undermining caring relations in society, but insularity of care may do the same. Communitarians and care ethicists fear society becoming a marketplace of atomistic, mutually uncaring individuals; but this can be contrasted with other dystopias, of small, jealously defended communal outposts, or a marketplace of atomistic, mutually uncaring dyadic units. As Plato suggested, dyadic marriage creates the conditions for a separation of individuals from the community. The nuclear family shuts members off physically from others in single-family homes and weakens other social bonds. Marriage marks off spouses from friends, family, and acquaintances, creating psychological conditions for division; in doing so, it can simply extend the scope of selfishness to embrace the spouse, rather than quelling selfishness. The retreat into marriage may enable, not cure, the alleged pathology of contemporary American culture, the investment of the self in the private, at the cost of public, goods or public engagement.[14] Marriage is arguably a paradigmatic form of retreat from the public, not a solution to social disconnectedness.

This compromises arguments that caring relationships in marriage support the state. Hegel argued that marriage habituated citizens to trust others and identify with a common good. Rawls's account of stability in *A Theory of Justice* holds that family attachments foster attachment to the principles of justice: "[O]nce the attitudes of love and trust, and of friendly feelings and mutual confidence, have been generated...then the recognition that we and those for whom we care are the beneficiaries of an established and enduring just institution tends to engender in us the corresponding sense of justice."[15] But partiality toward loved ones may also subvert justice. As Plato suggested, excessive care for one's own may cause the sacrifice of public goods and public life for private. This is a problem for Rawls where families interfere with equal opportunity by giving children unequal starting-points in life.[16] Marriage need not motivate spouses to seek the common good, and in fact it provides conflicting motivations.

However, there is a more important way in which current marriage, and the relationship ideal it promotes, threatens care.

III. AMATONORMATIVITY: HOW MARRIAGE THREATENS CARE

Aristophanes's myth of the origins of love in Plato's *Symposium* is refreshingly free of heterosexism. At the dawn of time, humans were rather like Siamese twins, with two bodies joined together; the gods split us apart, and erotic love is the search for our other half, a longing quelled only temporarily by sex. Some of these original beings were composed of two men joined together, some of two women, and some of one man and one woman, and this initial pairing determines whether our desire is same- or different-sex (the story cannot account for bisexuality!). But while this myth places same-sex and different-sex desire on the same footing, it elevates a dyadic, sexual love relationship above all others. To this extent, the story is amatonormative.

Just, caring relationships should be recognized as valuable, to the extent that they are valuable, whether in or out of marriage, and whatever form they take. But marriage promotes one form of caring relationship at the expense of many others. Our culture focuses on dyadic amorous relationships at the cost of recognizing friendships, care networks, urban tribes, and other intimate associations. Laura Kipnis points out that "we moderns" see "love as vital plasma," to a historically unusual degree.[17] The belief that marriage and companionate romantic love have special value leads to overlooking the value of other caring relationships. I call this disproportionate focus on marital and amorous love relationships as special sites of value, and the assumption that romantic love is a universal goal, "amatonormativity": This consists in the assumptions that a central, exclusive, amorous relationship is normal for humans, in that it is a universally shared goal, and that such a relationship is normative, in that it *should* be aimed at in preference to other relationship types.[18] The assumption that valuable relationships must be marital or amorous devalues friendships and other caring relationships, as recent manifestos by urban tribalists, quirkyalones, polyamorists, and asexuals have insisted. Amatonormativity prompts the sacrifice of other relationships to romantic love and marriage and relegates friendship and solitudinousness to cultural invisibility.

The coinage "amatonormativity" is modeled on the term "heteronormativity," which refers to the assumption of heterosexuality and gender difference as prescriptive norms. Because heteronormativity normalizes the gender roles that define heterosexuality, as well as heterosexuality itself, its critique emerges from feminist as well as queer theory. Critique of heteronormativity calls into question a wide range of social institutions, because sexuality and gender are assumed throughout the social system. Such critique attempts to make visible the cultural prevalence and effects of such assumptions. Heteronormativity not only marginalizes gays, lesbians, and bisexuals. It also marginalizes single parents by assuming that the reproductive family contains opposite-sex biological parents. "Compulsory heterosexuality" undermines strong relationships between women by drawing women's attention magnetically to their male partners.[19] Some critics of heteronormativity argue that the exclusive, dyadic relationship is a heterosexual ideal. Thus, marriage law that recognizes only exclusive dyads is heteronormative even if it recognizes same-sex marriage, and so heteronormativity marginalizes adult care networks.

To the extent that exclusive, dyadic relationships are a heterosexual ideal, amatonormativity overlaps with heteronormativity. Like heteronormativity, it can be found throughout social life, and it can be understood in relation to other systems of oppression, for example in its relation to gender roles (e.g., the stereotype of the single male differs from that of the single female, and men and women are understood as needing marriage for different reasons). Heteronormativity can be understood through considering what counts as violating it: the subversion of gender roles or displays of same-sex sexuality.[20] Violations of amatonormativity would include dining alone by choice, putting friendship above romance, bringing a friend to a formal event or attending alone, cohabiting with friends, or not searching for romance.

Through systematic discrimination, amatonormativity discourages investment in other kinds of caring relationships. Adults whose lives do not fit the amatonormative norm face discrimination, which benefits members of central, exclusive, sexual love relationships. Amatonormative discrimination is widely practiced. Its existence is not controversial. What is controversial is the claim that it is wrongful discrimination and not simply justified differential treatment—that it is arbitrary and hence, at least in law, unjust. I argue, first, that amatonormative judgments are false, and second, that discrimination on their basis is morally wrong for some of the same reasons that racial and sexual discrimination is wrong. It might be thought that, unlike racism and sexism, amatonormativity has relatively insignificant costs; to deflect this objection, I will begin by reviewing its costs.

a. Amatonormativity: Whom It Privileges, Whom It Penalizes, and How

Amatonormativity wrongly privileges the central, dyadic, exclusive, enduring amorous relationship associated with, but not limited to, marriage. By "central," I mean the relationship is prioritized by the partners over other relationships and projects. Such relationships tend to be characterized by sexual exclusivity, domesticity, and shared property, but need not be: Couples who maintain an enduring amorous relationship but refrain from sex, maintain separate domiciles, or keep their property disentangled, can still be recognized socially as amorous partners. Conversely, two friends who have sex, live together, or share property would not be privileged by amatonormativity if the friends did not present themselves as romantic partners. Thus, legal marriage, sex, shared domicile, or shared property are not necessary conditions for privilege; an amorous, enduring, central love relationship is. While marriage is not necessary for privilege, it is usually sufficient for it. While amorous love, endurance, and centrality are jointly sufficient for privilege, no one of these features is independently sufficient. A brief, amorous summer fling or extramarital affair would not be privileged, and friendships may be central and enduring but still not privileged.

Such amorous relationships are wrongly privileged over friendships, and their members wrongly privileged over "singles" (by which I mean the socially single, or "uncoupled," not the legally unmarried). Friendships and adult care networks are not accorded the social importance of marriages or marriage-like relationships, nor are they eligible for the legal benefits of marriage. However, for many people, friendships play a similar role in their lives, and have the same importance to them, as marriages or amorous relationships do for others. For some people, these friendships are explicitly seen as replacing, and preferable to, amorous relationships. Sasha Cagen writes that for "quirkyalones," "a community of like-minded souls is essential.... Instead of sacrificing our social constellation for the one all-consuming individual, we seek empathy from friends. We have significant *others*."[21] Ethan Watters hypothesizes that the growing prevalence of small close-knit groups of friends, which he calls urban tribes, reflects the fact that late-marrying urban professionals receive the support associated with marriage from friends. Cohabitation between friends is also increasing among Americans at or approaching retirement age.[22] Economic pressures also play a role in some friends' decision to cohabit family-style.

Such significant friendships, including groups of adults and shared child-rearing relationships, appear in the gay and lesbian community, African-American and Latin-American communities, among seniors, and unmarried urbanites. Recent demographic changes suggest that, increasingly, such friendships play the role associated with amorous relationships. Marriage rates have decreased; according to U.S. census data milestones, in 2005, 51 percent of women were "living without a spouse," and in 2010, married couples were for the first time a minority.[23] The shift away from marriage has been accompanied by a shift into new family forms, especially adult care networks, informal associations of friends or relatives who provide the reciprocal material and emotional support associated with marriage.[24]

The relationships penalized by amatonormativity may or may not involve sex and romantic love. Polyamorous relationships fail to meet the norm, just as groups of friends do. Polyamorists have multiple domestic or sexual partners, who in turn also typically have other partners, and these multiple relationships are characterized by affectionate bonds as well as sex (although there is some debate within the polyamorous community as to whether polyamory must involve love). Elizabeth Emens gives examples of the range of polyamorous configurations falling outside the norm of "compulsory monogamy" as well as amatonormativity: Mormon polygyny, an "ethical slut," a woman with two "husbands," and a four-partner family or "multiparty marriage." According to Emens, reflective polyamory is based on values of self-knowledge, honesty, undeceived consent based on full disclosure, self-possession, and prioritizing love and sex. Yet such "ethical nonmonogamy" or polyfidelity lacks the recognition received by monogamous relationships, and participants, judged to be immoral simply for their nonconforming relationships, face discrimination.[25] While my main focus is on discrimination against friends and nonamorous care networks, it is important to note that polyamory, which overlaps with care networks, also faces amatonormative discrimination.

One way of demarcating the privilege accorded by amatonormativity is that the privileged relationships are given family status. Family tends to be understood, for legal and census purposes, either by marriage or a marriage-like relationship (such as monogamous cohabitation or "common-law" marriage) or by the presence of children. Further, the reproductive family tends to be understood in marital terms. But the number of children born outside marriage has been steadily increasing (the U.S. Center for Disease Control found that almost 40 percent of births in 2007 were outside marriage, up from 34 percent in 2002), and this change is accompanied by a shift into new family forms, in which children born outside wedlock are increasingly reared by extended family members or household groups including a friend of the parent.[26] But while single parents and married or "common law" parents are recognized in law, extended-family or friend parental groups tend to remain invisible.

Increasingly, individuals live in adult and child-rearing support networks excluded by the understanding of family in terms of marriage or a central amorous relationship. This extends beyond legal categories to social norms: When, for instance, someone asks another person if she has a family or a relationship, he is not usually asking about her birth family—parents, siblings—nor her network of friends. The questions "Do you have a family?" or "Are you in a relationship?" understand family and relationships narrowly in amatonormative terms. Talking about one's friends would not usually be an appropriate answer to such questions. Similarly, the lesser importance socially accorded friendships is shown when they are not taken to give the same sort of social reasons that amatonormative relationships do.

The significant friendships that amatonormativity wrongly devalues serve many functions of traditional families—material support, emotional security, and frequent companionship. Urban tribe members, for instance, sometimes live together, most members meet with other members daily, and often the entire tribe meets on a weekly or monthly basis. The friends consistently take care of one another, and they acknowledge and take seriously responsibilities of mutual caretaking. In providing emotional security and material support, tribes play the role in members' lives that spouses or partners do for the married or coupled. It might be objected that tribes do not have legal support obligations, nor do they unite their finances as marital households do. But unmarried cohabitants or amorous couples, who are often treated socially on a par with married persons, can also lack such commitments. Tribes also differ from amorous relationships in that they are not exclusive. The tribe itself, rather than any individual member, tends to be central. But not all of the friendships which are wrongly devalued are tribe-like: Intimate two-person friendships closely resemble marriages in structure.

In what does the discrimination against friendships and care networks consist? One aspect consists in evaluative judgments regarding such friendships and their members. Urban tribespeople and quirkyalones report that their friendships are not treated as socially significant in the way that amorous partnerships are. This can mean that friendships are not seen as providing good social reasons. For example, Watters and Cagen provide accounts of how extended families of urban tribe members failed to recognize the significance of their friendships by refusing to accept plans with friends as good reasons to miss family events.

Moreover, persons outside amorous relationships are subjected to pervasive negative stereotyping. Members of urban tribes report being judged as incomplete, immature, and irresponsible because they are not in enduring amorous relationships. Their friendships are seen as symptomatic of an extended adolescence, rather than relationships with serious obligations. Watters writes:

To be an honorable spouse or a good father or mother seldom required heroics, but rather the steady demonstration of love, attention, and support.... Yet somehow the [similar] small things we did with our friends lacked the moral meaning those same acts might have in the context of a family. Cooking dinner and sharing time with one's children seemed like the act of someone who was living a good life. The act of cooking dinner for one's single friends did not carry the same weight. We seemed to lack the social narrative for how small good deeds shared among friends might be the central activity in praiseworthy lives.[27]

As Bella DePaulo puts it, "the caring that goes on within marriage and families is the only caring that truly counts" from the amatonormative perspective.[28] Such judgments might be defended on the grounds that child rearing is especially valuable due to the sacrifices involved, its social benefits, and so on; but childless marriages or amorous partnerships are accorded social status that friendships are not.

While the devaluation of caretaking outside amorous relationships simply fails to recognize an important feature of some friendships, there are also invidious stereotypes attached to adults who are long-term nonparticipants in amorous relationships. Such persons, although they may be members of adult care networks or urban tribes, are still socially classed as singles and, as such, subject to stereotyping—what DePaulo calls "singlism." Such stereotypes are recycled without comment in media outlets in which similar stereotypes about religion, race, gender, or disability would provoke an outcry. In Hollywood romantic comedies, for example, the single heterosexual man is stereotyped as an unkempt and irresponsible man-child, waiting for marriage to make him a responsible adult, whereas the unmarried woman is stereotyped as lonely, desperately seeking love, and filling her empty life with cats: "The years clock by, and the married people reap the rewards, while the single people buy cats and tell themselves they haven't missed anything. But they have."[29]

Singles are seen as lacking a sense of responsibility as well as having empty lives: One study found that test subjects judged people as "less socially mature, less well adjusted, and more self-centered when described as single than when described as married."[30] DePaulo describes an academic study of singles that asked what methods the subject had tried to end his or her singlehood, what qualities his or her ideal mate had, and whether or not singlehood was sad, shameful, and so on. The study offered the subject no opportunity to explain that she was single by choice, that her friends were more important than a mate, or that she found marriage sad, shameful, and so on.[31] These stereotypes of singles depend on devaluing friendships. To the extent that marriage and marriage-like relationships are seen as the "only relationships worth valuing," then it follows that those outside such relationships seem to lack an important source of value. To the extent that caretaking is only seen as valuable within marriages and families, caretaking within friendships doesn't count, and so singles are seen as selfish and irresponsible.[32]

Amatonormative discrimination does not consist merely in stereotyping and lack of social recognition. Much tangible discrimination attaches to marital status. Discrimination in housing, with preferential treatment for the married, is legally permitted in the United States, and is official government policy in military housing. An array of government benefits is accessible by the married, widowed, and divorced. Married or formerly married persons qualify for U.S. Social Security payments based on their spouse's employment. Married workers receive significantly higher benefit packages when these include spousal health insurance at a reduced rate, while unmarried persons receive no opportunity to purchase health insurance for a friend. Workplace discrimination is the apparent cause of the fact that married men receive significantly higher pay than their unmarried male peers with similar levels of achievement; moreover, singles widely report being expected to work evenings and holidays, to take on assignments involving extensive travel, and otherwise being treated by employers as if their nonwork commitments were less important than those of married co-workers. Physicians report providing better care to patients whom they saw as family members.[33] Finally, law enforces "compulsory monogamy" by imposing penalties—not just in criminal law penalizing adultery and bigamy, including bigamous cohabitation in some states, but through residential zoning laws limiting numbers of unrelated cohabitants and in child custody decisions. (For example, the child of a woman with two "husbands" was removed due to the judgment that her lifestyle was immoral.)[34]

At least some of this tangible discrimination originates in amatonormative judgments of those outside amorous relationships as lacking something valuable that is only attainable in amorous relationships. Amatonormativity assumes that an amorous relationship (typically marriage or cohabitation) should be sought in preference to other relationships, that the proper trajectory of a life is into such a romantic love relationship, and that romantic love is a universal goal, which those not in such relationships are seeking. By attributing a special value to exclusive amorous relationships, amatonormativity implies that alternatives such as celibacy, singledom, care networks, and friendships lack a central human good.

b. The Wrongness of Amatonormative Distinctions

Amatonormative evaluative distinctions between amorous relationships and friendships are false. Mutual caretaking in friendships or polyamory is just as valuable as that in exclusive amorous relationships. This parity may be easier to see in friendships that structurally resemble amorous relationships—that is, friendships which are central, dyadic, and exclusive. However, I will argue that mutual caretaking is as valuable in networks of multiple nonexclusive friendships as in dyads. What matters is that the relationships provide emotional support, caretaking, and intimacy. Below, I pose a simple bare difference argument challenging the reader to find morally relevant differences between a friendship and a valuable amorous relationship. Next, I argue that the false amatonormative evaluative distinctions are morally problematic. This is an important further step, as evaluative distinctions could be false yet not morally problematic (for example, some aesthetic judgments).

Friendships and adult care networks are on a par with amorous relationships in their function and emotional significance. Recall the distinctive feature of such friendships that I identified above: engaging in ongoing mutual caretaking and recognizing a responsibility to do so. The lack of amorous love, or the presence of multiple overlapping love relationships, does not make such caretaking, affection, and intimacy less valuable.

Consider a pair of long-term cohabiting friends who closely resemble long-married spouses in reciprocal affection and caretaking, prioritizing the relationship, and meeting each other's daily needs. Why would adding an amorous bond make such a friendship more valuable? The claim that an amorous relationship that resembles a friendship in all other significant ways has greater value than the friendship plausibly means one of two things: Either the amorous relationship is more valuable to its members (as in the stereotype that the lives of singles are empty) or caregiving within the amorous relationship has greater moral value (as in the stereotype that singles' mutual caregiving is less significant).

The first claim concerns the contribution yielded by different relationship types to members' welfare. But this should be easily refuted by considering the variety of relationship types that people claim to find fulfilling. It is not difficult to imagine someone for whom the intensities, demands, and jealousies of amorous love are draining, while the security and affection of friendship provide a satisfying emotional stability. While the friend is plausibly lacking a good—the intensity of amorous love, say—the lover is likewise lacking a good—calm nonpossessive friendship. It is implausible that the contented friend would be better off if he were in a love relationship of the kind he claims to find off-putting. Also, some long-married spouses are likely to have little more *amour* than a pair of old friends; their relationship might consist wholly in mutual caretaking and affection. Here again, there are no grounds to draw a distinction, although one relationship began in amorous love, and the other did not.

The second amatonormative distinction concerns the value of caretaking. Once again, it is not clear how an amorous dimension makes mutual caretaking more responsible or morally valuable. It might be suggested that child rearing, or the intent to rear children, is the ground for approbation. But (to repeat) many amorous relationships are childless. It might also be suggested that marriages carry legal obligations that distinguish them from friendships. However, in many circles, unmarried couples are accorded social recognition without such legal obligations. Once it is seen that friends can entertain serious, ongoing mutual caretaking responsibilities, there is no basis for morally distinguishing those responsibilities from those undertaken in amorous relationships. But what else, other than such mutual caretaking, could be the basis of attributing greater virtue to family members, understood as members of marriage-like relationships?

It might be thought that marriages, at least, involve lifelong commitment, and that amorous relationships naturally trend toward such commitment. However, friendships too can involve such an explicit lifelong commitment, and many may in fact be more enduring than marriages! In any case, amorous couples who have not made such a commitment still benefit from amatonormative privilege. Moreover, we must ask once again why a lifelong commitment is more valuable than a shorter or open-ended commitment (see Chapter 2).Temporary foster parenting deserves the same recognition and support as lifelong parenting. Why should this not be the case with relationships?

While long-term dyadic friendships closely resemble the amatonormative ideal except for their lack of romantic love and sex, adult care networks or urban tribes may seem too different from the ideal to be considered comparable. They lack the features of centrality and exclusivity. However, it is not clear why absolute priority toward a spouse or amorous partner makes the relationship more valuable or praiseworthy. The motivational and epistemic work of care can be shared among a number of people as well as directed at one. It might be claimed that prioritizing one other person is virtuously altruistic, treating another person's needs as one own. But, from the point of view of an urban tribesperson, it could be argued that giving one person absolute priority is limiting, cutting the individual off from community, enveloping the other in one's narcissism, as Freud would have it. In contrast to the stereotype of the irresponsible and self-centered single, members of care networks could be construed as less selfish than spouses; they share their friends, and they give care without expecting exclusive reciprocity.

Of course, such charges may be unfair to amorous dyads. Any given marriage or love relationship could be heavily invested in the surrounding community, just as much as it could be shut off from it. While modern North American marriage tends to supplant external social obligations, historically, marriage integrated the couple into the community.[35] The point is that this sort of generalization, charging all marriages with the faults of some, is just as suspect when applied to marriages as it should be when applied to care networks. Married people can be selfish or generous, community-spirited or insular—and so can members of care networks! Each friendship and marriage should be judged on its own merits, without generalizing that all care network members are more selfish or less responsible than all amorous love partners, or vice versa. The difference between caring for a single person or a group of people is morally irrelevant—plausibly, what matters is the agent's care for others.

The similarities between exclusive amorous relationships, friendships, and adult care networks provide reason for rejecting the amatonormative distinctions: All the arrangements can involve mutual support, intimacy, and caretaking that provide emotional fulfillment and are grounds for moral approbation. But not only do friendships and care networks lack social recognition, their members are systematically subjected to stereotyping and discrimination.

Amatonormative discrimination is morally wrong for the same reasons that other forms of arbitrary discrimination are wrong. First, social classifications that arbitrarily treat individuals unequally, harming some and benefitting others, involve a basic failure of equal respect. Systematic negative beliefs involved in stereotyping a socially defined group attach negative evaluations to individuals irrespective of their actual qualities. Like race, sex, and class, "single" or "coupled" status is an important social marker. Amatonormativity differs from racism and sexism in that racist and sexist stereotypes judge individuals as inferior due to a quality thought to be inherent (race or sex), whereas "singles" are judged inferior due to a relational quality. In this respect, "singlism" is like classism, in which individuals are judged inferior due to membership in a social class.

It might be responded that many social discriminations are made on the basis of convenience, efficiency, or familiarity, and such discrimination, though it may impose costs undeservingly, is not morally wrong in the way that racism and sexism are. For example, some people are naturally "night owls" and late sleepers. The 9-to-5 schedule of school, work, government offices, and many businesses has costs for such people; it is more onerous for them, through no fault of their own. Such people may also face stereotypes—when, for example, late sleepers are seen as lazy. Pet lovers are another example. Pet caregivers take on heavy responsibilities and derive great satisfaction from their interactions with their nonhuman companions, yet these relationships are not recognized as on a par with romantic dyads. Pet caregivers, too, may face stereotypes ("the crazy cat lady"). Yet it seems implausible to judge these cases as morally wrong discrimination of a kind with racism and sexism.[36]

However, first of all, these stereotypes are arguably morally problematic in certain cases. If an employee is passed up for promotion because it becomes known he is a natural night owl (though he always appears punctually in the morning), or because her multiple cat ownership triggers stereotypical assessments of her competence, this would be morally wrong discrimination. But while such stereotypes are problematic, there is arguably justification for the tangible burdens resulting from social organization borne by late sleepers and pet carers. For example, scheduling solves a coordination problem, and some sleep patterns will not conform; the exclusion of pets from some public places has a basis in public health concerns, and so on. These burdens are not arbitrary in the way I have been arguing that amatonormativity is; for I have been arguing that there is no justification for the differential treatment in this case. Moreover, amatonormativity targets singles as singles, whereas scheduling only burdens late sleepers as a side effect of coordinating activity. Most importantly, the costs of amatonormativity are especially significant and deep; I include the costs to women of vulnerability within amatonormative relationships (see Chapter 5.i).

Amatonormativity intersects with other forms of oppression, especially gay and lesbian oppression and women's oppression, to impose steep costs. Amatonormativity is itself systematic in a way characteristic of oppression: Legal penalties and discrimination interlock with social pressures and discrimination, stereotyping in the media, workplace discrimination, consumer pricing, and children's education.

Stereotypes are particularly pernicious when they operate in conjunction with social, legal, and economic structures to limit opportunities for members of one group while benefitting another. This is, roughly, one understanding of oppression within feminist theory.[37] Amatonormativity is oppressive when it privileges members of one form of caring relationship at the expense of nonconformists, whose opportunities are thereby significantly worsened. The opportunities of friends are limited in a number of ways: Not only are they subjected to the stereotyping and tangible costs discussed above, their ability to pursue their friendships is diminished. Just as heterosexism undermines strong relationships between women, amatonormativity undermines relationships other than amorous love and marriage by relegating them to cultural invisibility or second best. For example, at the conclusion of *Urban Tribes*, Watters describes how, when he married, he evicted his housemates—the other members of his urban tribe. As the ending to a book in which he has defended their long-standing importance in his life, this prompts the question as to why he must now evict them and diminish his role in the tribe. Why should long-standing friendships be downgraded on marriage? Amatonormativity sustains the belief that marital and amorous relationships should be valued over friendships, and this undermines the attempt to pursue enduring friendships (as Watters' housemates found out).

It might be responded that, despite such costs, there is a rationale for amatonormative discrimination. Helen Fisher has argued, on the basis of anthropological and biological evidence, that humans have a physiological drive to bond with a monogamous mating partner. Dyadic pair-bonding, with its characteristic stages of limerence ("being in love") and attachment, on her view, has a neurochemical basis. It is a drive analogous to hunger, thirst, sleep, the maternal instinct, and sex. This suggests a rationale for preferential treatment of amorous dyads:

> [O]ne might think that policy-makers would be well-advised to structure social arrangements so that they do not tend to frustrate the expression of this drive in behavior. Similar reasoning might be used to justify the inclusion of bathroom and meal breaks into an eight hour school day, or a ten hour factory shift. (Excretion-normativity? Nutrition-normativity?) Hindering the expression in behavior of human drives like hunger, the need to urinate, the need to sleep, and so on is likely to have predictable negative consequences. In this way, on a Fisher-type view of love, amato-normativity might be justified at the level of public policy as a rational response to the negative consequences of hindering people in the behavioral expression of a powerful and relatively implastic drive.[38]

We might go further and argue that amatonormative social pressures are beneficial because they guide us to satisfy this drive.

But even if we accept Fisher's controversial view, it would not justify amatonormativity. Fisher argues that humans are instinctually serial monogamists—her research suggests that the natural duration of a romantic love cycle is four years, corresponding to the normal gap between pregnancies in conditions without contraception and when women breastfeed. Moreover, she holds that extramarital sex has a physiological basis. Her account could not support the amatonormative preference for exclusive and enduring relationships. In fact, marriage and the amatonormative ideal would themselves frustrate the drives for serial monogamy and sexual variety. Furthermore, Fisher suggests that polygamy also has a physiological basis; while she sees it as a "secondary" strategy, she acknowledges that this is controversial—some anthropologists suggest that it is a dominant human urge. Finally, Fisher recognizes the emergence of a new family form, which she calls an "association"—"a brand-new web of kin based on friendship instead of blood."[39] This suggests that her view does allow some plasticity in the drive for companionship.

But let us imagine that society and policy develop "serial-amatonormativity," privileging, and pressuring people into and out of, four-year pair-bonding relationships. Marriage could have a four-year limit, and family and friends could express concern and disapproval when relationships lasted too long. Such discrimination would still be morally unjustified. There is ample evidence, already noted, of sexual minorities; privileging serial male-female monogamy would impose costs on these people unnecessarily. There is no need to privilege serial monogamy in order to remove barriers to it: To borrow a point from Mill, if the mating drive is so strong, then social pressure to mate is superfluous![40] All that is needed is to remove barriers that would frustrate pair bonding—but this can be done without privileging such relationships at the cost of others.

Rejecting amatonormativity does not mean discouraging amorous relationships; it means ceasing to encourage them at the expense of other caring relationships. Not only does privileging male-female monogamy impose costs on sexual minorities, it steers people into relationships that, though they may satisfy the mating drive, have other costs, such as domestic violence and inegalitarian gender roles. Male aggressiveness is also, according to Fisher, physiologically rooted; but due to its costs, society requires the suppression or channeling of this drive. Likewise, the potential costs of monogamy must also be weighed against the urgency of the (purported) drive. Finally, pair-bonding is not a drive like hunger or thirst, the frustration of which would be lethal. Many people choose, for all sorts of reasons, not to satisfy this drive; allowing such free choice is another good reason against paternalistic amatonormativity.

Amatonormativity does not simply discriminate against nonconforming relationships; it also precludes their formation by pressuring choice. Prizing dyadic relationships discourages the pursuit of others. Social judgments as to the possibility of fulfillment in friendships and care networks, and the invisibility or marginalization of these alternatives, make amorous love relationships "compulsory," as Rich famously claimed about heterosexuality.[41] Economic, legal, and social incentives exert great pressure to enter amorous love relationships, especially when other options appear less appealing and salient, as when singles are depicted as lonely rather than as surrounded by loving friends. The amatonormative assumption that "singles" are seeking romantic love, and are incomplete without it, parallels the confining assumptions of sexual "liberation": "The focus on 'sexual liberation' has always carried with it the assumption that the goal of such effort is to make it possible for individuals to engage in more and/or better sexual activity. Yet one assumption of sexual norms that many people find oppressive is the assumption that one 'should' be engaged in sexual activity."[42] Pressures to enter amorous love relationships likely result in individuals viewing friendships as less valuable than they might otherwise, and in some cases choosing less fulfilling relationships, given their idiosyncratic needs and preferences, than they otherwise might.

Friends and adult care networks are made less salient options through the lack of a social script to establish their significance. Entering a relationship with a romantic "life partner," commonly through marriage, is considered a significant social marker, denoting full adulthood and providing universally recognized social reasons, which do not meet with requests for further explanation. Some groups may accord this status only to marriage, others more broadly to cohabitants; but it is an evaluative social classification that friendships or, even more so, solitudinousness rarely breach. In a recent essay, Kate Parsons describes the confusion caused by her evasion of heteronormative terminology to describe her status when asked if she is married:

> I can say, "No, I'm single," and then wait for one of several reactions: pity, concern, envy (sometimes feigned, sometimes genuine), or the occasional interest in whether I am "available." Yet "single" is only true legally; I have a long-term domestic partner. I can opt to share more: "No, I'm not married, but I have a domestic partner and we've been together fourteen years." But this often plunges the conversation into loaded silence, leaving me wondering: Is this person just trying to formulate a follow-up question without a she/he pronoun? Does she disapprove of the same-sex partnership that I might have revealed with my term "partner"? Is she just embarrassed by the hetero-normative assumptions in her own question? Does she assume I am in a "dead-end" heterosexual relationship, pitiably "going nowhere" after fourteen years?[43]

Parsons and her partner have chosen not to marry due to the heterosexual privilege of marriage, which (where she lives) withholds its social and legal benefits from same-sex partners. The marginalization she experiences as a marriage boycotter and resister of heterosexual norms, the difficulty of communicating her status as clearly as using the term "husband" would, reminds her of this privilege.

But marriage law upholds amatonormative as well as heterosexist discrimination. If it is difficult, as Parsons reports, to convey that one is in a committed, mature relationship outside of marriage, how much more difficult is it to convey the strength and importance of one's attachment to close friends? Or that one's caregiving relationship, such as single parenting or caring for a friend with a disability, is rewarding? Or that such caregiving relationships are chosen rather than "second best"? The absence of a widely acknowledged script, or social markers, for such relationships creates day-to-day difficulties for members of adult care networks and close friendships. This is a further, subtle, way in which social norms make it more difficult to choose and live in such relationships.

These norms are undergirded by marriage promotion and abstinence education. They have been intensified by the "wedding-industrial complex," which broadcasts gendered promarriage propaganda through books, magazines, Hollywood movies, and advertising. Anne Kingston records "an upsurge in bridal publications" in the late 1990s; bridal magazines cover million-dollar weddings, such as Disneyland weddings where the price of a "Cinderella" cake "starts at $900"; the use of "Cinderella's glass coach," at $2500. Like other critics of the "wedding-industrial complex,"

Kingston sees commodification of marriage as obscuring deeper problems in the institution: confusion about its significance, socioeconomic obsolescence, emotional costs.[44] As I argue in the next chapter, these pressures have significant costs for women in particular; amatonormativity is not only oppressive in itself, it is a significant contributor to women's oppression.

It may also contribute to socioeconomic inequality. Martha Fineman argues that the focus on marriage in U.S. public policy has turned attention away from relationships of dependency. Marriage, in her view, privatizes care, placing its burdens on individual families, and marriage promotion precludes consideration of whether care for dependents is a social responsibility. Fineman argues on these grounds for the abolition of marriage.

But while agreeing with Fineman's goals, I would add that just, caring relationships are also a good that the state should support. When the state supports some caring relations at the expense of others, it is an injustice, as I argue in Part Two. Chapter 7 will propose a reformed marriage law that could offer support to all caring relationships without amatonormativity. Justice in such a law requires recognizing the diversity of caring relationships.

IV. CARE AND CONTRACT: THEIR COMPATIBILITY

Before proceeding, I will address three common criticisms of contract made by some care ethicists as well as communitarians. This looks back to my suggestion (in Chapter 2.iii) that women self-protectively negotiate egalitarian terms within marriage, and lays the groundwork for my marriage reform proposal, which treats some terms of marriage as contractual, and is grounded in a contractarian theory—Rawlsian liberalism. The first criticism is that contractarian theories such as Rawls's misrepresent human nature. The second charges that an insistence on justice threatens caring relationships, which are more valuable than justice. The third holds that self-interested contractual negotiation is an inappropriate tool within caring relationships.[45]

The disputed liberal conception of the individual is that of the independent and unaffiliated rational contractor. This, critics point out, is an inaccurate characterization of every human being who has been nurtured into adulthood. Benhabib takes as an example Hobbes, who invited us to "consider men...as if but even now sprung out of the earth, and suddenly, like mushrooms, come to full maturity, without all kind of engagement to each other."[46] More recently, Rawls's theory of justice imagines rational and mutually disinterested contractors behind a veil of ignorance blocking out their moral, religious, and interpersonal commitments. This model is said to misrepresent human experience, as individuals have attachments to one another and to moral and religious views. Agents may care more about the things the veil excludes than they do about justice. Taking the independent individual as paradigmatic overlooks the commitments fundamental to human experience.

Rawls's response is that he is not attempting to give a psychological "theory of human motivation," holding that humans are mutually disinterested and egoistic.[47] Nor is he suggesting that in ordinary settings these aspects of humans are the most important. Rather, our separateness and self-interest are salient within the circumstances of justice, which are characterized by conflict over scarce resources. Under such conditions, justice allocates rights and economic resources. Rawls's thought is that in choosing principles of justice, our capacities to have a sense of justice and a conception of the good are especially salient. He is not attempting to represent human nature, and so the charge of misrepresentation is misguided.

Rawls has also been criticized for assuming that autonomy and the principles of justice have an overriding importance. Indeed, he assigns justice preeminence among the social virtues. Critics have replied that this is an incorrect valuation which threatens the better goods of community and care. Thus, Michael Sandel writes that justice should dominate only where "nobler but rarer virtues"—such as generosity, benevolence, affection—are lacking.[48] Sandel gives the example of the family as an institution in which "affections may be engaged to such an extent that justice is scarcely engaged, much less as the 'first virtue.'"[49] Not only is justice superseded in families, but introducing justice into families or communities may "represent a moral loss" if it occasions the "breakdown of certain personal and civic attachments...[or] a rent in the fabric of implicit understandings and commitments."[50] Sandel imagines an ideal family in which generosity, not justice, prevails, so that individual rights are irrelevant. When domestic peace breaks up and affection fails, the family dutifully uses principles of justice to determine distributions. Sandel argues that the former scenario, in which the family naturally pulls for the same ends, is at least as valuable as the second. Its virtues were finer than justice.

The view that justice is unnecessary within the family has much precedent. Susan Moller Okin documented a long philosophical tradition of viewing the family as governed by affection rather than justice. On this view, the circumstances of justice—self-interested competition for scarce goods—do not apply, as there is an "identity of interests" among family members.[51] For instance, Hume wrote: "Betwixt marry'd persons, the cement of friendship is by the laws suppos'd so strong as to abolish all division of possessions; and has often, in reality, the force ascribed to it."[52] The thought is that there is no need for rights-based allocations within a family, since sentiment precludes conflict.

However, conflict over resources and the division of labor is certainly possible within families, as is violence. Family members, as citizens, have basic rights and liberties. Feminism has demonstrated why legal rights must reach inside families: Within them, individuals can suffer violence and sexual abuse, and dependent individuals can be neglected and mistreated.[53] Wives' deprivation of rights under coverture made them completely vulnerable to the whims or cruelty of their husbands. In the case of children, their vulnerability is well understood: No one suggests that children's rights are unnecessary, as their safety is secured by parental love. Thus, Okin responds to Sandel that associations displaying higher virtues are only "morally superior to associations which are *just* just only if they are firmly built on a foundation of justice."[54] Families can be dangerous places, and family members need legal protection and recourse.

Moreover, the picture of marriage as governed wholly by affection has always been disingenuous. The worry that rights possession is inimical to affection overlooks the fact that family members have possessed rights since Roman times. Of course, historically such rights have been unequal, favoring the husband under Roman *patria potestas* or English coverture. The state, while claiming to protect the private from interference, has structured it, determining who has the right to marry, to parent, and what further rights and responsibilities those activities entail. With this in mind, objections to rights-talk within marriage begin to seem like objections to talk of women's rights within marriage.

Sandel's family example suggests a scenario in which women's asserting rights to fairness and equal treatment within marriage corrodes trust and affection. But the absence of rights is even more problematic. In response to Sandel, John Tomasi imagines a family in which a servile, deferential wife takes her husband's goals as her own and has no sense of her own interests. Lack of a self-conception as an autonomous and rights-bearing individual is a greater evil than an excessive focus on such a self-conception. Analogously, in the larger polity, community without liberty is not better than liberty without community.

Some theorists have defended rights within marriage as a safeguard that is needed when care fails. Thus Jeremy Waldron argues that marital rights protect spouses in case of the breakdown of affection, which would otherwise protect their interests. As Pauline Kleingeld points out, Waldron assumes that rights claims are unnecessary in a "normal healthy marriage."[55] But Kleingeld argues that the choice between love and justice is a false dichotomy, and that marriage should be understood as a joint venture in which spouses pursue justice together. If love and justice are not complementary, spouses face a choice between self-protection and affection. But, as I argued above, morally educated love or care entails wanting justice for the other. Moreover, as Tomasi points out, justice is conceptually required for altruism. Altruistic actions are meaningful precisely because the agent had a right that she chose not to exercise.[56]

As I noted in Chapter 2.iii, feminist game theorists and contractarians have argued that women can use rational choice bargaining strategies to pursue fairness in their relationships. Jean Hampton argued that we can subject private relationships to a contractarian test for exploitation, asking ourselves: "Could both of us reasonably accept the distribution of costs and benefits (that is, the costs and benefits that are not themselves side effects of any affective or duty-based tie between us) if it were the subject of an informed, unforced agreement in which we think of ourselves as motivated solely by self-interest?"[57] By excluding affective benefits (such as the warmth one gets from nurturing another), the test ensures that emotions are not manipulated to exploit one party by deriving ongoing unreciprocated benefit. The test does not apply to relations with children or others who cannot reciprocate, where fairness does not apply, but between adults who can.

Hampton's test for exploitation accords with the reciprocity of caring, in which "carer and cared-for share an interest in their mutual well-being,"[58] but goes beyond it to demand fairness. Care must be compatible with self-respect. Self-abnegating care can be a form of self-harm: Consider the slavishly deferential wife. Costly and prolonged unidirectional caring for someone who can reciprocate, but chooses not to, involves a failure to be treated, and to treat oneself, as valuable. Hampton's contractarian approach reveals such exploitation by treating persons as separate, with possibly conflicting interests. Her point is not that relationships are self-interested contractual interactions, but that one test for their fairness is to consider them as if they were.

While Hampton's test applies to already existing relationships, game theorist Rhona Mahony argues for negotiating terms of relationships beforehand.[59] Like Okin, she assesses women's disempowerment within marriage as an effect of their earning less than their husbands and consequently sacrificing work to childcare, increasing the inequality in a vicious cycle. Mahony's solution, which involves individual empowerment rather than widespread social reform, is for women to use game-theoretical strategies: marrying men who earn less, increasing their own earning power, encouraging fathers to care for children. Although such strategies are no substitute for political justice, and may be difficult to employ against a background of economic inequality and hierarchical gender roles, they may be a useful tool enabling some women to protect themselves against economic vulnerability.

But other feminists argue that contract is an inappropriate tool for negotiating intimate relationships, and not just because women start with unequal bargaining power. A recurring worry is that treating marriage as a contract represents the contractor as a self-interested individual who can walk away at will from deep ties of care and intimacy. Martha Minow and Mary Lyndon Shanley write that "the model of a self-possessing individual linked to others only by agreement...fails to do justice to the complex interdependencies involved in family relations and child rearing."[60] Another theorist writes that contract suggests "individualism in the sense of selfishness."[61] But bargaining between caring partners does not reduce the relationship to a self-interested contract or imply that a relationship is essentially contractual. To see love and contractual bargaining as incompatible, one would have to think that love precludes self-interested thoughts. But healthy love and care depend on having a strong, protected self.

While Minow and Shanley are right that the accretions of relationships limit the power to exit, and hence to bargain, adults can, and should, be self-protective when entering marriage. Its possible economic disadvantages for women are severe. Women have good reason to negotiate the terms of their relationships—not just economically, but domestically. Partners who care about each other's welfare should for that reason care about fairness. This does not entail daily negotiation of household chores, but early articulation of fair and protective ground rules—whether legal financial agreements or domestic chore rotations. Such planning may seem to threaten trust. But, rather, it creates the conditions for trust by limiting risks. It allows both parties to relax their guard and obviates conflict by settling terms in advance. When parties agree on obligations in advance and can discuss them openly, open conflict and buried resentment are less, not more, likely.

Furthermore, as Tomasi suggests, fixing obligations allows spontaneous generosity. Consider Maushart's report in *Wifework* of women discussing their husbands' attitudes toward chores. When the husbands performed a small task, they would announce it proudly to their wives, expecting praise; but when their exasperated wives began to announce their much more extensive tasks as they completed them, they would receive blank looks, as if to say: "Why are you telling me that?" If men expect women to do housework as a matter of course, they are less likely to appreciate it; but if a clear rota of chores is established, the performance of a nonobligatory task becomes a gift. Just as justice is compatible with harmonious communities, contract is compatible with caring relationships.

Critics might entertain a more mundane concern that not all marital activities should be arranged in detail. Legal prenuptial agreements concerning dishwashing, dog walking, and so on, seem overly rigid. Some activities should allow for spontaneity. But such agreements don't fall within the remit of legal contract. Contract requires that "enforcement would not impose inordinate difficulties on the legal system" and matters are "capable of rational management and planning."[62] However, agreeing informally in general terms on such matters as housework, sex, reproduction, and money may be a precondition of harmony as well as justice. Doing so need not threaten day-to-day spontaneity.

Justice and care are of varying salience in different aspects and spheres of life. We may appropriately be more inclined to see and treat others as liberal rights-bearers in the marketplace than at home, and we may appropriately be more inclined to act caringly at home than in the marketplace. We approach strangers with correct behavior in mind, including respect for their rights, but we see intimates in their particularity and neediness. But justice and care coexist in all these relationships. We remain rights-bearers within marriage; we face momentous economic decisions within it. Our roles as rights-bearers and contractors may only partially reflect our full human capabilities, but they are crucially important to their fulfillment. Nor should marketplace transactions or understandings of corporate responsibility be wholly uncaring. Justice should be enriched with care, and vice versa; care should not be left out of civil society any more than justice should be left out of the home.[63] At the same time, the principles that govern just distribution of benefits and burdens throughout society should apply to the way the state structures private relationships.

Part One has attempted to de-moralize marriage: It has no unique moral value, nor is it morally transformative, and its benefits must be weighed against substantial costs. Paradoxically, the argument has implied that the moral elements associated with marriage—promise, commitment, and care—are often taken too lightly. Promises made in marriage are weighty, though less extensive than often thought; commitments should be examined for their rationality; and care, in a context of justice, is valuable—but amatonormative marriage constrains its development in other relationship forms. Attributing special value to marriage, we have seen repeatedly, leads to problems. It discourages nonconformist relationships. The belief that marriage is morally transformative may encourage emotional complacency, diminishing responsiveness to real needs in the other person, and thereby making marriage a self-defeating precommitment strategy. Finally, when marriage is taken as a special relationship not admitting ordinary considerations of self-interest, it leads to grave threats for women. These are all good reasons to minimize the moral value attributed to marriage. Part Two turns to arguments to minimize the restrictions on marriage legally, democratizing it by opening it to diverse relationships.

PART TWO

Democratizing Marriage

5

CRITIQUES OF MARRIAGE
AN ESSENTIALLY UNJUST INSTITUTION?

Histories of marriage document its role in oppressing women, gays and lesbians, and racial and religious minorities.[1] Critics argue that marriage is essentially patriarchal, heteronormative, harmful, and an ownership relation, and that reform cannot excise its oppressive nature. Is marriage unjust in itself or has it only been contingently unjust?

Feminists disagree among themselves over marriage reform. Some argue for the abolition of what they see as an essentially unjust institution. But others argue that marriage law protects women and recognizes the significance of noncontractual, interdependent relationships. Likewise with theorists of gay and lesbian oppression: Some argue that marriage is essentially heteronormative, others that same-sex marriage rights will empower gays and lesbians and counteract social stigma against same-sex relationships.

Controversies over marriage are not merely academic. The U.S. Federal Government promotes "traditional" marriage. In the 2008 U.S. elections, three state bans on same-sex marriage were passed, and Arkansas banned anyone "cohabiting outside a valid marriage"—including male-female partners—from adopting or fostering children (despite the fact that the state had only a quarter of the foster parents needed for children in state custody).[2] In Canada, same-sex marriage was legally recognized nationally in 2005, and the Supreme Court is currently deliberating on whether polygamy should follow. A Marriage Boycott movement calls on couples to abstain from marriage until all couples can marry, the Alternatives to Marriage Project fights discrimination against the unmarried, and the idea of abolition has been aired in the *New York Times*.[3] Possibilities for legal reform are various, and in assessing them, the question of whether marriage can be liberated from its history of oppression is key.

The criticisms I survey in this chapter are crucial to my argument for marriage reform in two ways. The fact that there are competing ethical views over the meaning and value of marriage implies that the liberal state should deal evenhandedly with the various competitors. However, these critiques also suggest that marriage law sustains, and has sustained, unjust systematic discrimination. If these claims are correct, marriage law reform becomes a matter of equal opportunity and rectification, due to its contingent injustices. But I argue that marriage is contingently, not essentially, unjust, and so a just reform is possible.

I. FEMINIST CRITIQUE

Many feminists argue that marriage contributes to the systematic oppression of women. In the United States into the 1970s, marriage deprived wives of full human rights. Under the doctrine of coverture, adopted in the United States from English common law, a wife's legal personality was erased on marriage. As Sir William Blackstone explained in his eighteenth-century *Commentaries on the Laws of England*: "By marriage, the husband and wife are one person in law: that is, the very being or legal existence of the woman is suspended during the marriage, or at least is incorporated and consolidated into that of the husband."[4] Caroline Norton, in 1855, listed the effects of marriage on wives:

> A married woman in England has *no legal existence*: her being is absorbed in that of her husband. Years of separation or desertion cannot alter this position.... She has no possessions, unless by special settlement; her property is *his* property.... An English wife has no legal right even to her clothes or ornaments.... An English wife cannot make a will... cannot legally claim her own earnings... may not leave her husband's house. Not only can he sue her for "restitution of conjugal rights," but he has a right to enter the house of any friend or relation with whom she may take refuge... and carry her away by force, with or without the aid of police.... She cannot prosecute for a libel... cannot sign a lease, or transact responsible business... cannot claim support, as a matter of personal right, from her husband.... She cannot bind her husband by any agreement.... As *her husband*, he has a right to all that is hers; as *his wife*, she has no right to anything that is his.[5]

Coverture deprived women of full legal rights and left married women virtually powerless. Spousal abuse was either explicitly permitted (U.S. and English law allowed husbands to discipline their wives physically), or ignored by authorities. Because wives were seen as having given their husbands rights to sexual access and their bodies were viewed as their husbands' to use, marital rape was deemed legally impossible, and hence, not a crime. John Stuart Mill in *The Subjection of Women* compared wives' legal position under coverture to that of slaves, with the difference that wives were intimate with their "masters," whom they were internally motivated to please by ideological teachings about duty and by love and desire.[6]

Although coverture was dismantled in England and the United States during the nineteenth century, elements lingered in law. Spousal rape was not made a crime in all fifty U.S. states until 1993, and as of 1996, twenty-three state criminal codes mitigated charges or exempted spouses (and, in some cases, cohabitants) from ordinary sexual battery and assault laws.[7] Until the second half of the twentieth century, legal roles within marriage were defined on the basis of views about women's inferiority. Spouses could not alter legally imposed gendered duties—for the husband, financial support and decision-making power, for the wife, domestic and child care duties—entailing that wives were not entitled to their earnings for any work done in the home, including work such as taking in laundry, because their husbands owned their domestic labor.[8] Twentieth-century American courts struck down contracts between husband and wife regarding income and support: A contract between spouses "was regarded as an impossibility...because husband and wife were considered to be a single entity."[9] Spouses are still, today, exempt from U.S. labor law protections within marriage, despite the fact that they may work for one another. And in Britain, the social security system and divorce law assumed wives' roles as mothers and homemakers: The "one-third rule," allocating one-third of marital property to the wife on divorce, was defended by Lord Denning in 1973 on the grounds that the husband would bear greater expenses, since he "must get some woman to look after the house—either a wife...or a housekeeper."[10]

Legislatures also imposed gendered standards known as "head and master laws." As late as 1970, the Ohio Supreme Court declared that a wife was "at most a superior servant to her husband...only chattel with no personality, no property, and no legally recognized feelings or rights," and a 1974 Georgia statute defined the husband as "head of the family" and the wife as "subject to him; her legal existence...merged in the husband."[11] Until the 1960s, married women's legal domestic obligations were explicitly given as rationale for their exclusion from some private- and public-sector employment and education.[12] Until the 1970s, husbands could determine domicile and be required to give consent for their wives' loan or credit card applications.

Twentieth-century radical feminism—echoing Mill, who thought coverture had anciently originated in force—saw marriage as emerging from violent beginnings: "Marriage as an institution developed from rape as a practice....Marriage meant the taking was to extend in time, to be not only use of but possession of, or ownership."[13] While modern marriage was claimed to protect women by assigning support obligations to husbands, this "propaganda" covered up the fact that it was a form of "slavery," in which wives were legally obligated to live with and have sex with their husbands and perform unpaid domestic labor. This legal condition resembled slavery (again, as Mill had argued): "[T]he master is entitled to free use of the slave's labor, to deny the slave his human right to freedom of movement and control over his own body."[14] In this passage, Sheila Cronan refers to contemporaneous wives' lack of legal rights against spousal rape and sexual battery, as well as laws requiring spouses to cohabit in some states. Until recently, and in some jurisdictions still, wives lacked full legal protection of their bodily integrity, a basic human right.

Wives' legal status has changed considerably and much for the better. But marriage continues to perpetuate elements of women's oppression, understood as the diminishment of their life opportunities through the interaction of systematic legal, social, and economic forces. The signal problems are spousal violence and economic dependence derived from gendered spousal roles.

Spousal rape and abuse are epidemic in marriage and intimate partnerships. Two U.S. studies found rates of rape occurring at some point during a marriage was between 10 and 14 percent; in 2000, the U.S. Department of Justice National Violence Against Women Survey found that 7.7 percent of women surveyed reported rape by an intimate partner during their lifetime.[15] According to this survey, "Intimate partner violence is pervasive in U.S. society: nearly 25 percent of surveyed women and 7.6 percent of surveyed men said they were raped and/or physically assaulted by a current or former spouses, cohabiting partner, or date at some time in their lifetime."[16] According to the U.S. Department of Justice Family Violence Statistics, of the "roughly 3.5 million violent crimes committed against family members during 1998 to 2000...48.9 percent were crimes against a spouse." Eighty-four percent of victims of spousal abuse were female.[17] Myths surrounding marital rape continue to influence prosecution and make recovery difficult.[18] Intimate violence is also prevalent among unmarried cohabitants, reportedly at even higher rates; the National Violence against Women Survey findings "support previous research that shows unmarried couples are at greater risk of intimate partner violence than married couples."[19]

Violence against women contributes to women's oppression directly, through the harm to individual victims, and indirectly, by contributing to a culture of fear in which such violence is taken as normal or expected. This culture affects uncoupled as well as coupled women, inhibiting women's perceived freedom to walk alone at night or burdening the choice to stay in a relationship with a perceived male protector. To the extent that marriage enables a culture of violence against women, it contributes to women's oppression. But what is the link between marriage and violence?

The majority of marriages, of course, are not abusive, and as noted, abuse occurs at even higher rates in unmarried cohabitation. Correlation should not be confused with causation; just because abuse occurs within marriages does not show marriage causes it. Feminist theory diverges on explanations of male violence: violent pornography and the pornographic objectification of women; innate male aggressiveness, explained by evolutionary biology; a culture that valorizes war and violence in activities such as sports; male psychological resentment of women stemming from infant dependence on female caregivers or the repression of the sexual instinct; a misogynistic culture; or some combination of these with women's social and economic powerlessness, which facilitates abuse. The question is how far marriage enables abuse by contributing to women's vulnerability, and whether it inherently does so.

Critics of marriage point out that marital legal access rights to common property, or laws mitigating penalties for sexual assault within marriage, facilitate abuse.[20] Certainly, laws mitigating sexual battery or permitting abusers to access shared property can (and should) be excised, and expedited procedures to protect victims of violence can be devised. Legal rights facilitating abuse are not inherent to marriage; access rights, rather, follow from shared property ownership or domicile. What may appear to be inherent to marriage, however, is the kind of relationship in which abuse occurs. "Intimate violence" against women by men (and between same-sex partners, and sometimes against men by women) occurs in intimate, dyadic, exclusive relationships that provide conditions for abuse by hiding the couple in a materially and socially private sphere. Women have many incentives to enter and remain in such relationships. Current marriage law provides economic and legal incentives to enter and stay, and social pressure and economic dependency add to these. Thus, marriage may facilitate abuse by making exit difficult and by promoting exclusive dyadic relationships.

Legal structures shape our choices by shaping our default expectations, and—in the case of marriage—endorsing and incentivizing certain choices. Legal recognition of exclusive dyads, and only exclusive dyads, underwrites amatonormative social pressures. If alternatives to exclusive, intimate relationships with men were more salient and equally supported, women's power to leave exclusive dyadic relationships, or choose others in the first place, would be correspondingly increased. Abolishing marriage is one way to remove the state's *imprimatur* on it. But there is a way to increase choices even more: by recognizing and supporting a range of relationships, including networks or friendships, thereby—indirectly—creating new social scripts and making alternative relationships salient.

However, there is strong evidence that exit-burdening economic dependence, rather than legal or social pressure, is the major factor in facilitating abuse and spousal rape. A landmark study of rape in marriage found that "90 percent of wives who stayed with their husbands following a rape depended on the husband for money, whereas only 24 percent of those who left faced this financial constraint.... *100 percent* of those women who were the sole providers for their households at the time of the rape left their husbands following the act."[21] Addressing the contribution marriage makes to violence requires addressing economic dependence.

Women's economic dependence in marriage, and the associated difficulty of exit, is the second way in which marriage perpetuates women's oppression. Marriage is associated with a gendered division of labor, which contributes to economic dependency, leading to power inequality. Okin documented a vicious cycle of wives' economic dependency, which she called "vulnerability by marriage." Most married women work outside the home, but many work part-time or sacrifice career opportunities to support their husbands' careers or to give more energy to domestic responsibilities. Even women who work full-time outside the home face a "second shift" of housework, which affects their workplace competitiveness—they have less energy and time to work on projects at home or simply rest. The more women's earning opportunities and workplace competitiveness shrink, as they spend time away from the workforce or work part-time or low-paid jobs, the more rational it seems to deprioritize their paid work to support the higher-paid husband's career. The resulting earning gaps can make women economically dependent on their husbands to maintain their standard of living. This sketch should be complicated slightly: According to Anne Alstott, the larger gap in earnings is not between married and unmarried women, but women with and without children. However, the gap between men and women is significant: Women's overall earnings in 2010 were only 81.2 percent of men's earnings.[22] Economic inequality between spouses produces power inequality. Decision-making power within marriage is tied to earning power, because for the economically dependent, divorce is a difficult option.[23]

The gendered division of labor in marriage has psychological and physical costs for women in addition to economic costs. Susan Maushart calls "the myriad tasks of physical and emotional nurture" expected of married women "wifework." Wifework consists not only in child care and the "second shift" of domestic labor, but attending to a husband's emotional and sexual needs, his health, nutrition, scheduling, laundry, wardrobe, social life, sending cards on his behalf and reminding him of birthdays, paying attention to him, and even laughing at his jokes: "Wifework includes what Virginia Woolf called 'reflecting a man at twice his normal size.'"[24]

Maushart argues that wifework accounts for emotional and psychological (as well as economic and physical) hazards of marriage for women. Men, it is widely reported, benefit psychologically from marriage. According to Maushart, women do not: "Wives report levels of depression two to three times higher than unmarried women, and, if they are unhappily married, three times higher than that of their husbands."

Married women, compared with single women, suffer "more nervous breakdowns, inertia, loneliness, unhappiness with their looks; more insomnia, heart palpitations, nervousness, and nightmares; more phobias; more feelings of incompetence, guilt, shame, and low self-esteem."[25]

Just as spousal violence contributes to a wider culture of violence against women, affecting unmarried women, the effects of gendered spousal roles extend to unmarried women too. A long tradition of feminist criticism examines the effects of the pursuit of romantic love and marriage on women's aspirations. Simone de Beauvoir wrote that marriage "is the destiny traditionally offered to women by society," leading women to focus on capturing a husband rather than pouring their energies into other—more creative and rewarding—vocations.[26] Similarly, Okin argued that the cycle of vulnerability by marriage begins long before marriage, as social pressures surrounding marriage and romantic love make women economically "vulnerable by anticipation" of marriage. A society which teaches girls that their highest purpose is to be wives and mothers, that the demands of wifework will squeeze out other roles, and that a good husband will be an economic provider, constrains women's ambitions and self-conceptions.

Such pressures are by no means obsolete. In U.S. public schools, abstinence education promotes a "marriage message," one which is, in some curricula, gendered. Congressman Henry Waxman's investigation into federally funded abstinence education curricula found that some "treat stereotypes about girls and boys as scientific fact. One curriculum teaches that women need 'financial support,' while men need 'admiration.' Another instructs: 'Women gauge their happiness and judge their success on their relationships. Men's happiness and success hinge on their accomplishments.'" Some curricula reinforce the gendered division of labor, teaching that men need "domestic support," and some reinforce the belief that adult women need male protection: "The father gives the bride to the groom because he is the one man who has had the responsibility of protecting her throughout her life. He is now giving his daughter to the only other man who will take over this protective role."[27]

In the last chapter, I argued that amatonormativity is oppressive because it penalizes singles and friends and reduces their opportunities to pursue their relationships. Amatonormativity also contributes to women's oppression. The wedding-industrial complex broadcasts amatonormative promarriage propaganda through books, magazines, movies, and advertising, targeting females from young girls to mature "career women." This media bombardment fuels women's vulnerability by anticipation of marriage by intensifying pressures to marry, and, even worse, obscuring the unglamorous side of marriage and its costs. This does women the disservice of drawing attention to the wedding itself and away from the more significant long-term concerns of wifework and the need to be self-supporting if the marriage deteriorates.

Within a society structured by gender roles that limit women's life chances relative to men's, the desire for romantic love and marriage may lead women to make disadvantageous life choices. It is not that interpersonal relationships are not valuable. But the amatonormativity of contemporary North American society—hot-housed by the wedding-industrial complex and popular entertainment—sells love and marriage as a valuable commodity for which women are willing to trade more basic goods. Men may be encouraged to trade a month's salary for a diamond ring, but society encourages women to make sacrifices with much steeper long-term costs: putting their husband's career first, downgrading their career expectations, choosing less well-paid part-time work. These choices lead to gaps in earnings and power within marriages, and children learn gender roles, perpetuating patterns of gender inequality in the next generation. Given current gender roles, amatonormativity has a disparate impact on women.

Gendered spousal roles are maintained today through social pressures and expectations rather than through legal prescription. Marriage does not legally require that wives take on gendered homemaker roles. But in considering how the state has structured the background expectations that shape our lives, it should give us pause that it did so require well into the twentieth century and that such roles are still being taught in some public schools. Marriage is still associated with gendered role expectations. But once again, abolishing marriage does not seem to be the only, or best, way to address this. Rather than placing marriage into the private sphere, legally removing gender from marriage—by recognizing same-sex marriage, where it is not already recognized—and removing the amatonormative structure of marriage may use law to combat gendered expectations.

This approach is controversial. Feminists disagree on whether reform or abolition of marriage will best serve women. Some feminists, like Cronan and Claudia Card, have called for abolishing marriage to weaken social pressures to marry and to weaken gendered spousal role expectations, but others argue that reform can serve these purposes. Ann Ferguson has argued that recognizing same-sex marriage will help undermine belief in gender difference (as well as gendered spousal roles), because marriage is the primary institution that supports such beliefs. I argue, below, that the symbolism of marriage can be altered to undermine the heteronormative and patriarchal social pressures it has previously supported.

Another question concerns how property division on divorce, and its reform, affects women. Okin and Mary Lyndon Shanley have argued that marriage is an important legal tool to protect the vulnerable; recognizing gender-structured marriage is necessary to compensate for inequities arising from it. Thus, legal recognition of marriage is necessitated by justice until a truly gender-neutral society is achieved.[28] Okin, for instance, proposes that, to recognize the value of unpaid house-work, all wages be equally held by the wage-earner and the unpaid homemaker. She also proposes that divorce law correct inequities arising from gender roles, ensuring that both parties have the same standard of living and that alimony lasts as long as the domestic labor did. These reforms address the inequities of gender-structured marriage, but they do not address social pressures and gender roles leading to the unequal division of domestic labor. Such legislation presents a dilemma, because by recognizing unequal marriages in order to protect the vulnerable, it may actually encourage women to become dependent. These questions are vital to the issue of exit from abusive marriages as well, since alimony protections give women greater power to leave; these issues are addressed in Chapter 8. Marriage reform requires good exit strategies.

Marriage presents two interrelated problems for women. It creates economic dependence, which reduces women's power and facilitates abuse, and it sustains gendered roles and amatonormative social pressures. A marriage law that is not gendered or amatonormative, recognizing a wide range of relationships, may help to address gendered spousal roles as well as giving women better alternatives. However, it might be objected that marriage, with its patriarchal symbolism, cannot be detached from hierarchical gender roles.

It might be thought that marriage, betraying origins in force, is essentially an ownership relation, in which men own women. Thus, any marriage law is inherently patriarchal. However, it is difficult to see why a reformed law of marriage can never escape its historical origins in patriarchal force. Let us consider one such genealogical critique of marriage and contract. Carole Pateman has argued that the contracting agent is inherently and tacitly defined as male, and that "[c]ontract...is...the mainstay of patriarchy."[29] In her reconstruction of the social contract tradition, women were excluded from the social contract by an earlier, sexual, contract, in which men agreed to confine women to marriage and the private sphere. The marriage contract, creating the private and subordinating women to men, is, in her view, the origin of modern patriarchy. Because the sexual contract is fundamental, and excludes women, contract is defined in terms of sex difference: The contracting individual in the social contract tradition is conceived as male, and maleness is conceived as possessing power over a woman, through marriage. However, while Pateman accurately accuses the social contract tradition of sexism, contracts, as state-enforced bargains between different self-interested individuals, do not necessarily presuppose male contractors. While it is true that married women were banned from contracting under coverture, this was remedied by enabling them to make contracts. Indeed, it is difficult to see what alternative remedy there could have been to the unjust exclusion of wives from making contracts—abolishing contract itself? A contract is a legally defined tool, which can be employed in a gender-neutral way and can serve women's interests when law allows them access to it.

Similarly, marriage is not essentially an ownership relation; its legal terms can be, and have been, redefined. Theorists who view marriage as essentially patriarchal point to its history and continuing morally laden and gendered meaning. However, citizenship provides a good analogy. When citizenship was held only by white males, it was contingently racist and sexist. In U.S. law, for instance, the citizen historically was defined as a male husband and head of family (as Pateman argues the contractor was), and law broadly reflected this assumption.[30] But citizenship has been redefined. The history of marriage is undoubtedly patriarchal; but it, too, can be redefined in law. Of course, this does not give sufficient reason for retaining marriage rather than abolishing it—there are alternatives, such as civil union. In the following chapters, I continue to develop a case for minimizing, rather than abolishing, marriage.

II. SAME-SEX MARRIAGE, THE "MONOGAMY STRAIGHTJACKET," AND FREE LOVE

The comparative merits of abolition and reform are also the subject of debate among theorists of gay and lesbian oppression. Some defenses of same-sex marriage have focused on the value of chaste, exclusive, sexual dyads. For example, Stephen Macedo defended same-sex marriage on the grounds that, by discouraging promiscuity, it would encourage gays and lesbians to lead better lives.[31] In contrast to such sexually conservative arguments, some theorists of lesbian, gay, and bisexual oppression have rejected same-sex marriage altogether, arguing that the marital ideal is a heterosexual paradigm. Gays and lesbians have often chosen less possessive and insular, more flexible and open, relationships. Thus Paula Ettelbrick asks, "Since when is marriage a path to liberation?" She argues that instead of affirming difference, same-sex marriage would assimilate lesbian and gay relationships into the heterosexual model—the "monogamy straightjacket," in Claudia Card's phrase.[32] According to Ettelbrick, same-sex marriage would undermine the goals of gay liberation: affirming gay and lesbian identity and relationship diversity.

Marriage, by legally distinguishing legitimate and illegitimate relationships, wrongly discourages relationship diversity; it encourages only one kind. Card compares the legal recognition of marriage to the defunct practice of marking birth certificates as "legitimate" or "illegitimate."[33] Relationships, like infants, should not be subjected to such legal distinctions. To Ettelbrick and Card, this classification is in itself an unjust discrimination, and it also serves as the basis for further unjust discrimination between the married and the unmarried. Card compares the gay and lesbian fight for same-sex marriage to a demand by a group excluded from slaveowning for the right to own slaves. She argues that the legal and economic incentives of marriage are inherently unjust, for a number of reasons. First, as discussed in the last section, the benefits attached to marriage and the difficulty of divorce burden the choice to marry or stay married with extraneous considerations. The reduction of exit options facilitates abuse and violence, as do spouses' legal access rights to each others' bodies and homes. Because these features enable abuse, marriage, according to Card, is an evil, insofar as it "facilitates…reasonably foreseeable intolerable harm"; same-sex marriage is undesirable because it would lead to abuse and avoidable deaths.[34] This evil, however, is not, as I argued above, inherent to marriage. Legal access rights and provisions mitigating spousal violence can be removed from marriage law. In addition, marriage reform responsive to the threat of violence can ensure adequate exit options, in light of economic dependence and dependence on marriage for benefits such as health care; I postpone this topic to Chapter 8.

Second, Card argues that distributing benefits such as health care through marriage is unjust because health care is a universal entitlement, which should not depend on marital status. This raises the question of whether legal distinctions and entitlements on the basis of marriage can be justified. Same-sex marriage advocates have argued that extending benefits such as health care and pension rights, custody and inheritance rights, tax and immigration status, and legal recognition of intimate relationships will benefit lesbians and gays. Even if excluding the unmarried from some of these goods is unjust, the exclusion of all gays and lesbians is a further injustice. Extending these benefits through same-sex marriage will combat lesbian and gay oppression and move closer to the goal of universal health care and pensions.[35] In an unjust system, one reform may not alleviate all injustices; but doing nothing, or abolishing marriage without implementing universal health care and pensions, would also result in injustice, and result in more people being deprived of health care and pensions.

However, even if providing such benefits through marriage can somehow be justified politically, will their provision through marriage serve gay liberation or force gay assimilation into the heteronormative mainstream? Some same-sex marriage advocates have argued that marriage would counteract stigmas against lesbians, gays, and bisexuals, thereby making society more accepting of diversity and the mainstream less heteronormative.[36] But can marriage law symbolize that same-sex lovers have equal worth, without also symbolically implying that some relationships are more valuable than others? By Card's and Ettelbrick's reasoning, same-sex marriage does not even symbolically express the equal worth of gays and lesbians; it fails to treat gays and lesbians equally because it fails to recognize their different modes of relationship. Admitting gays and lesbians into a heteronormative institution of marriage does not treat gays and lesbians equally. But Richard Mohr points out that same-sex marriage and relationship diversity are not incompatible: Marriage need not entail monogamy. Indeed, same-sex marriage may teach different-sex spouses that neither unchosen gender roles nor monogamy are essential to marriage.[37]

Card and Ettelbrick criticize the classification of relationships as "legitimate" and "illegitimate." However, it is precisely because marriage confers legitimacy that same-sex marriage is seen as an important symbolic goal for gay rights activists. Excluding gays and lesbians from marriage, they argue, is one of the primary ways in which society marks them as inferior. Thus Mohr argues that society denies gays and lesbians dignity by excluding them from marriage. The offer of "civil unions" replicates this inferiority—it "serves…to degrade gay men and lesbians by denying them one of the chief social forms by access to which America marks out membership in full humanity."[38] Card, too—who argues for abolishing all marriage—has more recently conceded the symbolic importance of same-sex marriage so long as different-sex marriage exists: Her opposition to same-sex marriage does not entail endorsing legislation banning it, such as the Defense of Marriage Act. She compares such legislation to the Nuremburg laws prohibiting intermarriage between Germans and non-Germans, suggesting that marriage bars may pave the way for other forms of legal discrimination.

Developing a theory of gay and lesbian oppression as distinct from other forms of oppression, Cheshire Calhoun has argued that marriage bars play a crucial role in the distinctive feature of such oppression, displacement from public life. The right to marry is at the heart of concepts of good citizenship: "[B]eing fit for marriage is intimately bound up with our cultural conception of what it means to be a citizen…because marriage is culturally conceived as playing a uniquely foundational role in sustaining civil society."[39] Excluding gays and lesbians from this institution displaces them from the center of political life and from status as full and equal citizens. Same-sex marriage is, on this view, essential to gay liberation.

However, Card's and Ettelbrick's point could be reformulated: Marriage may indeed be seen as a criterion for full citizenship, but wrongly so. Indeed, on this criterion, all unmarried persons, the divorced, and polygamists also fail to realize their capacities for citizenship. Citizens should not be graded on their marital status, or relationships on their supposed legitimacy. What is needed is not an extension of marriage but a transformation of the national imagination. The fundamental questions are whether marriage relationships can be recognized without quelling diversity, and whether any relationships deserve state support. In Chapter 7, I argue that there is political justification for state support for caring relationships. As I argue, Card is correct in rejecting state legitimization of relationships; where relationships between adults are concerned the only markers of legitimacy, from the state's perspective, should be mutual consent and compatibility with justice. But support for some relationships can be distinguished from classifying relationships into legitimate and illegitimate; the practical difference depends on clarifying the reasons for supporting them.

To foreshadow, one reason for reforming, rather than abolishing, marriage is that state definition of marriage will allow public rectification of past injustices. Abolishing marriage might seem to achieve equality by placing everyone in the same legal position. However, this would cede control of this still socially powerful institution to the churches and other private-sector groups. Abolition would allow private-sector providers to deny entry, with no countervailing public message of equality whereas reform would send an unequivocal message of equality. Ensuring equal access to a broadly recognized institution of marriage requires state involvement.

Just as Calhoun and Mohr argue that same-sex marriage will combat discrimination against gays and lesbians, some feminists have argued that same-sex marriage will combat gender roles. The critics' worry is that same-sex marriage will simply extend eligibility for patriarchal gender-structured marriage. But it is difficult to see how a marriage without gender difference can be inherently gender-structured. In itself, as Ferguson argues, "gay marriage *does* undermine the traditional patriarchal model" because different-sex marriage is the primary support of belief in naturally given gender roles.[40] The possibility of marriage without gender difference opens the possibility, for everyone, of marriage without gendered spousal roles. Criticism of marriage as inherently patriarchal or heteronormative suggests a false choice between superficial reform and abolition. Just as past marriage reform has ended women's legal subordination and race-based marriage bars, a restructured institution of marriage could challenge "the monogamy straightjacket" by recognizing diverse relationships, and thereby avoiding amatonormativity and heteronormativity.

A final aspect of Card's argument against marriage recalls the nineteenth-century free love tradition. Card suggests that the economic and legal incentives to marry burden the choice with extraneous considerations and make it unfree. This reflects a justice-related concern about burdening exit, but it may also reflect skepticism about institutionalizing love with legal obligations, and letting economic or practical considerations affect decisions about love, sex, and relationships.

Free lover and anarchist Emma Goldman wrote, "Every love relation should by its very nature remain an absolutely private affair. Neither the State, the Church, morality, or people should meddle with it."[41] But this should be considered in light of the twentieth-century feminist insight that the personal is political. We are taught how to love and the proper objects of love by social pressures and the state. Material conditions, determining where we can meet and where we can be alone, constrain love. In modern society, the state is always already involved. State noninterference would simply shift the construction of love wholly to cultural, social, corporate, and religious pressures. Love would be shaped by the machinations of the market and the mass media. Rather than withdrawing from protecting love relationships, the state could respect their "privacy" by providing a variety of options to support them. It is constraint on choice that constitutes "meddling"; supporting an array of relationships would not constrain, but empower, choice, and supporting all caring relationships would provide a strong counterbalance to the romantic-love-obsessed mass media and consumer culture.

A second free love worry is that love and sex should not be contaminated with economic or other material concerns. As the phrase "free love" suggests, a key idea of the movement was that the spontaneous character of love meant it could only be given freely, without compulsion or obligation. Stephen Pearl Andrews argued against marriage on the grounds that sexual relations were debased, like prostitution, by its legal bond. Free love must be authentic and spontaneous, given without thought of duty or benefit; Andrews defined adultery (drawing on its connotation of immoral sex) as any "sexual union, induced by any other motive...than that mutual love which by nature prompts the amative conjunction of the sexes."[42]

However, it is either naive or disingenuous to suggest that practical considerations should not shape decisions about love and sex. For one thing, the success of relationships may depend on material conditions, and for another, people may have other goods to weigh against entering a relationship, such as where they live, pursuing an education or career, or having resources for other projects. Moreover, the free love view entails that it is immoral to make a long-term commitment because that might require one to remain in the relationship, at times, for reasons other than spontaneous love. In my view, one cannot be obligated to love, but it is not morally wrong to persist through difficult periods based on a long-term shared project. People seek many goods in love relationships, including companionship, domesticity, reproduction, and so on, and may be willing to subordinate spontaneity and passion to their pursuit.

The correct kernel of the free love opposition to marriage bonds is their problematic imposition of one norm for everyone; as Andrews argued, different modes of association will suit different persons, and so if only one type of marriage is the norm, its constraints will be burdensome for many. But while Andrews questioned the norm of monogamy, he didn't question the centrality of love and sex to human life—indeed, he opened his unpublished *Love, Marriage, and the Condition of Woman* by asserting its centrality. The free love view, while proposing diversity in relationship structures, is still amatonormative in taking a certain kind of spontaneous, romantic, sexual love as the human goal! Someone who wants to settle down with a good friend for stable companionship, or enter an arranged marriage for reproduction, is simply seeking a different good from the ones that the free lovers prized.

Truly free love (understanding "free" as the free lovers themselves do) requires structures that permit easy exit—freedom to leave is the only way to ensure that staying is free. It also requires social structures that permit relationship diversity, including the choice to opt out of romantic love altogether, in friendships or care networks. A single form of marriage does not simply deny benefits to nonconformists; it also affects what people pursue. Recognizing one relationship in law discourages pursuing other kinds.

Andrews imagined that a society based on free love principles would permit a variety of amorous relations: monogamy, serial monogamy, polygamy. But abandoning amatonormativity might allow individuals to see their sexual relationships differently, not expecting emotional, erotic, intellectual, and leisure companionship all in one sexual partner, but recognizing the value of multiple relationships that carry warmth and affection, mental stimulation, and creaturely companionship. Where marriage and romantic love are not hegemonic, each individual might have a greater chance of discovering what suits her best. Once again, rejecting amatonormativity does not mean prohibiting or discouraging sexual and romantic relationships; it means ceasing to encourage them at the expense of relationship diversity and the marginalization of other caring relationships.

III. RACE

Marriage played a significant role in North American colonialism, racist nation building, and racial slavery and its aftermath. Early settlers condemned Native American family practices, some of which allowed polygamy, divorce, greater gender equality, and same-sex marriage. Settlers, missionaries, educators, and the law imposed an imported European Christian form of marriage on Natives. Family policy was used eugenically; Enakshi Dua writes that North American "projects of nation-building were constituted on a discourse of race, the nuclear family organized gender and sexual relations to ensure a racialized nation."[43] From the beginning of the colonial era until the end of antimiscegenation laws, marriage was used as a eugenic tool and tool of racial subordination, targeted especially at Native Americans, Asian immigrants and Asian-Americans, and African Americans. Racism dictated who had the legal right to marry and who could marry whom, while the imposition of eurocentric marriage law penalized the different practices of Natives, Asian immigrants, and African Americans.

In U.S. slavery, enslaved persons did not have the right to marry. Their informal families were torn apart, their children and partners removed and sold. Slaveholders forced breeding among enslaved persons in order to produce offspring who would themselves be enslaved, and they sexually used and assaulted enslaved females.

After Emancipation and the Civil War, enslaved persons embraced the right to marry as symbolic of civic equality. But a racist discourse sprung up among some chaplains, Freedmen's Bureau workers, and in the press, imputing innate promiscuity to persons of African descent—sometimes on the basis of habits formed as a result of slavery. During this period, formerly enslaved persons were arrested for unmarried cohabitation (which had been widely tolerated among whites up to this point) and other violations of the law of monogamy.[44]

Antimiscegenation law proliferated after the Civil War, once African Americans had gained the right to marry. The law did not so much prevent actual miscegenation as it excluded women of color and their children from the benefits of marriage, including social legitimacy. An exchange in George Washington Cable's 1879 story, "Madame Delphine," illustrates this. Madame Delphine, a "quadroon" with an "octoroon" daughter, asks her priest why inter-racial marriage is prohibited. The priest responds: "To keep the two races separate." The "quadroon" mistress of a white man responds "They do not want to keep us separated! They want to keep us despised.... from which race do they want to keep my daughter separate? She is seven parts white! The law did not stop her from being that; and now, when she wants to be a white man's good and honest wife, shall that law stop her?"[45] Antimiscegenation law helped maintain the fiction of racial difference and hierarchy by creating artificial divisions between socially defined races.

A specious argument used to defend antimiscegenation law was that both African Americans and whites were treated equally in both being forbidden to marry members of the other race. Of course, the law was grounded in beliefs about racial inferiority—the worry that intermarriage would sully the "purity" of the white race—and it served white privilege. It did not truly treat African Americans and whites equally, either symbolically, or, in many cases, materially. Antimiscegenation law also prohibited marriages between whites and Asians, largely in western states where anti-Asian sentiment was virulent.

This legacy still affects race relations and racial inequality. The symbolism of segregating marriage has been a powerful tool of racism. While laws prohibiting inter-racial marriage were struck down in 1967 by the U.S. Supreme Court in *Loving v. Virginia*, many state governments ignored the decision, and some judges sporadically enforced unconstitutional laws, remaining in state law, against interracial marriage. The state constitutions of Alabama and South Carolina contained such laws until 2000 and 1998, respectively. In a 2000 referendum, Alabama voters repealed the state's unconstitutional ban on interracial marriage—60 to 40 percent. But statistical analysis of voting demographics suggests that roughly half of white Alabama voters opposed repealing the ban.[46] Disapproval of interracial marriage reportedly continued at "around 30 percent" of Americans in the early 2000s.[47]

These astounding statistics point to the importance some Americans still invest in segregating marriage. Marriage bans play an important symbolic role in maintaining views of racial difference and hierarchy. Patricia Hill Collins has argued that marriage is associated with racism in more subtle ways. For instance, she argues, the American "imagined traditional family ideal" is racialized, as when the "typical family" is presented as white. Furthermore, the gender-structured male-headed family teaches hierarchy, a hierarchy sometimes used to "justify" racial inequality by analogy, as, for instance, when African American adults are portrayed as childlike (a discourse drawn on in justifying slavery, in which enslaved persons were compared with children, or naturally obedient and dependent wives). The ideal of biological kinship legitimated through marriage also lends support to ideas of belonging based on bloodlines and racial purity.[48]

The nineteenth- and twentieth-century U.S. construction of marriage law repudiated non-Christian practices, often in explicitly racist and ethnocentric terms. In public political discourse, polygamy was associated with Muslims, Jews, and Asians. Japanese and Korean "picture marriage" or "proxy marriage" was treated as invalid (in which a woman married a "proxy" in Japan, before traveling to the United States to meet her actual husband), and arranged marriage, which was associated with Asians, came under suspicion. Nonwhites were stigmatized as failing to conform to monogamous marriage, while marriage practices of some nonwhites were not only not recognized, but criminalized. The connection between monogamous Christian marriage and citizenship was so tight that at different times both marrying a prostitute and polygamy were suggested as grounds for stripping male citizens of citizenship.[49] Marriage law continues to be ethnocentric, enshrining an ideal handed down from European Christians, spread around the world by nineteenth-century missionaries, and built, in the United States, on the extermination or criminalization of Native American marriage practices, as well as, for that matter, nonconforming practices of immigrants or persons brought from Africa.[50]

The legacies of slavery and antimiscegenation law, and other effects of systemic racism, such as race-based poverty and unemployment, low wages, and high rates of incarceration of African American men, continue to shape African American marriage patterns. These patterns provide a good example of how marriage law and policy continue to treat as illegitimate practices associated with nonwhites. Like the Reconstruction officials who criticized the practices of former enslaved persons, state officials have continued to draw moralistic attention to African American marriage patterns. The infamous 1965 U.S. Moynihan Report criticized "Negro" families as too matriarchal, citing reversed gender roles within marriage as well as absent fathers. However, while some of the causes of these patterns are deplorable, the fact that families are female-headed is not in itself cause for negative evaluation.

In African American communities, practices of shared child rearing have proliferated. According to Collins, African American families have traditionally shared child rearing, reflecting "a continuation of West African cultural values" as well as "functional adaptations to race and gender oppression": "African and African American communities have...recognized that vesting one person with full responsibility for mothering a child may not be possible or wise. As a result, othermothers—women who assist bloodmothers by sharing mothering responsibilities—traditionally have been central to the institution of Black motherhood."[51] Othermothering builds networks of relationships between women of different generations. bell hooks argues that such "revolutionary parenting" represents a feminist ideal possible precluded, in the mainstream, by parental possessiveness.[52] If researchers and government agencies did not assume such practices to be defective, they would be able to recognize the successes of African American families—including single-parent families and othermothering—where they have occurred and understand better how to support these care networks.

Contemporary marriage law recognizes and benefits a eurocentric form of marriage that is less prevalent among African Americans than among white Americans. Benefitting this form of marriage therefore disproportionately benefits whites and excludes from benefits relationships more prevalent among African Americans. The U.S. government has responded to these patterns by encouraging African Americans to marry. But this overlooks the reasons for different marriage patterns and for poverty, failing to address root causes of poverty in systemic racism.[53] Moreover, it fails to recognize the success of alternative family structures such as othermothering. This critique is structurally parallel to Card's and Ettelbrick's critique of same-sex marriage—rather than recognizing different, but valuable, African American family patterns, the state has tried to encourage African Americans to enter the only form of marriage available.

This pattern continues today. The U.S. Healthy Marriage Initiative, which carries out marriage promotion, is racially targeted: There is an African American Healthy Marriage Initiative (AAHMI), Hispanic Healthy Marriage Initiative (HHMI), and Native American Healthy Marriage Initiative (NAHMI). The AAHMI claims to respond to "Crisis-level statistics" among African Americans: for instance, "42 percent of African American adults are married, compared to 61 percent of whites & 59 percent of Hispanics," and "68 percent of AA [sic] births are to unmarried women, compared to 29 percent for whites and 44 percent for Hispanics."[54] The relational presentation of these numbers is striking. African Americans have *lower* marriage rates and *higher* rates of out-of-wedlock pregnancy. In the statistics presented in this AAHMI Fact Sheet, the highest where high is seen as desirable, the lowest where low is seen as desirable (excepting divorce) is attached to whites.

The evidence that African Americans are in crisis is that their marriage rate is lower than that of whites. White rates are taken as normative.[55] (That white is also taken as normal is reflected in the fact that there is AAHMI, HHMI, and NAHMI, but no WHMI. The generic HMI is presumably for whites.) The AAHMI itself admits a problem with its racially targeted mission: The bulk of studies showing "the benefits of marriage have been conducted on white marriages rather than black marriages."[56] This suggests that the AAHMI rests on the assumption that correlation between marriage and benefits among whites will also hold for African Americans, who face racial discrimination and the complicated legacy of such discrimination.

Moreover, this taxonomy seems arbitrary in choosing race as the relevant category. A marriage map of the United States shows higher marriage rates in the South. Instead of being targeted racially, the HMIs could target Northerners, urbanites, or atheists. The choice to racially segregate the HMIs also assumes that marriages will be intraracial, not interracial; the taxonomy precludes a focus on interracial marriages. Choosing a racial taxonomy is also significant because marriage promotion has moralistic overtones. For example, George W. Bush, who founded the HMI, referred in a State of the Union address to the "moral tradition that defines marriage."[57] The Social Security Act criteria for abstinence-only education present marriage as the norm, the appropriate context for sexual activity. By its very rationale in this Act, the HMI implies that those with lower marriage rates have not lived up to society's norms, so the choice to present data on racial lines may encourage racist stereotypes.

As noted, this critique of marriage law as racially biased parallels the critique of it as heteronormative; the two critiques also intersect. Sarah Lucia Hoagland has argued that heterosexism and white supremacy are mutually reinforcing, that race and gender are constructed mutually in interlocking systems of oppression. For example, the sexuality of white women and women of color is portrayed oppositionally, so that the hierarchies among relationships that marriage defines also underlie racial hierarchies.[58] While this analysis may explain many social phenomena, it is not necessary to make the case that marriage reform is a matter of racial justice. To make that case, we need only show that different racial and ethnic groups have different marriage rates and different family structures, and marriage law disproportionately and arbitrarily benefits some groups over others in ways that reinforce patterns of discrimination and inequality. Once again, this injustice is not essential to marriage, but can be remedied by restructuring marriage to recognize different practices, so long as they are compatible with justice.

IV. SOCIOECONOMIC CLASS

Contemporary Marxists have updated Marx's criticism of marriage as an inherently capitalist institution that creates the conditions for private property, including property in women (which also influenced feminist accounts, discussed above, of marriage as an inherently unjust property relation). The claim is that marriage, as "the maintenance by one man or woman of the effective right to exclude indefinitely all others from erotic access to the conjugal partner," is "simply a form of private property."[59] However, this allegedly inherent injustice, it seems to me, can be eliminated by eliminating legal rights that make marriage akin to property. In practice, marriage need not be sexually exclusive—or dyadic.

But by supporting private property, marriage is said to underlie socioeconomic class stratification. Marriage, one Marxist argues, is "indispensable to the persistence of the capitalist order," ideologically and in numerous psychological and material ways.[60] Most notable is the claim that marriage supports the idea that the basic relationship between persons and need-satisfying things (including other persons) is ownership. But marriage, it is claimed, also supports capitalism by separating families as economic units, regulating inheritance, encouraging expenditures on weddings and single-family homes, and keeping divorce lawyers employed. Since the version of egalitarian liberalism I will be employing in later chapters is compatible with capitalism, I won't address these concerns about capitalism.

However, exclusive, dyadic marriage may well, as Plato argued, orientate resources to private goods rather than to the public good, and, as Fineman argued, away from collective responsibility for dependency.[61] Moreover, it has been argued that marriage is a tool by which employers control the proletariat. In *Against Love*, Laura Kipnis argues that marriages, with their inevitable compromises, quenchings of desire, and hard work, create a docile, cowed, workforce and electorate, who are habituated to settle for less than they want. She writes that marriages are "domestic gulags": "[W]hat current social institution is more enclosed than modern domesticity? What offers greater regulation of movement and time, or more precise surveillance of body and thought?"[62] On this noteworthy, though difficult to assess, view, marriage is a social control mechanism habituating spouses to accept authority and sacrifice their desires.

Setting aside these ideas as beyond the scope of this project, there are straightforwardly documented connections between marriage and socioeconomic class. Census data show a socioeconomic gap between the married and unmarried. One reason may be that men, who previously tended to "marry down," now tend to marry their peers in education and employment. Working-class women wait longer to marry; one possible explanation is that they envision that their pay will plateau once they have a child and so postpone marriage (and child bearing). Another possible explanation is that people wait to marry until they are financially stable.[63] These trends suggest that marriage consolidates capital, matching spouses economically and thereby entrenching inequalities. Presumably these effects will be compounded in the next generation, especially where college educations are expensive. Moreover, it means the benefits attached to marriage are disproportionately benefiting those already better off.

If marriage markets are entrenching economic inequality and eroding equal opportunity, this suggests a conflict with principles of justice. In *A Theory of Justice*, Rawls mentioned the possibility that equal opportunity might require abolishing the family to give children equal starts in life, but dismissed it; however, different family backgrounds do affect children's life chances. Rawls's critic Robert Nozick attempted a *reductio* of economic redistribution by imagining a society in which a central agency distributed mates.[64] However, unjust consequences of marriage, such as stratification of wealth and reductions in equal opportunity, could be corrected without arranging marriages, for instance, through inheritance tax and education.

Another explanation of the socioeconomic marriage gap is that impediments to marriage and intimate relationships are a hidden cost of poverty, homelessness, or unemployment. The unattainable luxury for the worst-off members of society is not the expensive destination wedding, but the stability, privacy, and heated room of one's own that marriage—or cohabitation, or intimate companionship—requires. Marriage is a less likely prospect for those living with their parents, in a motel or shared room, or where both parties have insecure employment.[65] Cohabitation is only an economy of scale for those who can afford to live alone in the first place, and thereby save by sharing the costs of housing. Poverty may also undermine marriages: Financial stress causes marital problems.[66] While I have argued against the amatonormative assumption that everyone wants such relationships, it is also an injustice that the poor should face impediments to relationships and marriage; this too conflicts with ensuring a range of relationship options. However, this also suggests that poverty is not best addressed by marriage promotion.

In the first half of this chapter, I argued that two important elements of marriage law reform are that it recognize relationship diversity and provide good exit options. This will be the subject of a proposal developed in Chapters 7 and 8. One further lesson of this chapter has been that current marriage law has been constructed by arbitrarily (from the perspective of justice) excluding competing forms of marriage. Contemporary marriage law in any particular jurisdiction is only one facet of this multiform institution. In considering reform, it is worth remembering how diverse forms of marriage are, and how greatly marriage law has been constructed, and reconstructed, by legislative fiat. To begin the political argument for reform, I will examine, in Chapter 6, how political liberal arguments for same-sex marriage have had hidden amatonormative assumptions.

6

DEFINING MARRIAGE
POLITICAL LIBERALISM AND THE
SAME-SEX MARRIAGE DEBATES

Southern Baptists define marriage as a union between one man and one woman in which the wife's role is to submit to her husband's "leadership." Openly gay Episcopalian bishop Gene Robinson describes his family as "mainstream" and says of his marriage to another man that their "relationship is one of mutual support, love, care . . . the way a marriage ought to be."[1] Robinson cites emotional qualities, not sex difference, in defining marriage. Which definition is correct?

There is controversy over the nature and purpose of marriage—especially whether it is primarily for recognition of intimate adult relationships or for reproduction and child rearing. In Part One, I criticized influential moral arguments, such as those of natural law, that marriage has a morally fixed purpose and, accordingly, essential features such as male-female monogamy. And I have emphasized that, historically and culturally, marriage has been highly variable. Marriage is a constantly evolving legal and social institution that has been structured in many complex ways for a variety of purposes; its essential features are not fixed by its history. However, in any case, as I explain below, neither moral arguments nor historical record should define marriage law in a liberal society

In disputed cases, the definition of marriage cannot be resolved by appeal to previous legal definitions, because the justice of that definition itself is under dispute; in any case legal definitions are often unhelpfully circular, defining "marriage" in terms of "spouses" and "spouses" in terms of "marriage," for example.[2] Nor can the definition of marriage be resolved by appeal to social definitions. Existing social understandings of marriage in liberal societies are fragmented; the common denominator might be, at most, that marriage involves an intimate relationship recognized by some authority. Even if there were a shared definition, social conventions are not necessarily a basis for law; social conventions may be themselves inegalitarian or unfair. Moreover, even widely shared and innocuous social practices might be unjust as the basis of law; for example, rules of etiquette. Most such practices fall within protected liberties, so that basing law or policy on them would be unjust. That it is a social norm is not enough reason to legislate a particular definition of marriage.

Defining marriage is not simply a matter of checking a dictionary. Philosophers have typically appealed to fundamental normative principles to make the case for particular definitions. In Part One, I argued that certain moral arguments that marriage has an essential purpose were unsuccessful; in Part Two, I begin with the point that political, not moral, principles ought to govern marriage law. Legal marriage design depends on what marriage is "for," and the question of what it is "for" will have to be settled by looking at independent political reasons for what institutions there should be, not some independently fixed definition of marriage.

In this chapter, I address the political definition of marriage by examining liberal debates over same-sex marriage. Same-sex marriage advocates have argued that it is unjust to define marriage legally on the basis of contested moral views regarding same-sex activity. I agree, but I also argue that these arguments have failed to follow the implications of such neutral or political liberal reasoning to the extreme conclusion. Some philosophers, marriage contractualists, have tried to take such reasoning further, arguing that the neutral or political liberal principles employed in some arguments for same-sex marriage imply instead that the state should not recognize marriage at all. In contrast, I argue that these principles require a radical restructuring of marriage that recognizes the many forms of caring relationship.

This proposal sometimes meets the objection that the changed institution would not be marriage, because marriage is by definition different-sex, monogamous, reproductive, and so on. On this point, two Canadian philosophers of language submitted affidavits to a Canadian court considering same-sex marriage. Robert Stainton argued that "marriage" is by definition different-sex, just as a bachelor is by definition an unmarried man, so that "same-sex marriage" is an impossibility, like a married bachelor. But Adèle Mercier responded that this confuses meaning and reference. Stainton's argument, she points out, would imply that the meaning of the word "lawyer" changed when women were admitted to the Bar. Past applications of a term need not yield necessary and sufficient criteria for applying it: "Marriage" (like "citizen" or "lawyer") may be extended to new cases without thereby changing its meaning.[3] Past applications of "marriage" should not present a conceptual hurdle to our investigation.

I will tackle the question of defining marriage in law by asking what just rationale for marriage law, as we have it, there could be. I begin by explaining how political liberalism constrains the legal definition of marriage.

I. LAW, MORALITY, AND POLITICAL LIBERALISM

The legal definition of marriage should be guided by the legal rationale of marriage law. This rationale should, in turn, be guided by political principles that generally govern legislation. In other words, marriage law should not be treated as a special case, but like any other part of the basic structure of society. In this and the next two chapters, I develop a liberal feminist account of marriage law within the constraints of political liberalism. In this section, I focus on explaining those constraints themselves.

We can see the force of such constraints by examining a few views that would violate them. It is a cliché of contemporary political discourse that the state should protect marriage because it is a moral norm. One philosopher who propounded such a view was Patrick Devlin, who took marriage as a prime example of a moral norm that the state ought to protect. According to his theory of legal moralism, the state should legally protect society's moral norms to preserve the existence of society itself: "[A]n established morality is as necessary as good government to the welfare of society."[4] Society must protect itself against disintegration due to changing mores. While Devlin accepted that the state should not legislate particular religious views, he held that his society possessed a common morality such that "the right-thinking man in western society accepts a Christian notion of marriage as the ideal and would not dispute that the law should be based on it."[5] The protection of marriage was especially important, in Devlin's view, because its reproductive role made it essential to handing down other moral norms.

There are many obvious problems with this argument. Contemporary liberal societies, characterized by a pluralism of practices, lack homogeneous marital norms to protect.[6] Even if a shared norm existed, it might be unjust to enforce it, if, for example, it involved inegalitarian gender roles the legal enforcement of which would violate liberties. But for a political liberal, there is a deeper problem with legal moralism: The state should not base law and policy on norms drawn from comprehensive moral views, views concerning conduct and ideals in areas of life outside the narrowly political. Political liberalism resists state promotion of morality by requiring that public reasons, reasons acceptable to citizens with differing moral and religious views, be available for policy and legislation.

Political liberalism can also be contrasted with the views of contemporary conservatives and natural lawyers such as John Finnis, Robert George, and Roger

Scruton, who argue that law should teach moral norms. As we saw in Chapter 3, they argue that by recognizing marriage, law conveys its value and thereby guides citizens' choices toward their own good. Law serves a morally educational purpose in guiding citizens to choose the good according to new natural law or virtue theory. These arguments, since they depend on comprehensive moral doctrines, do not provide public reasons.

Some liberals, known as perfectionist liberals, also hold that the state should frame laws according to judgments about valuable lives and human excellences. The most influential proponent of this view, Joseph Raz, grounds liberalism in the value of autonomy. According to his value-pluralist perfectionism, protecting autonomy requires that the state ensure that there are a range of valuable options available; value-pluralism allows that there are a variety of valuable choices. Raz gives monogamous marriage as an example. Assuming that it is a valuable form of life, Raz argues that state recognition of monogamy is necessary to preserve this valuable option. Legal reforms—permitting polygamy, for example—will not simply increase available options, but will change the pattern of people's choices, eroding the valuable option of monogamous marriage.[7] Protecting monogamous marriage is needed to keep this valuable option available. While Raz does not defend the value of monogamy, Stephen Macedo gives a fuller perfectionist rationale for the claim that marriage is valuable: Control of sexuality is part of the self-control needed for a "healthy and happy life." State support for such self-control, through incentives to enter stable marital commitments, helps people lead better lives.[8]

However, from a politically liberal perspective, such views inappropriately insert comprehensive moral doctrines into political life. In *Political Liberalism*, Rawls describes liberalism as historically emerging from the need for states to accommodate competing religious views. The protected liberties at the heart of liberalism—freedom of conscience and of religion—are in tension with theocracy; an ideal liberal state would not support any particular religion. State action is implicitly coercive; even if support for a religion does not involve legal requirements or prohibitions (such as mandatory prayer or tithing), funding for such support must come from taxes paid under threat of the state's coercive power. In contemporary political liberalism, this separation of the state from religion has been extended to the competing moral doctrines found in society. Law and policy have costs; costs imposed on citizens through coercive taxation should be justifiable to them without expecting them to share a contested moral or religious view. Political liberalism prohibits policy and legislation, at least in important matters of justice, from being based solely on controversial moral or religious norms—they must also be justifiable in public reason.

In Rawls's political liberalism, public reason requires that in deciding public matters, especially "matters of fundamental justice," and in the political sphere (the courts and the legislature), citizens must give reasons which they could reasonably expect those with different conceptions of the good (views of what is good or valuable) drawn from different comprehensive moral, philosophical, or religious doctrines to accept. Rawls draws a crucial distinction between narrowly political views, such as the theory of justice, and comprehensive doctrines, which concern all areas of life. In the political sphere, public reason allows the giving of reasons from within comprehensive religious, philosophical, or moral doctrines only if a justification that respects public reason is also available. Thus, Martin Luther King's use of Christian themes in his speeches met this standard because his calls for racial equality could also be justified through public reason.[9]

While some liberal arguments for same-sex marriage have appealed to public reason, others have appealed to the related doctrine of neutrality—roughly, that "political decisions must be, so far as is possible, independent of any particular conception of the good life, or of what gives value to life."[10] For neutralists, the state should remain neutral between conceptions of the good that are found in comprehensive religious, philosophical, or moral doctrines, excepting any conflicting with justice.[11] Many versions of this principle have been defended; here, I introduce Rawls' later formulation, which complements his account of public reason. As Rawls formulates the principle, "the state is not to do anything intended to favor or promote any particular comprehensive doctrine rather than another, or to give greater assistance to those who pursue it." More broadly, "basic institutions and public policy . . . are neutral in the sense that they can be endorsed by citizens generally as within the scope of a public political conception."[12]

This conception requires neutrality of aim, or justificatory neutrality, in framing the law, not the outrageously demanding neutrality of effect, which would require that states ensure policies have equal effect on which conceptions are adopted or even ensure substantive equal opportunity to pursue different conceptions.[13] The less demanding neutrality of aim, or justificatory neutrality, to which Rawls's theory of justice as fairness is committed, requires that the state not justify law or policy by appeal to a conception of the good within a comprehensive doctrine, such as judgments about valuable lives, virtues, excellences, and so on.

Neutrality, like public reason, constrains political decision making by excluding the giving of certain reasons for institutions and policy; it excludes conceptions of the good drawn from comprehensive doctrines. This constraint applies to the state, in the person of legislators and public officers, and to all citizens in political contexts.[14] It prevents lawmakers from prohibiting actions, providing subsidies, or framing institutions for the purpose of promoting any such conceptions. As George Sher puts it, one "way of promoting the good is just to provide the right sorts of options," as by funding museums and universities, or "deciding which agreements [the state] will and will not enforce," such as marriage.[15]

Thus neutrality opposes perfectionism. A strictly neutral state cannot fund the arts on the grounds that painting is superior to televised wrestling. It cannot ban activities such as pornography, prostitution, or gambling, on the grounds of their moral turpitude. But it could admit other grounds for so doing: For example, if pornography violates women's free speech or arts education inculcates political virtue. However, in *Political Liberalism* Rawls suggests restricting the application of neutrality only to matters of fundamental justice, thus allowing, for instance, funding for the arts or environmental protections.

Within political liberalism, the scope of public reason and neutrality is a crucial question. If these constraints apply only to constitutional essentials or basic matters of justice, it might be thought that they would not apply to marriage law.[16] However, this thought would be mistaken. Rawls makes clear in "The Idea of Public Reason Revisited" that the state's "legitimate interest" in marriage and the family is constrained by public reason: "[A]ppeals to monogamy as such, or against same-sex marriages, as within the government's legitimate interest in the family, would reflect religious or comprehensive moral doctrines. Accordingly, that interest would appear improperly specified."[17] Family law must be justified with reference to political values (such as children's welfare and women's equality). Public reason applies to the family because the family, as one of "society's main institutions," is part of the basic structure of society, and hence, a "matter for political justice."[18] In light of Rawls' comments, it is clear that public reason applies to marriage and family law as part of the basic structure. However, Rawls—like some other theorists—claims that the state's main interest in marriage and family law is reproduction. In this and the ensuing chapter, I will make a case for separating frameworks for adult caring relationships from parenting frameworks, and argue that matters of fundamental justice are at stake in both.

Two further considerations in favor of the constraints of public reason and neutrality apply to marriage. State action is implicitly coercive, so state endorsement of ethical views from which citizens reasonably differ fails to respect their liberty.[19] In the context of neutrality, this was expressed as the intuitive idea that neutrality is required "to treat . . . citizens as equals"—not because all conceptions of the good are equally valid, but because reasonable people hold different religious or ethical ideals and have a liberty right to pursue them.[20] These considerations are especially compelling when it comes to relationships, where there is deep disagreement and a strong liberty interest.

Second, state promotion of comprehensive moral, religious, or philosophical conceptions of the good in this area runs practical risks. It would require civil servants of extraordinary sensitivity, sophistication, self-awareness, and philosophical acumen. As Ackerman writes, "Love, friendship, and the like are not readily susceptible of mass production."[21] A special danger is that ethical views can reflect self-interest or class interest. The relation between restrictive sexual codes and the oppression of women is a good example. Rawls notes this problem:

> When it is said, for example, that certain kinds of sexual relationships are degrading and shameful, and should be prohibited on this basis, . . . it is often because a reasonable case can not be made in terms of the principles of justice. Instead we fall back on ideas of excellence. But in these matters we are likely to be influenced by subtle aesthetic preferences and personal feelings of propriety; and individual, class, and group differences are often sharp and irreconcilable.[22]

Risks of such fallibility are especially high in the case of marriage, where religion, culture, and sexual, heterosexual, and amatonormative privilege combine to encourage investment in beliefs about the excellence of "traditional" marriage.

Under the constraints of public reason, the reasons given for marriage law must meet a certain standard. Political liberalism precludes defining marriage law or policy on the basis of comprehensive religious, philosophical, or moral views. The application of these constraints to marriage law suggests the following position. It is open to religions, wedding chapels, groups of friends, and so on, to define marriage as they please. So long as they respect rights, private definitions of marriage need not concern a liberal state. That is, so long as minors or kidnap victims are not being pressed into marriage, so long as all parties are competent and fully informed of their rights, so long as the rights of nonconsenting third parties are not infringed upon, the state should not intervene in these practices. But the *legal* definition of marriage must be politically justified. Marriage law must be justifiable within public reason, explaining why—without appeal to comprehensive doctrines—the state is using its monies and coercive powers for this purpose. The rationale of marriage law should figure larger than it has in the liberal discussion of marriage law up to now. Debates over same-sex marriage have addressed the question of whether its purpose is to support and recognize intimate adult partnerships or child- rearing units. However, why should the state be involved in supporting and recognizing either? In Chapter 7, I answer this fundamental question; first, I show how the debate so far has failed to answer it satisfactorily.

Before doing so, I should address one further objection that liberal principles of justice do not apply to marriage. As Susan Moller Okin has shown, political philosophers from Locke to Rawls have resisted the application of their own theories of justice to marriage and the family. However, as Okin, Veronique Munoz-Dardé, and Rawls himself (finally) have argued, the family is part of the basic structure of society and thus, within Rawlsian theory, subject to the principles of justice.[23] While there is controversy over what the compatibility of the family with equal opportunity implies, it is not controversial within liberalism that marriage and family *law* should conform to principles of justice. This means that there are no exemptions from respecting rights within marriage and that the legal rights and responsibilities of marriage must be compatible with the difference principle (Rawls' principle of economic redistribution) and fair equal opportunity. Thus legislation such as the Marital Rape Exemption or laws or private policies requiring female schoolteachers to resign on marriage is ruled out.

The burden of proof lies on those who would make exceptions to general political principles in the case of marriage. Libertarian Jennifer Morse has argued that "marriage is an organic, pre-political institution" based in nature, which the state must respect; it is thus exempt from general libertarian principles such as free contract.[24] But arguments from nature are dubious. For one thing, the metaphysics and epistemology of human nature are under dispute in ways that undermine such claims; as Mill argued in *The Subjection of Women*, socialization precludes knowledge of human nature. Anthropologically, the diversity of marriage institutions undermines the claim that only one is "natural": Prehistoric marriage involved an annual exchange of spouses between nomadic groups; "husband-visitor" societies like the Na in China are arranged around the female line; some Native American tribes recognized some same-sex marriages; historically, polygyny has been dominant. In light of this variety, claims that there is a single natural form should give us pause. Appeals to the traditions of American democracy are similarly problematic. These traditions include slavery, coverture, and interracial marriage bans; some traditions need reform.[25]

In any case, arguments from nature have no role to play in liberalism. Institutions are to be regulated by principles of justice; nature is not normative. Within liberalism, there are no theoretical resources to argue for the exemption of marriage law from justice.

II. NEUTRAL AND POLITICAL LIBERAL ARGUMENTS FOR SAME-SEX MARRIAGE

Many liberal arguments for same-sex marriage have invoked neutrality and public reason. I will contend that such neutral and political liberal arguments for same-sex marriage have failed, by and large, to follow their reasoning as far as it goes. Further, the discussion has not produced an underlying rationale for marriage law. But competing political liberal arguments for marriage abolition suggest such a rationale is needed.

An important starting-point in liberal arguments for same-sex marriage is the recognition that the state provides numerous benefits through marriage, such as eligibility for health insurance and pensions, privacy rights, immigration eligibility, and visiting rights, which are denied to same-sex relationships. Same-sex marriage advocates note cases where long-term same-sex couples' lack of legal status has led to partners being excluded from hospital visitation or from a shared household or funeral arrangements when one partner dies.[26] Principles of fairness and moral equality seem to condemn such inequitable arrangements. Why should different-sex relationships be eligible for special privileges? Why should some citizens receive special protections that others lack? Some conservatives give religious or moral reasons, often concerning the impermissibility of same-sex activity. But public reason excludes such moral considerations.

Typical defenses of same-sex marriage in terms of public reason and neutrality begin by characterizing marriage as providing a legislative framework for certain adult relationships. They proceed by showing that same-sex relationships exhibit the features of different-sex relationships formalized by such a framework.[27] This argumentative strategy suggests an objection that turns on the definition or purpose of marriage: Marriage should not be understood primarily in terms of adult relationships, but instead as an institution concerned with protecting the interests of children. In the next section, I will respond to such an objection, arguing that legal frameworks for adult relationships are best considered separately from legal frameworks for parenting. For the moment, I will accept this definition in order to review political liberal arguments for same-sex marriage.

Having first taken marriage as recognizing certain adult relationships, these arguments then show that same-sex relationships possess the relevant features of the different-sex relationships formalized by marriage. For instance, if marriage recognizes intimate, committed relationships between adults, then intimate, committed relationships between adults of the same sex should be eligible for recognition. The next argumentative move is to show that attempts to distinguish same-sex and different-sex relationships depend on comprehensive moral or religious views such as judgments about the inferiority of same-sex relationships to different-sex relationships. If so, then arguments against same-sex marriage depend on appeal to reasons inadmissible in political liberalism; if this is true of all such arguments, none can be successful within political liberalism. Thus, unless a public reason for distinguishing different-sex and same-sex relationships can be found, equal treatment requires legalizing same-sex marriage.

A characteristic list of the core features of marriage is given by Ralph Wedgwood. Marriage "typically involves sexual intimacy, economic and domestic cooperation, and a voluntary mutual commitment to sustaining this relationship."[28] These core features of marriage, Wedgwood argues, matter more than peripheral ones, such as monogamy and the sex of the spouses. Wedgwood proceeds to argue that reasons for recognizing different-sex marriage—essentially, citizens' desires to have their relationships recognized as marriages—extend to same-sex relationships that share the core features. However, relationships, or adult care networks, may be important without involving sexual intimacy or economic or domestic cooperation, and members of such networks may desire social recognition or other benefits of marriage. The question is why these aspects—sex, a shared household, and shared finances—are not themselves peripheral; might they not be, like monogamy or the different-sex condition, a holdover from an institution now irrelevant to many citizens' relationships? What we need—and what a political rationale will provide—is the means to distinguish the central and peripheral aspects of marriage.

Likewise, Adrian Wellington argues that the function of marriage is the recognition of voluntary intimate relationships. Same-sex relationships resemble different-sex relationships in intimacy and voluntariness. Thus, Wellington concludes, same-sex relationships functionally resemble marriages, and hence "same sex couples are entitled to the same state sponsorship as opposite sex couples."[29] Neutrality and equal treatment with regard to a legal framework for adult relationships require legally recognizing same-sex marriage because same-sex relationships are similar to different-sex relationships in the relevant respects.

However, the functional criteria Wellington gives could apply to some close friendships and urban tribes. As he admits, his description of the function of marriage would apply to configurations other than romantic couples. He follows this admission by immediately stipulating that marriage recognizes "couples" as distinct from "special friends." But by his own reasoning, "state sponsorship" for couples, as distinct from "special friends," ménages à trois, and other adult care networks or groups of friends, also runs afoul of neutrality. If marriage recognizes voluntary intimate or committed relationships, then neutrality requires that marriage eligibility be extended to voluntary intimate relationships of all kinds, including friendships and adult care networks. From the perspective of justice, the limitation to romantic couples appears arbitrary.

Wellington might respond that ménages à trois or friendships differ from same-sex and different-sex dyadic relationships in a relevant respect.[30] Since friendships and the group relationships at issue are voluntary, he would have to claim that they differ in intimacy. *Prima facie*, this objection has some plausibility: A cohabiting dyadic couple might be thought to experience greater intimacy than members of an adult care network living separately. However, this raises the question of what *type* of intimacy is at issue (emotional, sexual, domestic), and this leads back to the same problem. Friends or triads or networks can claim intimacy, too. Polyamorists, for example, claim to exercise greater honesty and openness, presumably a constituent of emotional intimacy. Conservative sexual ethicists might claim, in contrast, that intimacy requires exclusivity. Some philosophers have tried to make the case that intimacy must be dyadic; however, three—or more—people might claim that, whatever their arrangement lacks that dyads have, they gain in a different type of intimacy. Defining the relevant intimacy that qualifies relationships for recognition will inevitably appeal to inadmissible comprehensive moral and religious views.

Just as Wellington and Wedgwood argued that distinctions can only be drawn between different-sex and same-sex relationships by appeal to illegitimate comprehensive doctrines, so distinctions between the other relationship types—amorous relationships and friendships, dyads and groups—can only be justified by appeal to comprehensive doctrines regarding the value of dyads as opposed to networks, sexual as opposed to nonsexual relationships, and so on. Judgments regarding the comparative value of different relationship types are matters of comprehensive religious, moral, and philosophical doctrines, not public reason. Once again, we are drawn to the need for a politically liberal rationale for marriage law, which can explain why marriage has the features it does.

Wedgwood, unlike many writers, does attempt to provide a neutral rationale for marriage law: "Many couples have a serious desire to make a legally binding mutual commitment, of this uniquely familiar and widely-understood kind; so these couples need some assurance that this commitment will have a generally-understood social meaning of the relevant kind."[31] Marriage brings a social recognition and understanding that many couples want, and legal recognition of marriage reinforces this. Because it invokes citizens' desires, rather than an ideal relationship or moral norm, this rationale is neutral.

However, members of adult care networks may also desire to make a "legally binding mutual commitment" and gain access to "a generally-understood social meaning of the relevant kind." Presumably, what many same-sex couples want from marriage is recognition of the centrality of the relationship to their lives, their enduring commitment, and social visibility—not just recognition that they live together and share finances and have sex, because, after all, they might not. Indeed, some currently married couples do not meet the criteria! While allowing that married couples do not always meet all three criteria, Wedgwood suggests that they intend to enter a relationship that meets the criteria. As he notes, some couples might be prevented from meeting the criteria by practical impediments—as when one spouse is transferred by work to a different city, or when spouses refrain from sex for health reasons. But other couples might want to marry without intending ever to satisfy the criteria. They might prefer separate residences or bank accounts, or meet and marry while already living in different cities, with no plans to move. There are many reasons people might choose to refrain from sex, including religious belief or lack of desire. And while law usually divides marital property on divorce, currently married couples may still prefer to keep their bank accounts separate, or alter these terms through prenuptial agreements. Wedgwood does not consider recognizing relationships that intentionally lack the "core" of sex, shared finances, and cohabitation. But many people may be in relationships lacking these and yet still desire recognition of the special status of their relationship!

Wedgwood argues that a redefinition of marriage should not greatly alter its core meaning, which would undermine his rationale for marriage law, that is, enabling citizens to satisfy their desire to have their relationship recognized as having a certain social meaning. However, it is not clear that marriage does indeed have such a core meaning, as the competing attempts to define it suggest. What core meaning is shared by the Southern Baptists, natural lawyers, and same-sex marriage advocates? For Southern Baptists, the core involves divinely ordained gender difference; for natural lawyers, procreation. These examples could be easily multiplied when we consider the diverse religious and moral doctrines in a liberal, multicultural society—not to mention the critics of marriage discussed in the previous chapter. The essential social meaning of marriage is already fractured, too fractured to sustain Wedgwood's core definition across the many groups constituting society.

Moreover, even if marriage did have a shared and stable core meaning, the state should not recognize and benefit it if it conflicts with justice. Parties should not be able to claim state recognition and protection for their relationship as having a status with a core meaning that arbitrarily excludes some groups. It is pertinent here that opponents of same-sex marriage argue that its legal recognition will undermine the core meaning of marriage, as they understand it. Wedgwood's argument preempts this by presenting a core meaning that does not include gender difference. But it does include other criteria that limit eligibility amatonormatively, and hence, in the absence of public reason for amatonormativity, arbitrarily and unjustly. Once again, it seems as difficult to provide a public reason for amatonormative discrimination as it is for heterosexist discrimination.

Wedgwood argues that unsettling the core meaning of marriage would prevent citizens from being able to obtain the social recognition they desire from marriage. But from the perspective of Card and Ettelbrick (discussed in the previous chapter), the social meaning of marriage discourages diversity, and this is a reason to unsettle it. If marriage does indeed have an amatonormative core meaning, this is a reason either to cease recognizing it—because it discriminates arbitrarily— or to change the core meaning so that it does not discriminate arbitrarily. On Wedgwood's account of the rationale of marriage, changing the social meaning is not an option, since its rationale depends on citizens' desires to endow their relationships with this social meaning. However, in the next chapter, I will offer a different rationale and purpose for legal marriage, which is consistent with unsettling the core meaning.

This discussion of Wedgwood and Wellington suggests that once marriage is understood as a legal framework for intimate or committed or caring adult relationships, the implications of neutrality and political liberalism are much more far-reaching than has been generally recognized. Applied to such a framework, neutrality and political liberalism imply that law should not endorse an ideal of relationship on the basis of a comprehensive moral or religious doctrine. Excluding same-sex relationships appears to depend on doctrines regarding the value or permissibility of same-sex activity, as same-sex marriage advocates have argued. These doctrines cannot be given as public reasons against same-sex marriage. But defending the restriction of marriage to a cohabiting, financially entangled, sexual, monogamous, exclusive, romantic, central relationship also depends upon a view justifiable only from within comprehensive moral doctrines—amatonormativity. (Even attempts to defend amatonormativity in terms of biological science, as discussed in Chapter 4, depend upon a comprehensive ethical view of the human good, as rooted in biology.) Defenders of same-sex marriage have attacked current marriage law as defensible only by appeal to contested comprehensive moral judgments about same-sex relationships—but amatonormative marriage law is likewise only defensible by appeal to contested comprehensive moral judgments regarding the value of amorous dyads!

Excluding nondyads or nonamorous relationships from marriage has costs to their members beyond the financial benefits of marriage. Marriage exclusion also denies recognition—a point made by same-sex marriage advocates such as Wedgwood. Care networks, friends, and polyamorists can also employ this point. While extending marriage to such groups would alter the social meaning of marriage, it would extend state recognition to them on equal terms with other relationships. This might, in turn, gradually increase social recognition of diverse relationships.

Some defenders of same-sex marriage have acknowledged this point. Mohr, who argues that marriage bars perpetuate gay and lesbian oppression, has argued for recognition of the diverse sorts of relationships in which people pursue intimacy. Calhoun, too, has followed the implications of this argument for same-sex marriage: She argues that same-sex marriage advocates should accept the legalization of polygamy: The "disestablishment" of marriage requires the state to recognize a diversity of relationships.[32]

As Calhoun suggests, same-sex marriage advocates' resistance to defending polygamy and other diverse marital forms may be prompted by their opponents' strategy of arguing that recognizing same-sex marriage will initiate a slippery slope to recognizing polygamy, incest, pedophilia, and bestiality. Such arguments are found in the philosophical literature, but are also made by members of Congress and other public figures.[33] The slippery-slope worry is, in part, ludicrous: Nothing in arguments for same-sex marriage suggests the permissibility of sexual acts with minors, and neither minors nor nonhuman animals are competent to consent to contracts or hold the rights and responsibilities of marriage. Polygyny is a more difficult question, raising the issue of harmful effects for women, a discussion I postpone until Chapter 8. But many other forms of group marriage are possible, not to mention friendships and adult care networks. The logic of political liberalism demands a nonamatonormative rationale for excluding friendships, care networks, and groups from the benefits of marriage; in the absence of such a rationale, they should be eligible for the benefits of marriage if any relationships are. Rather than playing into the hands of same-sex marriage opponents, this might helpfully divert the discussion from the narrow focus on sex that their slippery slope arguments evince.

III. SEPARATING MARRIAGE AND PARENTING

Here we must return to a topic deferred in the last section: Reproduction and child welfare could provide public reasons for shaping marriage law. There are two challenges here: The first is the claim that marriage is essentially procreative, the second that child welfare requires hetero- or amatonormative discrimination in law. The first challenge would reject the starting point of the arguments discussed in the last section, which define marriage as primarily a vehicle for recognizing intimate adult partnerships. But a case needs to be made for this. Wellington argues that a legal understanding of marriage as essentially procreative would violate neutrality. Political liberalism does prohibit defining marriage as procreative exclusively on religious grounds or on the basis of ethical arguments such as those made by new natural lawyers and Scruton. But defining marriage as essentially procreative need not be nonneutral, if there is a neutral rationale for an institution that supports biological parents or pairs of adults rearing children together. Indeed, it might well be thought that the state's main interest in marriage is reproduction.

One reason often given for marriage is that it is "for" reproduction and child rearing; if this were the case, and "traditional" marriage were essential to child rearing, this could provide a justification for restrictive marriage laws in terms of public reason. If the rationale of marriage is rearing children produced biologically by the spouses, then it must be different-sex (except for stepfamilies), and so, the argument goes, excluding same-sex partners from marriage would not be an unjust denial of equal treatment. However, defenders of same-sex marriage have pointed out that biological procreation does not appear to be the rationale of current marriage law: Some spouses adopt, rear stepchildren, use gamete donors, or do not procreate.[34] Law permits the infertile, those past child-bearing age, and those who already have children to marry. Nor does child rearing (whatever the provenance of the children) appear to be the only purpose of marriage: Many marriages are childless, and marriages do not end when children leave home. Moreover, many persons in same-sex relationships or who may enter same-sex relationships have children; excluding them from marriage is at odds with the claim that marriage is essentially an institution for child rearing.

But this is too fast. An objector could admit that procreation, child rearing, and marriage are not congruent in our society, but insist that they should be. He might add that the deviation of some marriages from the institution's underlying rationale is irrelevant. After all, practice does not settle the normative question of what institutions we should have. The objector could insist that the design of marriage law should attend to its implications for child welfare, even if child rearing is not the primary purpose of marriage. For example, Rawls (without endorsing the view) suggests that child welfare could theoretically provide a public reason against same-sex marriage, although claims about sexual morality cannot.[35] Rawls's thought is that every reasonable moral or religious view can be expected to accept child welfare as a reason for legislation, while not every such view can be expected to agree on sexual morality. The objector could contend that marriage creates families in which children tend to be reared, and marriage law should be framed to promote optimal environments for children. Legally recognized same-sex marriage—let alone polygamy or other non-"traditional" arrangements—would affect people's choices, presumably decreasing the number of children reared by married biological parents, and this may affect child welfare. Such an objector will have to face questions about stepfamilies and artificial reproductive technologies (should those be prohibited to promote biological parenting?). But, moreover, there are serious problems with the claim that "traditional" marriage best promotes child welfare.

If child welfare were harmed by same-sex marriage, this could provide a public reason against it, while justifying heterosexual privilege in marriage for the infertile and childless. But claims that same-sex parenting is harmful have been found groundless. A Hawaii Court review of social science literature on same-sex parenting did not show significant differences. There is a "growing consensus among researchers that in terms of psychological adjustment there are no differences between children in planned lesbian families . . . and those raised in heterosexual families."[36]

However, the more subtle point is not that same-sex parenting would harm children, but that married biological parents provide the optimal child-rearing environment, and marriage law should promote only this optimal environment. This objection has three weaknesses: First, the nuances of the empirical evidence regarding child welfare suggest that there is no compelling reason to think that alternative marital forms would be more harmful than current marriage law; second, a parenting framework should not recognize only optimal parenting structures; third, reasons other than child welfare guide marriage legislation, for marriage has purposes other than child rearing.

A typical case for monogamous different-sex marriage points out that single-parent families have higher rates of poverty, and that children do best in low-conflict marriages with both biological parents.[37] However, empirical findings of the benefits of marriage are mixed: While low-conflict marriage appears to benefit children, the presence of step-parents does not, and children appear to benefit from divorce in high-conflict families, so much so that if "divorce were limited only to high-conflict marriages, then it would generally be in children's best interest."[38] In light of these mixed results, Marsha Garrison concludes that both critics and defenders of marriage have overstated their position: Marriage can benefit, but it can also harm. Moreover, we should approach correlations between marriage and child welfare with caution. Some apparent benefits can be explained by "selection bias"—the more educated and wealthier are likelier to have children within marriage. Correlation is not causation. Economist Gary Becker suggests a reason for caution: Studies showing children within marriage do better do "not tell us whether or not children of divorced parents would have done poorly even if their parents had stayed together."[39]

Consistency in designing a framework supporting only what these studies show is best for children would require doing away with heterosexual privilege and replacing it with low-conflict biological parent privilege. By this reasoning, high-conflict marriage should be discouraged (the studies cited showed no harm from same-sex parenting as compared with different-sex parenting, but did show high-conflict parenting to be detrimental). Step-parents (or other nonbiological parents, presumably, such as adoptive parents or users of gamete donors) should not be allowed entry into marriage, either. However, in designing a parenting framework, promoting the optimal must be balanced with protecting the many. A parenting framework does not simply promote family forms; it also confers protections and benefits. Promoting low-conflict marriage between biological parents by excluding other parents would entail excluding many parents whose children would benefit from the family's inclusion.

Furthermore, society does not and cannot require that parents be ideally suited to maximize children's well-being—there would not be enough parents. There is, rather, a high threshold requirement precluding abuse and neglect, and requiring nurturing. The objector who presses against including same-sex, polygamous, or single-parent families on child welfare grounds should consider whether he would press such an objection to interracial families (where children of such families were disadvantaged), socio-economically worse-off families, or parents who are junk-food eaters and couch potatoes. If not, his view incorporates an arbitrary bias.

Making the framework as inclusive as possible will help more children through the direct provision of benefits. Morever, a key factor in children's psychological development is continuity of care, which is available in same-sex—as well as polygamous, single-parent, and extended—families.[40] Polygamy, same-sex marriage, single parenting, and unmarried cohabitation can be as loving, caring, and stable as "traditional" marriage. Indeed, Bertrand Russell suggested that relaxing marital exclusivity (in contemporary terms, permitting polyamory) would benefit children by strengthening marriages, preventing couples from divorcing due to extramarital affairs. Emens similarly suggests that some polyamorous structures might provide more stability.[41]

Finally, the line of argument pressed as an objection to same-sex or nonamatonormative marriage—that marriage should be designed to promote child welfare—depends on two fundamental assumptions: first, that the state should provide a parenting framework, and second, that it should be bundled together in one legislative package with a framework recognizing adult relationships. To some, children are an expensive taste, which the state should not subsidize. Rearing children is indeed costly, in direct economic costs and indirect costs such as workplace competitiveness. However, many pursuits have costs, and the state does not subsidize them: For example, I may incur similar costs as a parent does by devoting myself to yachting, but no one seriously argues that the state should subsidize or support my yachting. Why is child rearing different?

There are a number of reasons not to treat children as an expensive taste. In Chapter 7, I will argue there is reason for the state to support dependency frameworks and caring relationships. A few other reasons should be briefly mentioned here. First, children are unlike other expensive tastes in that child rearing enables society to continue over time; unless overpopulation is a problem, children produce positive externalities—funding pensions for the retired, providing the next generation of citizens and workers. If the state has an interest in its own continuance, it has an interest in ensuring that its citizens are reproduced: For this reason, Rawls writes that "reproductive labor is socially necessary labor."[42]

Second, the state should protect the rights of its citizens, and it must make provision for those who cannot protect their own rights, such as children. But as children often cannot make their own complaints, and will die through neglect or abandonment, the state must legally assign parental duties and a mechanism for ensuring they are fulfilled. Through myriad choices in designing these duties and their assignment, the state structures the smaller groups within which children live.

Third, child rearing is entwined with equal opportunity in two ways. Children's development is affected by their families; design and oversight of child rearing structures is necessary to implement fair equal opportunity. Women's equal opportunity is also at issue, as child-rearing work continues to be performed disproportionately by women, at great cost. An institutional framework for parenting would address child protection and child welfare, parental assistance, and equal opportunity. It would also create binding parental legal obligations and define the extent of state noninterference.

Child welfare does not provide reasons against same-sex marriage or nonama-tonormative marriage. Indeed, as many same-sex partners or revolutionary parents wish to rear children, and the economic benefits of marriage might benefit their children, another argument for marriage reform could be mounted on this ground. However, in my view, there are several reasons to separate a legal framework designating and supporting adult caring relationships from one regulating and supporting parenting.

First, liberty requires that terms of adult relationships be chosen contractually, while parenting obligations should be imposed and standardized. Legal structures assigning parental obligations are needed between parent and child, not between parents. Securing parental obligations independently of marriage protects children in high-conflict marriages and marriages that end in divorce. Given abuse and conflict within marriage, women and children may often be better off outside marriage— high-conflict marriages are worse for children than stable single parents.[43]

Second, separating parenting and marriage framework allows providing benefits associated with marriage to children (one-third of U.S. children) outside marriages. Martha Fineman writes that " 'only one-fourth of U.S. households fit the 'norm' of a wage-earning husband and a homemaker wife living with children.' So, one might ask, as a sheer matter of practicality, what should 'family policy' have to say about all those others?"[44] Incentives for parents to marry or to stay married provide no assistance to children whose parents do not marry and may harm children in high-conflict marriages. Financial benefits and incentives to stability should attach to parenting, not marriage.

Ideally, independent parenting frameworks would provide support for parents, including economic assistance, informational resources, child care, and workplaces supportive of caregivers. They would protect family autonomy, allowing families to govern themselves without shielding abuse. The frameworks would also protect children by establishing and promulgating parental obligations and providing some mechanism for identifying children at risk. They should also set out the limits of parental "infusion" of children with beliefs the inculcation of which violates their autonomy or seriously damages their life chances. On equal opportunity grounds, the frameworks should offset the opportunity costs of child rearing for the primary caregiver, as Anne Alstott argues. Parental licensing might be implemented with fairly minimal criteria, such as screening out those with a history of violent child abuse or pedophilia.[45] Such parenting frameworks would stretch into many areas of law and policy, especially education and health.

Freestanding parenting frameworks would also contribute to other political goals. They would allow recognition of society's direct responsibility to vulnerable children rather than mediating it through marriage. Fineman argues for recognition of collective responsibility for dependency and gives this as a reason for abolishing marriage, which treats such care as private; but establishing independent parenting frameworks could serve the same purpose.[46] Separating marriage and parenting can also help to offset another kind of worry. Judith Butler has expressed concern that calls for state intervention in marriage will only increase state intervention in and regulation of relationships, discouraging diverse kinship structures. The concern relevant here is that recognition of same-sex adult relationships will prompt attacks on their members' custody rights and access to adoption and artificial reproductive technologies. She gives the example of France, where civil union legislation could only pass by denying joint adoption rights to civil union members.[47] Separating marriage and parenting frameworks might seem to reinforce Butler's worries, since it allows differential treatment of adult members between the two frameworks. However, given my arguments above concerning child welfare and parenting structures, neutrality and political liberalism imply that parenting frameworks should recognize diverse units, too—othermothers and revolutionary parents, care networks, same-sex parents, and single parents. Moreover, because separating the frameworks delinks marriage and parenthood, it has the side effect of combating the heteronormative assumption that social or legal parents are biological parents. As I argue in Chapter 8, state action combating the discriminatory beliefs that the state has supported is one way the state can rectify historical injustices.

Parenting frameworks could recognize parenting networks such as the othermothering in African-American communities described in Chapter 5.iv. Parenting law does need to assign responsibility to at least one guardian. However, child welfare will be improved if law recognizes and encourages the contributions othermothers, or friends and relations, can make in parenting. An extended-family model of parenting can benefit children by increasing the amount of support available for them. Such extended relations could be supported by law through recognition as child-adult, rather than adult-adult, bonds. This is in tension with the dominant nuclear family model of parenting, which is why bell hooks calls this model "revolutionary." But there are reasons for supporting such frameworks. Where they exist already, offering them support helps the children within them. Law should aim to support children and child care directly, rather than through the inefficient strategy of promoting marriage.[48] Finally, the statistics about child welfare hide the fact that some alternative families are better than some two-biological-parent families.

The foregoing considerations suggest that an independent parenting framework would be more just and more efficient in promoting child welfare. Another reason for separating the frameworks is that marriage has purposes other than creating a stable environment for child rearing, of which I will supply an account in Chapter 7. Marriage allows partners to signal the importance of their relationship, to gain access to legal entitlements, and to invoke legal and social safeguards of commitment. Since supporting the goods in adult relationships will require different policies than supporting child rearing, this is another reason to separate frameworks for adult caring relationships and for parenting.

In *Marriage and Morals*, Bertrand Russell predicted that a more rational (as he thought) attitude toward sex would lead to an increase in out-of-wedlock births, and that social philosophers would need to address this. He was right. A just society should have an institution ensuring the welfare and development of children and protecting their relationships with their parents, but this should not be marriage. Of course, one does not want to fall into the folly of Henry James's comical reformer Miss Birdseye, whose raison d'être was "to testify against the iniquity of most arrangements."[49] There are reasons for keeping institutions already in place. The familiarity of an institution should count for something when considering other equally good imaginary institutions. However, what is currently in place is not working well; divorce rates are high, and many children are being raised outside marriage. In the balance against the familiarity of our current system are the constraints of public reason, equal opportunity, equal treatment, and child welfare.

IV. POLITICAL LIBERALISM AGAINST MARRIAGE

Providing a politically liberal rationale for marriage law is challenging. If parenting frameworks are separated from marriage, why should the state recognize and support any relationships between adults? What rationale can public reason provide? There is an even stronger objection to legally recognizing marriage than the *absence* of a rationale in public reason: It has been argued that any marriage law at all will violate constraints of public reason and neutrality, because marriage is inherently controversial, or because it is essentially linked with comprehensive moral and religious doctrines.

One related argument holds that neutrality militates only against same-sex marriage while endorsing different-sex marriage. Jeff Jordan argues that recognizing same-sex marriage would take sides, rather than remaining neutral, on a controversial moral issue. Recognizing same-sex marriage, he argues, would force those who disapprove of it to partake, unwillingly, in a system that recognizes it. On his interpretation, neutrality requires that a liberal state should try to accommodate both sides in such public dilemmas. His proposed "accommodation" is that the state tolerate same-sex activity without legalizing same-sex marriage; this, supposedly, concedes something to each side in the debate.[50]

This suggested compromise is, of course, no compromise: It cedes everything to those who oppose same-sex marriage. More importantly, the argument misconstrues neutrality and political liberalism. Neutrality does not require that the state remain neutral between opposed policies *when one policy is unjust*. Political liberalism requires that one can provide public reasons which one can reasonably expect all *reasonable* comprehensive doctrines to accept. The example of interracial marriage shows the problem with arguments from controversy: Interracial marriage was (in fact, still is) controversial, reportedly more controversial in past decades than same-sex marriage is now. But the state is not required to be neutral in matters of justice, and racial marriage bars were unjust. The state was not required to be neutral regarding views that would wrongly deny some citizens the right to marry (as it was construed). In such matters, the claim to equal liberties, equal treatment, and equal opportunity trumps offense or controversy. The neutral state is not required to avoid controversial legislation when rights are at stake. If same-sex marriage is a matter of justice, its controversial nature should not prevent its legislation.[51]

However, while equality requires recognizing same-sex marriage if there is any law of marriage, other arguments hold that political liberalism requires the state to refrain from recognizing marriage at all. For example, Lawrence Torcello argues that any conception of marriage is inherently contested. Because both understandings of marriage, "traditional" and same-sex, are controversial, the state should recognize only civil unions and not marriages. A first problem with this argument is that it fails to provide a neutral rationale for civil unions. A public reason needs to be given as to why there should be a law of civil union at all. And by Torcello's own reasoning, civil union should be as problematic as marriage because it incorporates a controversial "union" conception of relationships, which some feminists, for instance, would reject. Finally, like Jordan's, this position misconstrues neutrality. Legislation is not non-neutral simply because the decision is controversial. It is the state's reasons for actions that neutrality constrains—not the outcome. If neutrality indeed required never legislating controversially, it would be overly restrictive: Almost any important political decision will take a course of action favored by some contested conception of the good.

A stronger neutrality case against marriage can be made. As Steve Vanderheiden puts it, legal marriage and civil unions both involve legal discrimination: The married (or united) are treated differently in terms of receiving benefits, under tax law, and so on. Such legal discrimination requires justification. Vanderheiden goes further to argue that neutrality precludes such justification, because it precludes the state from favoring any particular arrangements for love, intimacy, and sex. Instead, it should simply allow consenting adults to choose those arrangements that they prefer. Hence, the state should cease recognizing intimate relationships entirely. However, if a public reason for recognizing some relationships could be found, such recognition would be compatible with neutrality.[52]

Tamara Metz poses another challenge by arguing that marriage itself is essentially rooted in comprehensive moral and religious doctrines. Like Wedgwood, she draws attention to the social meaning of marriage, arguing that marriage is a "formal, comprehensive social institution" that transforms the self-understanding of individuals who enter it and connects them to the community.[53] This meaning requires that marriage be officiated by an ethical authority. But a liberal state cannot be such an authority, precisely because it should remain neutral between competing ethical and religious views. Metz shows how recent and historical U.S. judicial decisions have invoked the ethical meaning of marriage, especially its connection to ideals of character and conduct. If marriage is essentially a comprehensive ethical institution, it is very difficult to see how public reason could be given for it (although reasons could be given for institutions replacing marriage, like the intimate caregiving unions that Metz proposes). However, as I will argue in Chapter 7.iv, marriage, like other institutions, can be detached from its historical symbolism.

Torcello went wrong by assuming the inevitability of some marriage-like institution when his own political liberal premises should have called it into question. But neutrality and public reason make the very existence of a marriage-like institution problematic because they require excluding rationales drawn from comprehensive doctrines regarding the value of relationships, and because it appears rationales for marriage (once separated from parenting) would have to invoke some such doctrines. If reasons drawn from comprehensive doctrines are excluded, few avenues are left by which the political liberal can justify marriage law. It is not immediately clear what interest the state has in marriage, if parenting is shifted to another framework. There must be a publically acceptable rationale for legal marriage (or civil unions) in the first place.

Nicholas Buccola suggests a way around this: If the judgments of various religious and ethical views converge on legal recognition of intimate relationships, such an "overlapping consensus" could justify a law of marriage. (In Rawls's *Political Liberalism*, "overlapping consensus" refers to the agreement on key liberal principles between various competing comprehensive doctrines; for example, various religions, atheists, agnostics, and so on can all agree to religious liberty for different reasons.) But deep disagreements, especially over polygamy and same-sex marriage, seem to make this unlikely in the United States in the near future. Those for whom marriage is defined by sex difference are unlikely to reach a consensus with advocates of same-sex marriage. In the absence of such a consensus, political liberalism needs to find a rationale for marriage law.

This opens the door to the contractualist position that marriage should be, essentially, abolished and assimilated into the existing system of private contract.[54] This would continue the twentieth-century trend in which many aspects of marriage law moved toward the contract paradigm.[55] Gender roles in marriage are no longer legally defined, and prenuptial agreements allow parties to alter somewhat the terms of divorce. No-fault divorce also brings marriage close to ordinary contract, as opposed to fault-based divorce, which compelled performance in the absence of a narrow set of reasons for exit.[56] However, some features remain that make marriage an anomalous contract: "[T]here is no written document, each party gives up its right to self-protection, the terms of the contract cannot be re-negotiated, neither party need understand its terms, it must be between two and only two people, and these two people must be one man and one woman."[57] The state defines the rights, obligations, exit conditions, and other legal implications of marriage. Contractualists argue that the state lacks adequate justification for prescribing the terms of consensual legal relations between competent adults.

In many ways, the marriage "contract" has been more akin to status than contract. Historically, the marriage contract was "anomalous," "a legal fiction," "not a proper contract," "[u]nlike any other contract."[58] The U.S. Supreme Court noted in 1888 its atypicality: "[A] relation between the parties is created which they cannot change," while "[o]ther contracts may be modified, restricted, or enlarged, or entirely released upon the consent of the parties."[59] Moreover, under the doctrine of coverture, the wife contracted away her civil rights, as in a civil slave contract, up until a century after slavery was outlawed in Britain.[60] In 1861, Sir Henry Maine famously wrote that "the movement of progressive societies [has been] a movement from status to contract." Maine contrasted feudal orders, in which socially defined roles were assigned impersonally based on categories such as gender and caste, with contractual orders in which individuals could choose their roles and define their terms.[61] When the predetermined roles and obligations of marriage depended upon gender, it more closely resembled status in a feudal and caste system than contract in a society based on free exchange. Remaining aspects of marriage as a standardized preformed status are in tension with marriage as a contract between free individuals.

For contractualists, marriage should be regulated like any other legal relationship between adults—by freedom of contract. The state should not define the terms of such contracts unless some rationale can be given for treating marriage differently. A defense of marriage law must explain why the state has a right to interfere in the terms of a contract between consenting adults. Furthermore, as already emphasized, justification must be given for expenditure of government monies on marital benefits and for preferential treatment given the married. To paraphrase Catharine MacKinnon's remarks in another context, current marriage law is essentially an affirmative action plan for heterosexual monogamists; why do they deserve special treatment? Even if marriage were extended to same-sex couples or care networks, why should any relationships receive such benefits?

The next chapter takes up this challenge: Within the constraints of public reason, what rationale can be given for a law of marriage? Why should a political liberal state regulate, support, or legally recognize marriage-like relationships at all? And, if a politically liberal rationale can be found, what would the resulting law look like?

7

MINIMIZING MARRIAGE
WHAT POLITICAL LIBERALISM IMPLIES FOR MARRIAGE LAW

In this chapter, I take up the challenges posed in Chapters 5 and 6 by giving a politically liberal rationale for marriage law and showing that this rationale supports a marriage law that recognizes the diversity of relationships.[1] Taking to their appropriate conclusion the implications of political liberalism's commitment to excluding from the public forum arguments that depend on comprehensive doctrines entails that the state should support what I call "minimal marriage" and that any additional restrictions on marriage (by sex, gender, number of parties, amatory relationship, rights exchanged) are unjust. Minimal marriage allows individuals to select from the rights and responsibilities exchanged within marriage and exchange them with whomever they want, rather than exchanging a predefined bundle of rights and responsibilities with only one amatory partner. Through marriage law, the state shapes our understanding of family; I argue here for a law recognizing adult families that amatonormativity excludes.

Recent defenses of same-sex marriage, as we have seen, have invoked liberal neutrality and public reason.[2] Such reasoning is generally sound but does not go far enough in examining the implications of neutrality for marriage. Also, as we have seen, some philosophers have argued that neutrality and public reason require abolishing legal marriage and relegating marital agreements to private contract. It is true that many defenses of marriage illegitimately (to the political liberal) ground marriage law in comprehensive ethical claims about the value of relationships. However, I will argue that there is a rationale within public reason for a legal framework supporting nondependent caring relationships between adults ("marriage"), and that this framework is a fundamental matter of justice.

My argument has two stages. In section ii, I show that public reason, with its ban on arguments that depend on comprehensive religious, philosophical, or moral doctrines, cannot provide justification for more-than-minimal marriage. In section iii, I show that not only can minimal marriage be justified within public reason, but also that a liberal state is required to provide such a legislative framework for personal relationships. I do not argue for public reason here; my aim is to show how far-reaching its implications for marriage are. Indeed, some may take my conclusions as a *reductio* of public reason. But the perfectionist liberal cannot rest easy, for perfectionism that allows diversity in conceptions of good relationships has the same implications.

I open with a detailed proposal for a minimally restricted law of marriage. The central idea is that individuals can have legal marital relationships with more than one person, reciprocally or asymmetrically, themselves determining the sex and number of parties, the type of relationship involved, and which rights and responsibilities to exchange with each. For brevity, I call this "minimal marriage." This name for the proposal alludes to Nozick's minimal state (although the political framework here is liberal egalitarian, not libertarian). Just as Nozick describes the libertarian state as *minimal* in comparison with current welfare states, so minimal marriage has far fewer state-determined restrictions than current marriage. And just as Nozick's minimal state is, in his view, the most extensive state justifiable, these restrictions on marriage, so exiguous from the point of view of the current regime, are the most extensive that can be justified within political liberalism. This proposal applies to marriage law, not directly to private-sphere benefits or religious practice, although marriage reform would alter the implications of statutes prohibiting discrimination on the basis of marital status and entitlements to third-party benefits.

My focus on marriage as a legal contract threatens to trigger long-standing debates over an alleged tension between contract and care. Few propose an inherent tension between care and the legal structuring of marriage—law can support caring relationships (as parental rights support parental care). It is contractual bargaining that is seen as inappropriate. A familiar statement of this tension is that contract presupposes self-interest and choice, whereas care, and hence marriage, presupposes altruism and commitment.[3] (See further discussion in Chapter 4.iii.) But the alleged tension is sometimes overstated: Attention to the contractual elements of marriage does not imply that the marriage relationship is essentially contractual. Nor is it obvious that care and contract are opposed, empirically speaking. For instance, chosen obligations may be more agreeable than imposed obligations, and spouses' careful long-term planning does not entail that they view each other as competitors.

However, I assume that the basic structure of society must be just, and accordingly my view might be crudely presented as entailing that justice trumps care. An objector might charge that if it turns out that contractual bargaining does threaten care, I would still be committed to contractual liberty. But I envision a deeper connection between justice and care. I argue that supporting caring relationships is an important matter of justice and that a rationale exists for this within constraints of public reason.

Discussions of marriage reform are also met with the objection that they wrongly treat marriage as a constructed, not a natural or prepolitical, relationship. As I argued earlier (Chapters 4.iii and 6.i), there are empirical and theoretical problems with claiming that a certain form of marriage is "natural," and throughout I have emphasized the legal construction of modern marriage (especially in the Introduction and Chapter 5). But even were marriage "natural" in some sense relevant to institutional design in some political theory, its "natural" features could not specify its legal framework, because this is a complicated mechanism reaching into many areas of law. In the next section, I review some of the more than 1,000 legal implications of marriage in the United States. What these suggest—like the variability of marriage throughout history and the more local history of its construction in the United States—is that a legal marriage framework makes many decisions about the boundaries of marriage and its constituent legal powers, responsibilities, entitlements, and so on, which cannot be read off "nature."

I. MINIMAL MARRIAGE

Minimal marriage institutes the most extensive set of restrictions on marriage compatible with political liberalism. It is *minimal* in that limiting the institutional framework to only what is so compatible entails a significant reduction of the restrictions placed on marriage. It might also be described as marital pluralism or disestablishment. I argue that a liberal state can set no principled restrictions on the sex or number of spouses and the nature and purpose of their relationships, except that they be caring relationships. Moreover, the state cannot require exchanges of marital rights (shorthand for various entitlements, powers, obligations) to be reciprocal and complete, as opposed to asymmetrical and divided. In an ideal liberal state, minimal marriage would also reduce the marital entitlements available; in the next chapter, I will discuss the transitional problems arising in our nonideal world, where abolishing marital entitlements to health care or pension benefits would cause grave hardship and injustice.

To show what is at stake in marriage law reform, I will review some of the numerous entitlements, liabilities, permissions, and powers currently exchanged reciprocally and as a complete package in marriage. In U.S. federal law alone, there are "1,138 federal statutory provisions...in which marital status is a factor in determining or receiving benefits, rights, and privileges."[4] Laws concerning property, inheritance, and divorce are additional, falling under state jurisdiction.

Marriage entails rights "to be on each others' health, disability, life insurance, and pension plans," "jointly [to] own real and personal property, an arrangement which protects their marital estate from each other's creditors," and to automatic inheritance if a spouse dies intestate. Spouses have rights in one another's property in marriage and on divorce. They are designated next-of-kin "in case of death, medical emergency, or mental incapacity," and for prison visitation and military personnel arrangements.[5] They qualify for special tax and immigration status and survivor, disability, Social Security, and veterans' benefits.

Marital status is implicated throughout U.S. federal law—in "Indian" affairs, homestead rights, taxes, trade and commerce, financial disclosure and conflict of interest, federal family violence law, immigration, employment benefits, federal natural resources law, federal loans and guarantees, and payments in agriculture. Marital status also confers parental rights and responsibilities—assignment of legal paternity, joint parenting and adoption rights, and legal status with regard to stepchildren. Marriage brings entitlements to third-party benefits as well as to governmental rights and privileges; Mary Anne Case argues that its "principal legal function" is not to structure relationships between spouses "but instead to structure their relations with third parties" through the "designation, without elaborate contracting, of a single other person third parties can look to in a variety of legal contexts," especially in distributing benefits.[6] While this may be an efficient system, it is not, I argue, currently just.

The large array of marriage rights can be roughly taxonomized according to function, a taxonomy I will employ later in explaining the implications of my proposal. Some marriage rights are entitlements to direct governmental financial benefits: West Virginia's cash payouts on marriage, increased Social Security disability payments for married persons, and increased disability pensions for married veterans and federal employees.[7] Married soldiers can receive family separation allowance and increased housing allowance.[8] Tax benefits "permit married couples to transfer substantial sums to one another, and to third parties, without tax liability in circumstances in which single people would not enjoy the same privilege." Old Age, Survivors, and Disability Insurance (Social Security) "is written in terms of the rights of husbands and wives, and widows and widowers," and spouses may qualify for Medicaid, housing assistance, loans, food stamps, and military commissary benefits.[9] Many of these entitlements appear to reflect an assumption of a "traditional" single-breadwinner model, in which one spouse, not working outside the home, depends entirely on the other for health insurance and income.[10]

Other rights facilitate day-to-day maintenance of a relationship or enable spouses to play significant roles in one another's lives. Special consideration for immigration is an example: Spouses cannot share daily life if they are in different countries. Civil service and military spouses may receive employment and relocation assistance and preferential hiring. Out-of-state spouses may qualify for in-state tuition. Other examples are spousal immunity from testifying, spousal care leave entitlement, hospital and prison visiting rights, entitlement to burial with one's spouse in a veterans' cemetery, and emergency decision-making powers. Through such entitlements and through status designation, marriage allows spouses to express and act on their care for one another.

Another function of marriage is to serve as an insurance scheme for the divorced or widowed. It entitles survivors to funeral and bereavement leave, pensions and health care, the right to sue for a spouse's wrongful death, automatic precedence for life insurance payouts and final paychecks, control of copyright, and automatic rights to inherit if the spouse dies intestate and to make decisions about disposal of the body. Marriage law also provides protection for spouses on divorce. In some states, such as North Carolina, deserted spouses can sue third parties for "alienation of affection."

In an ideal liberal egalitarian society, minimal marriage would consist only in rights that recognize (e.g., status designation for third parties, burial rights, bereavement leave) and support (e.g., immigration rights, care-taking leave) *caring relationships*. Caring relationships may include friendships, urban tribes, and care networks as well as polyamorous or monogamous different-sex relationships. Care, broadly construed, may involve physical or emotional care taking or simply a caring attitude (an attitude of concern for a particular other). Parties to such a relationship know and are known to one another, have ongoing direct contact, and share a history. I will argue that a law performing the functions of designating, recognizing, and supporting caring relationships is justifiable, even required.

Rather than giving a detailed legal proposal, my defense of minimal marriage is intended to provide a philosophical justification, within political liberalism, for a set of legal rights whose purpose is to support caring relationships. I will argue that, contrary to the privatization view, a liberal state is required to provide legal supports for caring relationships. These supports, or minimal marriage rights, are juridical rights designed to support caring relationships. They protect such relationships through entitlements facilitating relationship maintenance and by giving their members a way to signal to the institutions shaping their lives (employers, government, hospitals, states, and so on) which relationships should receive these protections.

Because the content of minimal marriage rights, or the rights needed to protect and support caring relationships, depends on the social context in which they are enacted, it is impossible to specify them fully in the abstract. For instance, the legal marital entitlements currently needed in Canada—with universal health care—will differ from those needed in the United States—where many depend upon legal marital entitlements for basic health insurance. Furthermore, the entitlements would differ in an ideal liberal egalitarian society and in a nonideal transitional stage. In an ideal liberal egalitarian society, the set of marital rights would be relatively small, consisting only in rights designed to support the maintenance of relationships or to enable spouses to play significant roles in one another's lives.

At any stage, the rights available through minimal marriage would be determined by their rationale. For instance, entitlements to direct financial assistance are not essential to supporting caring relationships; because they seem to presuppose, illegitimately, a relationship involving economic dependency, they would be difficult to justify in political liberalism. Similarly, the right to sue for alienation of affection presupposes a possessive model of relationship and is not essential to maintaining a caring relationship (suing the third party for damages will not help the relationship!).

While the rights cannot be specified antecedently or independent of a particular social context, the best candidates for such rights, in an ideal egalitarian society, would include eligibility for spousal immigration, employment and relocation assistance, and preferential hiring (currently offered to U.S. military and civil service spouses and by some private employers), residency (where relevant for in-state tuition, etc.), hospital and prison visiting rights, bereavement or spousal care leave, burial with one's spouse in a veterans' cemetery, spousal immunity from testifying, and status designation for the purpose of third parties offering other benefits (such as employment incentives or family rates).

Unlike current marriage, minimal marriage does not require that individuals exchange marital rights reciprocally and in complete bundles: It allows their disaggregation to support the numerous relationships, or adult care networks, that people may have. Minimal marriage would allow a person to exchange all her marital rights reciprocally with one other person or distribute them through her adult care network. It thus supports the variety of relationships excluded by amatonormative marriage law: friendships, urban tribes, overlapping networks, and polyamory.

Finally, parental rights and responsibilities should not automatically be conveyed through marriage but through assumption of a parental role. I argued in Chapter 6.iii that parenting frameworks should be separated from marriage. Legal parenting frameworks should be as capacious as minimal marriage, allowing inclusion of "othermothers" and "revolutionary parents," and secondary caretakers as well as primary guardians. Co-parents who wished could connect themselves to one another laterally through minimal marriage rights as well as establishing their roles relative to the child through parenting frameworks.

Minimal marriage is not the contractualization or privatization of marriage. As discussed in Chapter 6.iv, proponents of marriage contractualization argue that the state should not define the terms of marriage and should relegate such relationships to private contract. The contract paradigm is characterized by voluntariness and individualization, while status relations are standardized according to pre-existing social convention and often based on arbitrary or impersonal criteria such as caste. Contractualization tends toward the abolition of marriage as a legal category; if marriage were thoroughly assimilated to contract, no distinctive status elements would remain. Although I argue for reducing state restrictions on the terms of marriage, I also argue for retaining marriage as a distinctive legal category.

There are many reform possibilities that fall between full privatization and current law. As Ronald Den Otter writes, "No one other than the most libertarian of libertarians thinks that the disestablishment of marriage entails the end of state involvement."[11] Abolishing marriage could coexist with the introduction of new contractual tools to replace some of its functions, or new legal forms to support family structures such as the intimate caregiving union status proposed by Tamara Metz. To the extent that a proposal, such as mine, retains a distinctive status element, it falls further away from full contractualization along the continuum.

Minimal marriage consists in rights that recognize and support caring relationships. These rights designate a status, the status of being in a caring relationship with another person or persons, and their content is standardized accordingly. Many rights that facilitate or recognize relationships, are (roughly) currently available only through marriage, not through private contract: immigration privileges, automatic decision-making powers, residency qualifications. These are not easily assimilated to contractual individualization because their content is defined by their function—recognizing and supporting relationships. Contractual individualization here only means that each individual chooses to whom transfer the right.

Many current marriage rights would be eliminated in an ideal liberal egalitarian society. Such a society would not provide health care and basic income through marriage. Law should not assume dependency between spouses, because this presumes that they order their relationship according to a particular comprehensive doctrine, so most marital entitlements to direct financial assistance would be eliminated (except for those, such as in-state tuition eligibility, whose primary purpose is to enable relationship maintenance). Because the state would not assume dependency, property arrangements would be contractualized, allowing parties to decide property division, alimony, and inheritance, and to set conditional terms and specify penalties for default. Some "insurance" provisions—particularly those that reflect the significant relationship between the spouses in the case of death—would be maintained. (Property division in a nonideal society is discussed in the next chapter.)

Some currently protected marital "privacy" rights would be retained within minimal marriage, but others would not. "Privacy" rights that allow individuals to choose the terms of their relationships are, for the most part, entitlements under freedom of association. For example, as Mary Anne Case points out, marriage law, unlike most domestic partnership laws, does not require couples to cohabit or share finances; marriage thus protects spouses' "privacy" in these choices as the partnership laws do not.[12] But "privacy" rights within marriage conflict with justice when they override legal rights in other domains. For example, marriage currently carries involuntary exemptions from contract law, labor law, and criminal law. But exceptions to criminal law (as in exemptions for sexual battery within marriage) conflict with justice. Moreover, as the state cannot assume the nature of marriage relationships, it cannot automatically remove spouses' entitlements under tort and labor law. The test for whether any specific entitlement would be retained in minimal marriage in an ideal liberal egalitarian state is its rationale: Can it be justified as essential to support a caring relationship? Is it normally needed, in current circumstances, to sustain such relationships? Is it needed in special circumstances to allow day-to-day contact and relationship maintenance?

This proposal might seem overly complicated. But minimal marriage could be implemented in law by presenting spouses with a form giving prospective spouses a list of entitlements, indicating numerical limits. Spouses could tick off boxes to indicate the rights they chose to transfer to another person or persons. The complexity of choice might justify a waiting period and counseling, but the reduction in marital rights would simplify such a form. This approach would require spouses to know what legal rights and responsibilities they are taking on; in current marriage they take on an even more complicated set of rights and responsibilities, with the difference that law does not require them to know the terms to which they are agreeing.

At this point, an objector might suggest a *reductio*: This proposal will have to countenance immoral or ridiculous marriages.[13] But as minimal marriage complies with criminal law, it cannot permit rights violations. Actual marriage law has overridden human rights—under coverture, a wife lost her civil and legal rights for life and even now traces of the marital rape exemption linger in state criminal codes exempting spouses from sexual battery charges. Minimal marriage, which respects criminal law, could not countenance such exemptions, or, *a fortiori*, marital slave contracts. Pedophilia is ruled out on the same grounds. In addition, children and nonhuman animals cannot make marriage contracts because they cannot make any contracts. No one can marry unilaterally; minimal marriage status designations require consent from both parties, and minors are not legally competent to consent. Moreover, parents or guardians have rights regarding minors in their care, with which minimal marriage contracts might conflict.[14] Nonhuman animals cannot hold the rights or responsibilities exchanged in marriage. So marrying one's dog is a nonstarter. Minimal marriage would indeed allow adult siblings or first cousins to transfer rights; but because minimal marriage supports friendships and care networks, this does not imply or presuppose anything about the moral or legal status of sex or procreation between such relations. Answers to *those* questions would come from other areas of moral and political philosophy.

No one can marry unilaterally because minimal marriage rights would have an "uptake" requirement (i.e., that such rights not be transferred unilaterally). This would rule out "stalker" marriages (in which someone transfers marital rights to a nonconsenting person) as well as marriages to those not competent to consent. The rationale is that caring relationships are reciprocal; a friendship involves mutuality, for example, although it need not require a reciprocal exchange of rights for its continuance. "Uptake" is a criterion to insure that the relationship meets this reciprocity condition. A second reason for the uptake requirement is that some transfers may have costs to the recipient, by affecting the transferee's administrative status or eligibility for other such transfers. Such costs should not be imposed unilaterally. For some transfers there might be no significant cost—for instance, if Judith Jarvis Thomson wished to transfer hospital visiting rights unilaterally to Henry Fonda, this doesn't burden him because he doesn't have to use them and, presumably, they will not reduce his eligibility for other such transfers. But in other cases unilateral transfers might cause administrative chaos—if, for example, Judith Jarvis Thomson were to designate Henry Fonda a Boston resident—or deprive the transferee of the opportunity to receive another numerically restricted transfer of the same kind—for example, relocation expense eligibility might be capped for reasons of efficiency, so that Thomson's transfer would prevent Fonda from receiving such a transfer from his actual partner.

Ludicrously large marriages are another potential *reductio*. Could Hugh Hefner marry his top fifty Playmates? Could a hundred cult members marry? No. The restriction to caring relationships imposes practical limits, for there are psychological and material limits on the relationships one can sustain. Caring relationships require that parties be known personally to one another, share history, interact regularly, and have detailed knowledge of one another. However, should a surprisingly large number of people genuinely sustain personal relationships, there is no principled reason to deny them distributable benefits such as visiting rights (though they may be required to alternate, cut visits short, and so on), though other entitlements might be limited in number on grounds of feasibility.

Once again, my purpose is not to provide a detailed legal proposal but rather to give a philosophical justification for a more flexible law supporting a variety of relationships. Because minimal marriage rights differ in kind and are implicated in different areas of law and policy, a general prescription as to their institutional design is not appropriate; different rights will involve different specific considerations. Issues such as the appropriateness of self-designation and the feasibility of multiple transfers will depend on the particular entitlement and institutions. Some rights, like hospital visitation, may be transferred to a number of parties; other rights, like immigration eligibility, may be capped. Further, to a great extent, institutional design will depend on social background conditions.[15]

It might be thought that it would be too difficult to police minimal marriage by determining whether an actual caring relationship existed, and that this would encourage marriage fraud. But this objection assumes that marriage comes with the extensive entitlements that it brings now. For most relationship-maintaining rights, self-designation is usually appropriate.[16] Entitlements that burden the state little and whose primary function is to support a relationship—for example, visitation rights—make self-designation of a caring relationship feasible. In such cases abuse of the right would have no major costs, and there is little motivation to abuse. Others—for example, immigration eligibility—might be more ripe for fraud, and hence would require greater scrutiny. In such cases, greater bureaucratic oversight, such as an interview to determine that parties do actually know each other and (so far as can be determined!) care for one another may be appropriate. But this would differ little from investigations in immigration cases now; presumably, tests like those now used by immigration officials to determine whether spouses are in an intimate relationship could be devised to determine whether parties are in a caring relationship. Further, entitlements costly to the state (presumably those most tempting for fraudsters) would be limited on grounds of feasibility (in light of limited resources). Where self-designation is not appropriate, procedures will fall within the remit of relevant institutional frameworks (such as immigration law). It is worth emphasizing here that the various rights would be overseen by the appropriate governmental agencies and integrated into their existing policies. Further, while individuals would have the option of a status designation, they could transfer some marital rights without officially designating their relationship a minimal marriage. This is another choice, one which I will discuss below.

It might also be objected that the criterion of a caring relationship raises the bar as contrasted with current marriage. But current marriage does require an intimate relationship, which spouses are required to document in immigration cases. Although it would be impractical and invasive for the state to undertake such investigations in every case, it does not seem undesirable, in theory, to make such a relationship a criterion for legal marriage (ruling out, for instance, mail-order brides who will be treated uncaringly as servants).

But the requirement that relationships be caring should not be taken to rule out arranged marriage, where that is fully consensual and in other ways compatible with justice: Within some comprehensive doctrines, arranged marriage may be the only entry into a certain kind of caring relationship, and this method of creating a caring relationship should not be excluded. So long as the marriage is intended to produce such a relationship, it would employ minimal marriage rights for their intended purpose.

So far, the proposal might seem extravagantly removed from real life. But consider the case of Rose. Rose lives with Octavian, sharing household expenses. To facilitate this *ménage*, Rose and Octavian form a legal entity for certain purposes—jointly owned property, bank account access, homeowner and car insurance, and so on. The arrangement is long-term, but not permanent. Octavian's company will relocate him in five years, and Rose will not move—but they agree to cohabit until then. They even discuss how to divide property when the household dissolves, and agree that if either moves out sooner, the defaulter will pay the other compensation and costs. (This arrangement is not punitive, merely protective.)

Rose's only living relative, Aunt Alice, lives nearby. Alice lives in genteel poverty, and Rose feels a filial responsibility toward her. Rose's employer provides excellent health care benefits, for which any spouse of Rose's is eligible (at a small cost), and other spousal perks such as reduced costs for its products. Octavian is a well-off professional and doesn't need these benefits—he has his own—but Alice needs access to good health care and, should Rose die, could use the federal pension that would go to Rose's surviving spouse if she had one. Assuming that such entitlements comport with justice, minimal marriage would allow Rose to transfer the eligibility for these entitlements to Alice.

While Rose enjoys Octavian's company, and has affection for Alice, only Marcel truly understands her. Marcel is, like Rose, a bioethicist, and understands her complex views on end-of-life decision making. Rose wants to transfer powers of executorship and emergency decision-making to him. In addition, Marcel and Rose spend a lot of time together, discussing philosophy while enjoying recreational activities, and would like eligibility for "family rates" at tourist attractions, health clubs, and resorts. Their local city gym, for instance, has a special rate for married couples, but they don't qualify.

There could be more people in Rose's life who occupy a role usually associated with spouses. Rose might share custody of a child with an ex. Or she might cohabit platonically with Octavian, living separately from the long-term love of her life, Stella. She could also cohabit in a small polyamorous family unit of three or four persons, or live separately from the other members of her adult care network.

In all of these scenarios, there is no single person with whom Rose wants or needs to exchange the whole package of marital rights and entitlements. In fact, doing so would be inconvenient, requiring her to make additional contracts to override the default terms of marriage. Even worse, marrying any one person would expose her to undesired legal liabilities such as obligatory property division and could interfere with her eligibility for some loans and government programs. But Rose wants and needs to exchange some marital rights with several different people.

Of course, Rose can already do some of this. She can nominate an executor and emergency decision maker and transfer property. This flexibility recognizes that individuals do not all have the same needs; even current marriage law recognizes the possibility that one person might not meet all the other's needs. But the current marriage regime doesn't flex very far. It opens spouses to undesired legal obligations, restricts choice of partners, and holds a monopoly on some powers and permissions.

Rose's ménage might seem strange to some—though investing all one's eggs in one basket might seem equally strange to Rose! It's certainly not obvious that each person will find one other person with whom their major emotional, economic, and social needs permanently mesh. But minimal marriage does not take sides on this. It allows "traditionalists" and romantic lovers to exchange their complete sets of marital rights reciprocally, while Rose and others like her distribute and receive marital rights as needed. Minimal marriage is a law of adult care networks, including "traditional" marriages.

I offer a two-stage defense of minimal marriage. In section ii below, I argue that any restrictions more extensive than those of minimal marriage cannot be justified within public reason. In section iii, I will argue that minimal marriage is required by liberal conceptions of justice.

II. WHY MORE-THAN-MINIMAL MARRIAGE IS INCOMPATIBLE WITH POLITICAL LIBERALISM

Minimal marriage, and no more extensive or restrictive law, is consistent with political liberalism. The ban on arguments that depend on comprehensive conceptions of the good precludes appeal to the special value of long-term dyadic sexual relationships. Without such amatonormative appeal, I will argue, restriction of marriage to such relationships cannot be justified.

As discussed in Chapter 6.i, liberal societies are characterized by a pluralism of reasonable comprehensive religious, philosophical, and moral doctrines. In such societies, legislators should refrain from enacting law and policy, especially in basic matters of justice, exclusively on the basis of comprehensive moral or religious views that many citizens may not accept. In public reason, legislators give reasons for law and policy that those with differing comprehensive doctrines may be reasonably expected to accept; public reason excludes reasons that depend entirely on comprehensive religious, moral, and philosophical doctrines.[17] For my argument, it is sufficient that public reason applies to lawmakers and government officials acting in a public capacity, that it applies to matters of basic justice, and that it requires refraining from arguments that depend on contested comprehensive doctrines. Thus, I can avoid some of the debates over the scope of public reason.

Public reason requires that lawmakers not appeal to reasons depending on comprehensive moral, religious, or philosophical doctrines in framing marriage law—that is, a legal framework designating and supporting adult caring relationships. More fundamentally, as I argued in the previous chapter, it requires publicly justifiable grounds for there being marriage law at all. In the previous chapter, I also argued for separating legal frameworks designating and supporting adult caring relationships and regulating and supporting parenting. Thus, minimal marriage would be framed as a law supporting adult, not parental, relationships, so the state interest in reproduction would not provide a rationale for it.

Assuming for the moment that a legal framework for adult caring relationships is justified, public reason implies that such a framework should not endorse an ideal of relationship depending on a comprehensive doctrine—but this is just what the monogamous, amatonormative ideal of marriage, gay or straight, is. As I showed in Chapter 6.ii, some defenses of same-sex marriage have smuggled in amatonormative assumptions. Cheshire Calhoun has argued that liberal same-sex marriage advocates should recognize that their reasoning extends to polygamy and "marital disestablishment." As she writes, defenders of same-sex marriage have failed to demand "that the law be neutral with respect to competing conceptions of how people can best satisfy their needs for emotional and sexual intimacy, care-taking, reproduction, and child-rearing."[18] Once it is noticed how many varying conceptions of good relationships exist within different comprehensive doctrines, it is clear that public reason and neutrality imply that marriage should not presuppose sexual or romantic relationships, shared domicile or finances, aspirations to permanence or exclusivity, or a full reciprocal exchange of marital rights, just as it should not presuppose gendered spousal roles or the sex of the parties. These understandings of relationships are drawn from within comprehensive doctrines, and it is difficult to see, as I suggested at the end of the last chapter, how narrowly political values could weigh in on such aspects of relationships.

Marriage, including same-sex marriage, currently recognizes a single central exclusive relationship of a certain priority and duration, often associated with an aspiration to "union." But this ignores alternative ideals of relationship discussed in Chapter 4.iii: close dyadic friendships, small group family units, or networks of multiple, significant, nonexclusive relationships that provide emotional support, caretaking, and intimacy and are not (all) romantic or sexual. In Chapter 4, I argued that any law which treated such relationships differently from dyadic sexual relationships was an instance of unjust amatonormative discrimination. Minimal marriage is free of amatonormativity.

In Chapter 5, I introduced critiques of marriage drawn from different comprehensive doctrines. Some gay and lesbian theorists and feminists have criticized the central, exclusive relationship ideal as a heteronormative paradigm. They point out that gays and lesbians often choose relationships that are more flexible and less possessive, exclusive, and insular. Some gay and lesbian theorists have argued against same-sex marriage on the grounds that instead of affirming difference, it will assimilate lesbian and gay relationships into the heterosexual model.[19] But this concern rather implies that marriage law should be reframed to accommodate difference. This is what minimal marriage does: It allows the relationship diversity that Ettelbrick associated with gay and lesbian liberation.

Different conceptions of good relationships are not exclusive to the gay and lesbian community. They are drawn from a variety of comprehensive doctrines, discussed in Chapters 4 and 5. Polyamorists (gay, straight, and bisexual) ground polyamory, or engagement in multiple love relationships, in values of honesty, autonomy, love, and sex. They see exclusive marriage as promoting a psychologically unhealthy norm of possessiveness, what Laura Kipnis calls the "domestic gulag." Kipnis, like some Romantics and free lovers, sees exclusive monogamy as destroying passion and spontaneity.[20] Other social critics attack "traditional" marriage as incompatible with ideals of equality. Some feminists have criticized the idea of marriage as union insofar as women have lost their identity in the union, and some understand marriage as ownership of women. Adrienne Rich argues that the exclusive, prioritized relationship of heterosexual marriage undermines strong relationships between women. Some race theorists see "traditional" marriage as ethnocentric and the "traditional" family ideal as helping to perpetuate racism. For all of these theorists, "traditional" marriage is grounded in an ideal drawn from a comprehensive doctrine that they reject. Minimal marriage is not.

Other groups emphasize the importance of adult care networks rather than critiquing marriage. Quirkyalones and urban tribalists hold ideals of sociability that reach beyond an isolated dyad. The quirkyalone movement began in one woman's public musing that her friends played the role in her life that marriage or coupledom does for many, which produced a flood of responses from like-minded readers. Quirkyalones want respect for their choice to be "single"; in their experience, as reported in Chapter 4.iii, society treats the unmarried or uncoupled as incomplete and immature, however old or accomplished the individuals may be, and fails to recognize non-"traditional" relationships.[21] For different reasons, many people today find the ideal of a central, exclusive relationship irrelevant. The conceptions of good relationships within their comprehensive doctrines involve networks "tribes," or groups of friends, and they defend these conceptions on ethical grounds and by appeal to other values.

Some theorists write as if critiques of marriage reflect academic theories removed from real life. Yet quirkyalones and urban tribalists have been vocal in their calls for recognition, and there have been widespread calls in the queer community for recognition of adult care networks.[22] Evidence suggests that many contemporaries live outside marriage, many in alternative care networks—and many by choice. Quirkyalones are typically young urban professionals, but, as noted in Chapter 4, frustration with the hegemony of marriage is not limited to the privileged. Patricia Collins and bell hooks describe alternative family models that reflect the working-class African American experience. Minority communities or communities in economic difficulty may produce strong intergenerational ties between women or in extended families. These networks help their members face challenges such as combining paid work and child care; they may also, as hooks argues, reflect different values from those enshrined by the nuclear family.[23] Adult caretaking networks also appear among seniors.

The monogamous central relationship ideal is only one contested ideal among many. Framing marriage law in a way that presupposes such a relationship favors one contested conception of the good and thereby fails to respect public reason and reasonable pluralism. In the absence of a public reason for defining marital relationships as different-sex, monogamous, exclusive, durable, romantic or passionate, and so on, the state must recognize and support all relationships—same-sex, polygamous, polyamorous, urban tribes—if it recognizes and supports any. As political values generally do not speak to these comprehensive choices, a public reason for amatonormative or heteronormative discrimination is unlikely to be forthcoming. And as I argued in Chapter 6.iii, minimal marriage is separate from the legal parenting framework, so the state's interest in reproduction and child welfare is muted here; anyway, as I argued there, this interest does not support heteronormative and amatonormative discrimination. Because the state cannot assume that spouses must relate in a certain way, it cannot assume one set of one-size-fits-all marital rights. What it can do is make available a number of rights that designate and support relationships which individuals can use as they wish.

The argument has been framed in terms of public reason. However, it could also be framed in terms of value-pluralist perfectionism. It is true that a value-pluralist perfectionist liberalism—as opposed to a narrowly sectarian perfectionist politics—could consistently deny the value of adult care networks. But in light of the idiosyncrasy and variability of relationships, it would be odd for a value pluralist to impose a single norm in this particular area. Raz's suggested argument for marriage could thus be extended to adult care networks; to do so, a case would have to be made that monogamy is not the only valuable form of marriage, and that autonomy requires that individuals have valuable options in this area (and not simply the single option of monogamy).[24] While a value pluralist could reject this approach, value-pluralist perfectionism gains appeal by avoiding narrow, restrictive views of the good, so value-pluralists would strengthen their theory by taking a more inclusive view of the value of caring relationships.

It might be objected that minimal marriage is non-neutral toward "traditional" ideals, just as some "traditionalists" complain that same-sex marriage violates neutrality (see Chapter 6.iv). But this objection is confused. Minimal marriage does not endorse any contested conception of the good; rather, it refrains from endorsing any, because its rationale, as I will argue, is based in the theory of primary goods, not in a particular comprehensive doctrine. Furthermore, as the neutrality in question is not of effect but of aim (that is, justificatory neutrality), it cannot be an objection on grounds of neutrality that minimal marriage will decrease the number of "traditional" marriages. Moreover, the objector's rights are not infringed in the same way that those of gays and lesbians, polyamorists, or care networks prohibited from marrying are infringed. Anyone who claims that affront to "traditionalists" is reason against minimal marriage should reflect on the implications of his views given continuing disapproval of interracial marriage.[25]

Finally, although, as I pointed out in Chapter 6.i, Rawlsian political liberalism does not aspire to the outrageously demanding principle of neutrality of effect, it has been argued that ideal neutrality does indeed require neutrality of effect.[26] Even if this principle is impossible to implement, the state could implement second-best measures if moral equality indeed requires that the state give citizens substantive equal opportunity to pursue their conceptions of the good. For example, the state could subsidize unpopular conceptions of the good or compensate people unable to pursue their ideals as a result of state action or inaction. Such a requirement would have interesting implications for marriage. For example, it might require the state to subsidize the most unpopular caring networks or compensate those who could not pursue their ideal of relationship. On the other hand, bureaucratic interference here might be inefficient: "Love, friendship, and the like are not readily susceptible of mass production."[27] For this reason, I set this complication aside.

III. WHY A LIBERAL STATE SHOULD RECOGNIZE MINIMAL MARRIAGE

I now take up the challenge postponed from Chapter 6. Why should the state recognize and support any relationships? How can a framework for adult relationships be justified within political liberalism? Two cases need to be made here. First, a publicly justifiable rationale for marriage law must be given, one that can be defended within public reason. Second, it must be shown that marriage law serves a purpose that private contracts alone, and rights to privacy and association, cannot, and thus that there is reason to legislate marriage.[28] Many current functions of marriage can be carried out through private contract: wills, property settlements, executorships. Why need the state provide specific marital rights? I will begin by considering three proposed neutral rationales for marriage law that, in my view, fail to make the case for amatonormative marriage.

State stability might seem to provide public reason for marriage law. Rawls writes that a "conception of justice is more stable than another if the sense of justice that it tends to generate is stronger and more likely to override disruptive inclinations and if the institutions it allows foster weaker impulses and temptations to act unjustly."[29] In Rawls's own account, the family is key to developing the sense of justice. More recently, some liberals have pursued the connection between marriage and stability by appealing to the psychological and economic effects on children of single-parent families.[30] While stability is a neutral rationale, this defense faces a number of problems in showing that "traditional" marriage promotes it. First, domestic violence and exploitation within "traditional" marriage teach children injustice and are thus by definition destabilizing.[31] Second, insofar as stability provides a rationale for marriage, it provides a rationale for supporting all configurations that can provide children with support networks—as minimal marriage, in conjunction with a parenting framework, does. Finally, stability gives a reason to choose between two equally just schemes; if justice requires minimal marriage, or no marriage law, stability cannot itself justify "traditional" marriage.

A second possible neutral justification for marriage law is that it satisfies citizens' preferences. Wedgwood argues that marriage law can be justified neutrally as satisfying citizens' desires to have their relationships recognized as marriages: The essential rationale of marriage law is that people want to marry. This avoids appeal to a contested conception of the good by simply appealing to people's wants. The legislative rationale is facilitating the satisfaction of wants, not promoting a conception of the good. However, this rationale faces problems. Preferences are shaped by existing social practices and so may reflect oppressive power structures. I have argued that satisfying wants for a narrow amatonormative or gender-structured marriage law would conflict with justice. Satisfying the preference that only "traditional" relationships be recognized as marriages in law, or the preference to enter a form of marriage that excludes nontraditional caring relationships, would sustain unjust discrimination against other forms of caring relationships. Moreover, insofar as preference satisfaction is reason for law and policy, it supports minimal marriage, which better accords with citizens' diverse preferences than current marriage law does.[32]

However, preference-satisfaction is not a strong enough rationale, in that it does not make marriage a matter of justice. Preference satisfaction does not give sufficient reason for legislation. Consumers may want various and plentiful cheap goods, but this does not give legislators decisive reason to use the coercive powers of the state or taxpayer monies to create a framework providing them; this does not show such law is a matter of justice. I will argue that marriage rights are a fundamental matter of justice, as the social bases of the primary good of caring relationships. This status makes such rights subject to claims of justice. In my view, a narrow set of rights—hospital and prison visiting rights, special consideration for immigration eligibility, bereavement and caretaking leave—are appropriate subjects for claims of justice; the state cannot ignore claims to such rights.

Finally, Christopher Bennett has offered a purportedly neutral justification of "traditional Western marriage" in terms of autonomy. Drawing on Hegel's account of recognition, he argues that intimate relationships provide a mutual recognition that secures individual autonomy, and that the exclusivity of conjugal love is especially important for this. While this strategy addresses the need for a neutral rationale, the exclusivity requirement appears ad hoc; as Deidre Golash responded, small groups may be more successful in securing autonomy (as might close friendships), and thus Bennett's reasoning would imply recognizing relationships other than "traditional" marriage. In addition, if gender-structured marriage decreases the options and self-esteem of many women, it thereby threatens their autonomy.[33]

There is a stronger rationale for minimal marriage law: The social bases of caring relationships are social primary goods. In light of its importance in human life, the omission of care from the account of primary goods is striking. Its inclusion has far-reaching implications: Primary goods specify citizens' needs "when questions of justice arise." Because they are bases for claims of justice, the state must distribute them according to the principles of justice.[34]

Primary goods are introduced in *Theory of Justice* as a basis for interpersonal comparison of resources, specifying persons' wants, whatever plans of life they may have. They are, roughly, all-purpose goods that people are assumed to want whatever their plans: "[W]ith more of these goods men can generally be assured of greater success in carrying out their intentions and in advancing their ends, whatever these ends may be."[35] As developed in *Political Liberalism*, the idea of primary goods provides a "political understanding of what is to be publicly recognized as citizens' needs," and hence, one admissible in public reason.[36] In this later work, primary goods are defined in terms of the needs of citizens understood under the political conception of persons. This conception defines persons in terms of their moral powers (capacities for a sense of justice and a conception of the good), and hence primary goods are those goods essential to the development and exercise of the moral powers and to the pursuit of varied conceptions of the good: "To identify the primary goods we look to social background conditions and general all-purpose means normally needed for developing and exercising the two moral powers and for effectively pursuing conceptions of the good with widely different contents."[37]

Rawls divides primary goods into two classes: social and natural. The former include goods that society can distribute: liberties, opportunities, income, wealth, and the social bases of self-respect. The latter include goods whose distribution society can influence, but not directly control, such as health. Only the former are subject to claims of justice. I will show that minimal marriage is publically justifiable, and a matter of justice, by arguing that the social bases of caring relationships and material caretaking are, like the social bases of self-respect, social primary goods, and that minimal marriage rights just are the social bases of caring relationships.

As discussed in Chapter 4.i, care has different aspects. Material caregiving, which might include basic tending such as feeding and dressing, or activities designed to cheer or stimulate the cared-for such as grooming, playing games, or chatting, can be done by a paid caregiver. Another aspect of care is attitudinal care. Caring relationships involve attitudinal care; they exist between parties who know one another, take an interest in one another as persons, and share some history.

In practice, separating the two aspects of care is difficult. Caring relationships may exist between persons who are also related in other ways, as between a paid caregiver and cared-for. And caring attitudes tend to prompt material caregiving in relationships. Children need both material caregiving and caring relationships to develop physically and psychologically. Adults are liable to need material care throughout their lives, when incapacitated, and such caregiving is generally done better in caring relationships. While paid caregiving can meet this need, material caregiving tasks that could in theory be performed by anonymous paid caregivers are often done much better with a detailed knowledge of the cared-for, and nonurgent aid is made more likely by the motivating concern that springs from caring relationships.

Much material caregiving for dependent adults is done in the context of unpaid caring relationships—and because it has costs, and the bulk of it is done by women, this is of concern to feminists. However, showing that such care is a primary good would ground an argument that the state should provide structures to protect caregiving and those who do it. Dependency frameworks, such as those proposed by Martha Fineman, could regulate and protect practices of caring, while providing state support for caregiving.

In what follows, I will argue briefly that material caregiving for children and dependents is a primary good. Insofar as it can be distributed and compared interpersonally (through the allocation of care workers, for example), it is a social primary good. Dependency frameworks would be the social bases of that good. However, my main focus concerns caring relationships between adults, which need not involve material caregiving for dependents. I will argue that such relationships themselves are primary goods, but not social primary goods. As with the primary good of self-respect, the state cannot distribute them directly, nor are they good bases for interpersonal comparisons. However, the social bases of caring relationships are social primary goods, which the state can distribute, and which are subject to claims of justice; once again, these social bases of caring relationships just are minimal marriage rights—rights supporting, protecting, and recognizing caring relationships.

Material caregiving clearly falls under the definition of primary goods, as goods essential to the development and exercise of the moral powers and pursuit of varied conceptions of the good.[38] None of us would have moral powers or conceptions of the good to pursue were it not for such care as children. Throughout our lives, during periods of illness or incapacity, we are liable to need such care in order to sustain and develop our moral powers. Material caregiving is a primary good for dependents of all ages because it is necessary for the development and exercise of their moral powers; for those whose dependency prevents them from taking care of themselves (children, some persons with disabilities or illnesses), it is necessary for survival.

Further, caring relationships are primary goods for children because their normal psychological development depends on them. In *Theory of Justice*, Rawls recognizes the connection of caring relationships to the moral powers in his account of moral development; the sense of justice is developed in the family.[39] On the other hand, while caregiving is generally done better within caring relationships, the privacy of the home can hide dysfunction and abuse. The status of caring relationships for dependents as a primary good, and the private provision of much material caregiving, is reason for the liberal egalitarian to accept legal dependency frameworks supportive of otherwise unpaid caretakers in personal relationships, and regulating, educating, and protecting carers and dependents against abuse or neglect. (A vulnerable carer might be abused by the dependent, or by those around them.)

The primary good status of material caregiving provides an indirect rationale for minimal marriage. Minimal marriage is not a dependency framework but rather a framework for adult caring relationships that do not necessarily involve material caregiving for dependents (although they may do so). However, there is an overlap between dependent and nondependent relationships. As children develop or adults age or fall ill, relationships will shift from dependence to nondependence or vice versa. From day to day, even within a relationship between adults who can generally care for themselves, needs and burdens of care may shift back and forth. One party may fall ill. Because independent adults can (and often do) become dependent, relationships between independent parties lay epistemic and motivational foundations for future material caregiving. State support for caring relationships not involving dependency is continuous, in other words, with state support for caring relationships involving dependency. There are differences: Extensive state support that would be appropriate for givers of unidirectional major care would not be appropriate in caring relationships not involving dependency. But as the latter often lay the grounds for dependent adult caring relationships, supporting the former supports and promotes the latter. This in itself is a strong reason to support adult caring relationships not involving dependency.

On this rationale, minimal marriage would be an indirect social basis for the primary good of material caregiving—indirect because of the long timespan involved, and because in many cases parties to minimal marriages will not actually realize this good within the marriage. Moreover, because material caregiving can be had without caring relationships, minimal marriage is not essential to it, weakening this rationale. To provide a stronger rationale, I will argue that caring relationships in general (not just for dependents and children) are primary goods. This will provide a rationale for minimal marriage as the social basis of this primary good.

It might be objected straightaway that caring relationships lack two important features of social primary goods: being distributable and providing a simple, objective basis for comparison. Material caregiving is distributable and a basis for comparison (in terms of hours of care, for example), but caring relationships are not. Their just and efficient distribution results from personal choice, protected under liberties of association and privacy. They cannot be distributed. Nor do they provide a good basis for interpersonal comparison, due to differing individual needs for care and intimacy. Thus it might be thought that their inclusion would undermine the appealing simplicity of the account of primary goods.

However, self-respect is not in itself distributable, nor is it a good basis for interpersonal comparison. Just as the social bases of self-respect are the social primary good related to self-respect, so there are social primary goods related to caring relationships that can be distributed and objectively compared: the social bases of caring relationships, that is, the social conditions for their existence and continuation. These are the rights identified above as distinctive to minimal marriage, which designate and enable day-to-day maintenance of relationship. Insofar as caring relationships depend on social arrangements for their existence and continuation, their social bases—the socially distributable conditions for such relationships, or the legal frameworks designating and supporting them—are subject to claims of justice. The status of caring relationships as a primary good, combined with the diversity of such relationships, provides a publically justifiable rationale for a capacious, flexible legal framework supporting them. Minimal marriage just is this framework.

The first reason that caring relationships in themselves, dependent or not, are primary goods is that they are essential to developing and exercising the moral powers. Caring relationships are almost universally a context in which individuals do so. Most people simply do not and cannot develop and exercise those powers in isolation, but do so in relationships with other people. We form our conceptions of the good in colloquy with significant others and exercise our sense of justice in relationships. Rawls's own account of moral development in *Theory of Justice*, as noted, includes attachment to family and friends. It might be objected that one can exercise moral powers with strangers, or without caring relationships, in settings such as communes or churches, Internet chat rooms or philosophy colloquia, and that one can form a conception of the good through solitary philosophical reflection or impersonal dialogue. However, it might equally be objected that one could develop and exercise the moral powers without using the liberties or money. Caring relationships are normally an ongoing site of development and exercise of the moral powers, and normally as essential as money in so doing.

Further, caring relationships are "all-purpose means normally needed" in the pursuit of different conceptions of the good. Caring relationships are comparable to the good of self-respect: They provide psychological, emotional, and even health benefits that enable parties to pursue their varied goals. Of course, individual needs for intimacy and care differ, which is one reason the social bases of such relationships should be flexible. And a cautionary note must be sounded: Some relationships are oppressive, exploitative, and abusive. Bad relationships can devastate; but the fact that bad food can destroy one's health does not make good food any less essential. What this implies is the need for their legal framework to include easy exit options; the state should not pressure or incentivize staying in interpersonal relationships, due to their dangers. Its role is limited to protecting them and facilitating their existence when necessary.

The comparison with self-respect is instructive. Rawls says that "perhaps the most important primary good" is self-respect, or self-esteem, because without it, "nothing may seem worth doing, or if some things have value for us, we lack the will to strive for them."[40] There are clear connections between close interpersonal relationships and mental (as well as physical) health.[41] These connections suggest that caring relationships are comparable to self-respect in psychologically supporting individuals in their plans of life.

Indeed, caring relationships may even be intimately connected to self-respect. There is controversy over Rawls's account of self-respect, which he conflated with self-esteem. Self-esteem, or a positive appraisal of one's abilities and plans, is vulnerable to inequalities of degree and so does not comport easily with the difference principle, which allows some economic inequalities.[42] The other salient option for defining self-respect is recognition self-respect, that is, recognition of oneself as a free and equal citizen possessed of the moral powers. But it is more difficult to show why recognition self-respect is a primary good, supporting the pursuit of one's goals. One possible solution is to acknowledge an emotional dimension of self-respect, akin to a sense of entitlement, associated with recognition self-respect.[43] Caring relationships could contribute to this sense of valuing oneself and perceiving oneself as valuable because they involve another person, with detailed knowledge of one's particularity, perceiving one as valuable. Caring relationships in large part consist in such valuing of a particular other. This valuing plausibly underlies some of the benefits of caring relationships reported in psychological research, and explains why those relationships, like self-respect, are a primary good: They provide an important condition of pursuing one's plans, that is, a sense of one's value and the derivative sense that one's plans are worth pursuing.

A number of objections to the claim that caring relationships are primary goods may present themselves. First, some people may not need caring relationships to value themselves or to develop their moral powers. They may have a strong independent sense of self-worth, and espouse an ideal of rugged individualism. However, as I argue below, the fact that some people do not need a certain primary good to pursue their conception of the good is going to be a problem for any account of primary goods. In part, this objection depends on the numbers of people who do eschew caring relationships. A second objection is that some people need relationships to develop their powers and sense of self-worth, but not adult caring relationships: They derive the relevant benefits in relationships with dependents who cannot reciprocate or with nonhuman pets, or they derive them from groups or teams in the workplace, at church, in clubs, or in school. Finally, it might be objected that such benefits alone do not a primary good make; spa treatments, for example, might have benefits (relaxation, radiant skin) that help one in pursuit of various conceptions of the good, but it would be absurd to consider them primary goods.

In responding to these objections, three features of care are noteworthy. First, caring relationships are themselves important to most humans. They are normally involved in plans of life and conceptions of the good. Unlike spa treatments or caring for pets, they are widespread contexts for the exercise of moral powers and recognition of one's value. Second, their benefits are not negligible or superficial, like those of spa treatments, but "crucial to our well-being."[44] These benefits are not commonly obtainable through substitutes, although, as the objection presses, some people may derive them from other relationships, or without relationships. Like self-respect, caring relationships are an essential—irreplaceable for many or most—support in the pursuit of our projects. Psychologically, they are normally ingredients in, as opposed to mere means to, mental health and the sense of one's value (to adopt Mill's distinction). The close connection between caring relationships and such objective benefits is widespread.[45] Citizens, under the political conception of persons as having plans of life, normally need caring relationships to carry out their plans of life—and hence they are primary goods.

However, including caring relationships in the thin theory of the good still prompts the "hermit objection": The hermit may protest that relationships are not essential to advancing his plan of life or exercising his moral powers. This recalls the criticism that Rawls's list of primary goods is not neutral because it rules out antimaterialist ideals—such as monastic ideals of poverty. Defenders of Rawls respond that monks can use money to advance their ideals—perhaps by giving it away.[46] However, some conceptions of the good, such as communism, do conflict with private property. The hermit objection is no more problematic than the monk objection. As both hermit and monk present a problem for the Rawlsian, anyone who wishes to defend a Rawlsian theory of justice will need to respond to an objection structurally similar to the hermit objection. In my view, the appropriate response is to admit that the thin theory of the good reflects goods almost, but not quite, universally useful.

Rawls himself says that we can identify the primary goods by considering "social background conditions and general all-purpose means *normally needed*" to exercise the powers and pursue plans of life.[47] They are not absolute but vary with social background conditions. Moreover, without much explanation, Rawls says such goods are "normally," not always, needed. Some counterexamples, then, are consistent with the designation of a primary good; such goods are not always or universally required to pursue plans of life, as we can see by considering individuals who do so without liberties or money. But this raises the difficult question of what "normally" means here—what is the threshold for normalcy? Psychologists hypothesizing that humans have a drive to establish ongoing caring relationships argue that substantial empirical evidence confirms the hypothesis that such a drive is "extremely pervasive" and central to human life.[48]

If this empirical claim is correct, could it establish that caring relationships are a primary good? In Chapter 4, I argued that even if Fisher's hypothesis that humans have a cyclical drive to mate is correct, it cannot justify amatonormative discrimination which would exclude sexual minorities from benefits, and that valuing such a drive depends on comprehensive conceptions of the good. Many individuals do not conform to the four-year pair bonding cycle, which Fisher suggests is an innate drive. However, the psychological literature suggests that the drive to form caring relationships is more widespread, and it has close connections to self-respect and to other all-purpose means for pursuing plans of life. If the true hermit or isolated individualist is as rare as the peripatetic monk or communist (a condition that depends on the social background conditions and is subject to empirical assessment), then caring relationships are "normally" needed as much as money is "normally" needed.

But what of individuals whose primary caring relationships are not with other reciprocating adults? Because minimal marriage, as I have described it, is integrated with dependency frameworks and parenting frameworks, dependent and parental caring relationships would receive support within the appropriate frameworks, specifically designed to support them, and so minimal marriage does not unjustly discriminate against them. But does minimal marriage unjustly discriminate against relationships with nonhuman animals, such as pets? While these relationships may be a source of benefits for the human, they differ relevantly from adult caring relationships, the interpersonal cognitive dimensions of which are likely significant to their confirmation of self-worth. Adult caring relationships involve detailed reciprocal knowledge and communication typically greater than that had with pets. The reciprocal knowledge and communication that is possible between humans likely accounts for some of the psychological benefits of caring relationships. Being known and cared about as a particular other is important in confirming the sense of self-worth and the derivative sense of the worth of one's plans; one's sense of one's own value is normally enhanced when one can communicate one's complex projects or characteristics to another person who understands and cares about them. (I don't mean to be speciesist; if a particular nonhuman animal could engage in such a relationship of complex interpersonal recognition and communication, then the state might extend relevant rights—relocation assistance, visitation rights—if possible.)

Another objection is that some people may derive a sense of value from, and exercise their moral powers in, groups without caring bonds. Group membership may be beneficial without involving affective bonds, personal interaction, and reciprocal knowledge and care, as in a philosophy colloquium, an academic department, a sports team, a church, an Alcoholics Anonymous meeting, a workplace, a monastic religious order. But even if such group membership is a primary good for the same reason as caring relationships, such impersonal groups are not unjustly discriminated against by being excluded from minimal marriage. Each relationship—dependency, parental, adult caring, impersonal groups—is protected and supported by different rights, reflecting their different institutional needs, and thus they have different legal frameworks. Minimal marriage rights are designed to protect continuing caring relationships where people are known in their particularity and interact regularly as particular others; parties to the relationship are not fungible. But protecting and supporting groups requires different rights; normally, rights to association and privacy suffice to allow members to meet and interact. Minimal marriage rights would not be appropriate, because the group, not the particular individuals within it, matters as an entity; this is shown by the fact that the group persists while individuals exit and enter it. Particular individuals would be (in this very limited context!) fungible. The more ongoing interpersonal bonds of affection and friendship develop, and the less fungible people within the group become, the more the group comes to resemble a caring relationship. Uncaring groups are adequately protected by rights to privacy and association; but caring relationships are not.

The next question, in defending minimal marriage, is why caring relationships need the minimal marriage framework for protection and support. Presumably, people will enter such relationships whether or not there are frameworks to support them. Once again, the same might be said of self-respect; it can be attained without institutional support, yet given its importance as a primary good, the principles of justice require that institutions be selected with an eye toward the equal distribution of the social bases of self-respect. Self-respect is affected by social arrangements—and so are caring relationships. The basic structure affects the type and distribution and the number of caring relationships; amatonormativity, for instance, burdens some caring relationships. If they are primary goods, the principles require that the basic structure ensure the fair distribution of their social bases. But, once again, what essential role do the social bases play in supporting them that private contract and rights to privacy and association do not already play?

First, three kinds of minimal marriage rights cannot currently be attained through private contract nor rights to privacy and association. These are, first, entitlements to special eligibility for immigration or legal residency (which has concrete implications for, e.g., in-state tuition and taxation); second, entitlements against employers for care taking or bereavement leave and designation as a spouse for spousal relocation and hiring policies; third, hospital and prison visitation rights.

Second, the social bases of caring relationships are needed *in occasional but not unusual circumstances*—not in all cases—to maintain those relationships. Finally, these entitlements are such that either only the state can provide them or the state is best placed to so do in an effective way. To be sure, many relationships might at times depend for their continuance on therapy, relaxing vacations, and so on; but what distinguishes minimal marriage rights such as immigration and residence, leave entitlements, and visitation is that they are legal rights, which the state constructs and enforces. These rights depend on the state for their existence. The state also, in large part, makes them necessary. The many ways in which the state and its institutions are constructed—for example, borders carry implications for residency, work, tuition, taxation, and so on—create impediments to relationships, burdening them with financial or opportunity costs. Because institutions can create such burdens, people under certain circumstances need protective rights just to continue a relationship without unreasonable burdens, rights allowing them to live and work in the same place.[49]

Caring relationships sometimes need support and protection that the state is uniquely able to provide and is best placed to orchestrate. Even caring relationships between independent adults sometimes require some legal machinery; some entitlements needed for their maintenance are available only through law or state policy. Maintaining such relationships normally requires frequent contact and shared experiences. Thus, institutional design should attend to the social conditions for such access, that is, the social bases of caring relationships.

These social bases fall into two groups: those that would be available in an ideal liberal egalitarian society and those that would not be but might be appropriate in actual societies. Marriage rights in an ideal liberal egalitarian society would perform functions of status designation and facilitating the day-to-day conduct of the relationship. The rationale for minimal marital entitlements is not, as in current marriage law, that the designee(s) is the only source of emotional and material support for the other, but that she is party to a caring relationship that deserves protection.

Above, I noted that some marital rights facilitate day-to-day maintenance of a relationship and enable spouses to play significant roles in one another's lives: These include entitlements to special consideration for immigration, eligibility for spousal employment and relocation assistance and preferential hiring (offered to U.S. military and civil service spouses), residency (where relevant for tuition, taxation, etc.), hospital and prison visiting rights, bereavement or spousal care leave, burial with one's spouse in a veterans' cemetery, spousal immunity from testifying, and status designation for the purpose of third parties offering private benefits (such as spousal hiring, employment incentives and family rates). Some relationships depend for their continuance on such entitlements because they greatly facilitate spousal contact. In the modern world, caring relationships sometimes require practical support such as visiting rights, leave, immigration eligibility, and relocation assistance; individuals need a way to signal to the vast institutions shaping their lives (including employers) which relationships should receive these protections.

The state and other large institutions shape our lives by determining geographic boundaries, permissions to work, and various types of institutional access. Again, many impediments to relationships are in fact created by the state—immigration restrictions, relocation of civil servants and military personnel, prisons. Others arise from circumstances of contemporary society, in which vast institutions (hospitals and workplaces) affect individual lives with little regard for particularity. Marital rights signal which relationships such institutions are required to recognize as relevant in visitation, caretaking leave, or spousal hiring and relocation. These entitlements are the social bases of caring relationships. They are not available within private contract, nor are they covered by rights to privacy and association; they extend special support to relationships and can only be used in that capacity. Furthermore, they lie outside the contract paradigm because their content is shaped by the nature of caring relationships; they designate a status—that of being in a caring relationship—which must be treated as salient in institutional decisions with significant implications for individual lives.

Because caring relationships are primary goods, the provision of these entitlements should not be left to the marketplace; their legislation is a matter of justice. The state can require employers to provide entitlements, such as caretaking leave, and not to discriminate between different caring relationships where such entitlements are concerned. Practically, the state must play a large role in structuring these entitlements, for the state itself creates relationship-threatening geographical divisions, designs labor law (and is a major employer), and determines immigration eligibility. Enforcement of visitation rights and determination of immigration or residency eligibility can only be done by the state. Moreover, because it is enduring, centralized, and not subject to market pressures, the state is in the best position to register marriages to prove eligibility for third-party benefits. Employers, insurers, and others may still use marriage as a means to establish entitlements, and, while status designations could be sold by private companies or religious organizations, the state is in a position to record and authenticate such designations.

Further, as many conservative defenders of marriage have noted, and as discussed in Chapters 2 and 4, marriage law does not simply allow access to legal entitlements, but lends the state's authority to designating eligibility for marital status. Feminists and political liberals are right to be wary of such designations because of their historical association with racism, sexism, heterosexism, and amatonormativity. However, if legal recognition is extended to diverse relationships, it can combat heterosexism and amatonormativity, by making alternatives more familiar and signaling their equality under the law. As conservatives have noted, state recognition conveys a unique authority for such purposes. As I will emphasize in the next section, the state should not designate such relationships as "legitimate" or having a comprehensive ethical value, but simply as equally eligible for protection.

State recognition also has implications for third-party benefit provision, a crucial function of marriage law. It designates a status for third parties who provide incentives and benefits, including health care, pensions, insurance, and so on. Without a status designating relevant relationships, third parties might discriminate unjustly, for instance, offering benefits only to different-sex couples or amatory partners. Marital status guarantees that benefits offered on the basis of marriage will be offered without amatonormative discrimination. This is significant because many marital benefits derive from employers. If all caring relationships were eligible for "married" status, they would be protected from private-sphere discrimination. Because caring relationships are primary goods, the provision of these entitlements should not be left to the marketplace (at least, in the transitional stage). This means, where substantial benefits are provided with marriage, minimal marriage will provide real alternatives to "traditional" marriage. While, in an ideal liberal egalitarian society, social bases would be limited to status designation and facilitating day-to-day conduct of the relationship, in our actual society, further entitlements to social security programs, health care, and other government benefits are justified, as I will argue in the next chapter.

Someone might object that my view implies more: The state should help the friendless and loveless find caring relationships—by providing counseling, advice, dating, or friendship services and so on. Well, why not, so long as no one is coerced and state action is effective? But such measures are likely to be heavy-handed and inefficient. Increasing people's relationship fitness is not done well by government programs. However, more effective measures might seem less like a *reductio* and more like a good idea: The state should pursue an education policy that includes attention to the psychological and emotional bases of caring relationships in all their diversity. One function of schools is socialization. So if there is solid evidence regarding educational techniques that are likely to make children better able to form relationships later in life, these might be implemented in schools.

Within the Rawlsian framework, minimal marriage would be derived as follows. In *Theory of Justice*, Rawls imagines a four-stage implementation of the principles of justice. Leaving the original position, contractors reconvene in constitutional and legislative stages, gaining additional knowledge of their society at each stage before finally emerging fully from the veil of ignorance into courtrooms and public offices. Given the abstraction of principles chosen in the original position and the constitutional convention, it seems likely that marriage law would be enacted at the third, legislative stage. While ideal legislators know their social traditions, the condition that they do not know which ideals they espouse ensures neutrality among *contested* conceptions of the good.[50]

Behind this partial veil of ignorance, ideal legislators would choose to make the social bases of caring relationships, as social primary goods, available on an equal basis for all caring relationships. They would frame whatever laws are essential (in some cases) to pursuing relationships and cannot be provided privately. The social conditions for relationships in a given society (such as working conditions, borders, and so on), as revealed under the partial veil, would determine the content of these social bases. In societies like ours, they would consist in the designation and maintenance rights described. But because some relationships threaten autonomy and equal opportunity, legislators would view incentives to remain in relationships or reduced exit rights with suspicion. The resulting framework would be minimal marriage, which makes marital rights supporting relationships available to the many possible configurations of caring relationships.

Law affects choices. Principles governing the basic structure affect our motivations; this is acknowledged in Rawls's argument for the difference principle, and his account of stability. Communitarian and care ethicist critics of liberalism have charged that its individualism produces uncaring, self-centered citizens.[51] Pateman argued that the logic of contract, applied to marriage, will lead to a society in which short-term sexual contracts are the norm—essentially, marriage will be replaced by prostitution or promiscuity.[52] I have suggested that "traditional" marriage, with its focus on the nuclear family, could be seen as promoting a marketplace of dyads. Minimal marriage, in contrast, allows broader caring networks with friends or lovers. In response to worries about liberal atomism, it promotes care, while moving away from the ideal of nuclear family privacy.

This proposal can be distinguished from Tamara Metz's argument to abolish legal marriage and replace it with an "intimate caregiving union [ICGU] status."[53] Metz argues that marriage inherently conveys an ethical status; ICGUs, by contrast, are intended to support caregiving, without conveying an ethical status. They would confer bundles of privileges, such as next-of-kin rights and joint ownership rights, on caregiving unions. One difference between our views is that ICGUs, unlike minimal marriage, would assimilate parenting and adult relationships into one legal framework. ICGUs support all forms of caregiving. I argued that it is more efficient and just to separate parenting frameworks from minimal marriage (Chapter 6.iii). Also, ICGUs would not protect friendships, which lack, Metz suggests, the dependency and risk that caregiving involves. Yet, as I argued in Chapter 4, friendships can involve taking on substantial obligations—and anyway, minimal marriage's rationale, that caring relationships are primary goods, differs from Metz's rationale of protecting caregivers. Further, ICGU rights come in bundles; it's not clear how or whether such bundles can be distributed over networks, and whether specific rights can be waived, as in minimal marriage. Finally, Metz suggests that people must voluntarily register ICGUs, like marriages, but this requirement might undermine their stated rationale of protecting caregiving. Unregistered caregivers will remain unprotected. If ICGU status were conferred nonconsensually (like "common law marriage"), to protect unregistered caregivers, it might interfere with adults' liberties to choose the terms of their relationships. One strategy to avoid this dilemma, which I pursue in Chapter 8, is to separate the rights protecting relationships from those protecting caregivers themselves; rights protecting relationships—minimal marriage—should be conferred only voluntarily, rights protecting caregivers should be conferred by default.

IV. WHAT'S IN A NAME? MARRIAGE, SYMBOLISM, AND LEGITIMACY

It is important to emphasize that the above proposal need not be institutionalized as "marriage"; it could be called, for instance, "personal relationship law." But I can now state the reasons for calling the proposed legal framework "minimal *marriage*." Nomenclature matters: Political resistance to calling same-sex unions "marriages" is often an attempt to deny them full legitimacy and to retain a privileged status for different-sex partnerships. Extending the application of "marriage" is one way of rectifying past amatonormative and heteronormative discrimination. While this departs from current usage, the reference of "marriage" need not be determined by past use (though there is precedent in "Boston marriage," probably originating from Henry James' *Bostonians*, and referring to a companionate, possibly lesbian, relationship between "spinsters"!). The objective of calling a revised legal framework "minimal *marriage*" would be to rectify past state discrimination; such rectification might also take the form of an apology, reparations, or a monument to victims of discrimination on the basis of sexual orientation. If such measures were taken, it would be less important to retain the term "marriage," and in that case, it might be desirable to replace "marriage" as a legal term with "personal relationships" or "adult care networks."

As discussed in Chapter 5 and 6.iv, some critics argue that marriage is inherently patriarchal, ethnocentric, or comprehensive.[54] If so, as the name "marriage" is retained only to rectify unjust discrimination, the rationale for retaining the name would be undermined. Retaining the name depends on rebranding marriage. One reason to think that it can be rebranded is that many institutions with historically unjust or inegalitarian symbolism have altered their symbolism. In *The Sexual Contract*, Pateman shows that the historical "contractor" was male and defined in a way that presupposed domination of a woman—but this symbolism, as I argued in Chapter 5.i, does not inhere in contemporary contract. Similarly, in *Public Vows*, Nancy Cott shows that the concept of citizenship in the United States was at one time explicitly symbolically associated with male heads of households, and law was framed on this basis. But if "citizen" can lose its sexist symbolism, yet retain its other symbolism (such as being equal under law), it seems possible that "marriage" can do so.

It might be objected, as Metz argues, that marriage is, like prayer or baptism, an essentially comprehensive practice. But while legal marriage is still imbued with moral and religious symbolism, it has also become unmoored from comprehensive doctrines, reflected in the social confusion about what it means. Couples who write "personal" vows, have a civil ceremony without invoking the comprehensive symbolism, or say that they are getting married, "but just legally," demonstrate this shift. In contrast, outside philosophical examples, it is rare to find people who say they are praying, "but just in a secular way"!

It might be thought that even if the symbolism of marriage can be changed, there is no reason to attempt rebranding rather than simply abolishing it, and that the state should merely provide rights supporting personal relationships while "leaving the expressive domain to the religions and to other private groups."[55] But rebranding may be the best strategy to rectify the heteronormative and amatonormative discrimination of current marriage law. Abolishing marriage is one way to remove the state's endorsement of such discrimination. But by recognizing and supporting a diversity of relationships, including networks or friendships, the state may help to create new social scripts and make alternative relationships salient, by recognizing them as equal under law.

Abolishing marriage might seem to achieve equality by placing everyone in the same legal position. However, this would cede control of this still socially powerful institution to the churches and other private-sector groups, such as commercial "wedding chapels." State involvement makes equal access to marriage as a social status more likely. Abolition would allow private-sector providers to deny entry, whereas reform would send an unequivocal message of equal citizenship.[56]

This proposal would unsettle the current social meaning of marriage. But one purpose of the proposal is precisely *to* trouble that social meaning in order to improve the social standing of alternative relationship forms. By affirming difference, the state can denormalize the ideal of heterosexual monogamy. Insofar as this ideal presents sexual, cohabiting relationships as more valuable or more worthy of state support than other caring relationships, it sustains social discrimination against those other relationships.

However, the question of symbolism faces a dilemma. On the one hand, to rectify past discrimination, the symbolism of legal marriage must be strong enough that recognizing the marital status of same-sex relationships and networks has a corrective effect. On the other hand, the symbolism should not be so strong that children or adults outside minimal marriages face stigma! The state should not indirectly foster any symbolism that reinforces invidious comprehensive-doctrine-based distinctions between caring relationships in and out of marriage. However, the state can make minimal marriage rights available, stressing that all caring relationships are *eligible* to employ them, although some may not need to. Again, this would allow the state to lend its authority against private-sphere discrimination—a correction that, in this case, is politically justified because the state has sustained the discrimination through legal discrimination and penalties reinforcing amatonormativity.

Minimal marriage should not be intended to convey legitimacy, merely a status designation. Part of the political point of the proposal is to weaken the invidious and illiberal distinction between legitimate and illegitimate relationships. As noted in Chapter 5.i, Claudia Card wrote that distinguishing relationships as "legitimate" and "illegitimate" is just as wrong as distinguishing "legitimate" and "illegitimate" children. One can say that a birth certificate is legitimate, in the sense that it was correctly filled out, witnessed, and so on. But this is different from categorizing the infant as legitimate or illegitimate. In the same way, minimal marriage rights may be held legitimately (due procedures have been followed) without their marking the relationship as "legitimate." Procedural legitimacy is the only sense of legitimacy involved in minimal marriage.

However, though minimal marriage does not confer legitimacy in any substantive sense, it rectifies past discrimination against lesbians, gays, bisexuals, polyamorists, and care networks by placing all relationships on an equal footing under law. This avoids the problem identified by Michael Warner: Some

> advocates for gay marriage are seeking...a political shortcut to dignity and respect from straight people through the granting of marriage rights. Many people respect the consecration of marriage, in other words, and it is this respect that many gay people might be seeking, more than the consecration per se. The benefits of marriage will follow for them, not so much because they see the state as having intrinsic powers of consecration, but because so many other people in society view the state in this way. There is a kind of circularity in this thinking; and to argue for gay marriage on these grounds is to despair that respect can be compelled on any other terms.[57]

Minimal marriage does not seek to confer respect by drawing on the comprehensive expressive meanings of marriage, but rather to signal the injustice of drawing invidious distinctions under law. If the state simply withdraws from marriage, this may be interpreted as tacitly allowing such distinctions; it would have simply ceased to make them, rather than to correct them.

Perhaps the most common objection to "minimal marriage" is that it is simply not marriage. However, while the proposal does depart from current understandings of marriage, this response is reminiscent of a similar reaction to recognizing same-sex relationships: "Just don't call it marriage!" This proposal is not an attempt to redefine marriage conceptually. It reflects the fact that there are already a number of competing conceptions of marriage. In light of the competing conceptions of marriage and of valuable relationships, some of the legal supports for marriage should be stretched to include them all. The parties themselves can decide whether or not they consider their relationship a marriage, in the social or religious sense; the legal rights of minimal marriage exist to support caring relationships

I have argued that there is sufficient reason within liberal theory for legal frameworks for caring relationships between adults. In the next chapter, I examine the difficulties of implementing such a proposal in a nonideal society.

8

CHALLENGES FOR MINIMAL MARRIAGE
POVERTY, PROPERTY, POLYGYNY

So far, I have been considering what justice would imply in an ideally just society. But we do not live in one. In nonideal circumstances, it may be unjust to implement the results of ideal theory. Sexism, racism, heteronormativity, and amatonormativity must be addressed by any political theory aspiring to relevance. Ideal theory has been criticized for its failure to attend to the most challenging problems of contemporary liberal democracies. Even worse, it has been argued that ideal theory is structurally unable to address these problems. In this chapter, I address specific challenges marriage reform faces in actual societies and show how liberal egalitarianism can consistently address transitional problems of poverty, property division, and polygyny. The example of minimal marriage offers a partial response to feminist critics of liberalism by showing that the consistent application of liberal principles can yield a marriage law that no longer arbitrarily privileges some members of society. Liberal egalitarian principles, consistently applied, hold unappreciated possibilities for radical reform.

"Ideal theory" in ethics refers to theories that construct or derive moral principles through idealizations, such as the idealized autonomous rational contractor of Rawls's original position or Rawls's assumption of strict compliance.[1] Assuming ideal circumstances precludes generating principles directly responding to injustices such as slavery, segregation, the Trail of Tears, sexual harassment, domestic violence, and so on. Noting these ideal theoretical constraints, Charles Mills asks, "How in God's name could anybody think that this is the appropriate way to do ethics?"[2] Indeed, ethical or political theory that fails to address actual injustices is poorer for that omission, risking, as Mills charges, becoming ideological.

Rawls's theory of justice has been criticized for its inattention to real injustices. For example, Seana Shiffrin suggests that it is "surprising that the principles of justice do not directly protect against racial discrimination."[3] It has been suggested that his theory is systematically unable to address such issues. Rawls's characterization of the contractors as autonomous results in prioritizing the liberties and thereby precluding state interference in "private" sources of oppression.

However, the theory must be able to address actual injustices. Even were Rawls's two principles of justice implemented tomorrow, existing inequalities would continue to create further inequalities. Some individuals will always fail to comply, leading to the need to design new institutions to prevent and correct injustice. In any case, the principles are not likely to be implemented; reform comes piecemeal, and the ideal will always remain aspirational. Liberals need to be able to give a consistent account of how to respond to actual injustices.

Principles of justice derived from idealizations can be powerful tools for change. Despite their flaws, they reflect an ideal of moral equality and a fair bargaining situation unavailable in actuality and for this reason can suggest significant possibilities of reform. But taking the ideal as guide requires an account of how to move from the actual toward the ideal. Where reforms could cause new harms or injustices, there is reason for concern.

I. POVERTY

This section addresses concerns that minimal marriage would exacerbate poverty for women and children by ending "traditional" marriage promotion and benefits. As noted in the Introduction, U.S. federal law addresses the poverty of single mothers through marriage promotion policies such as state commissions and proclamations, divorce law, marriage "education," state tax policies and cash assistance, Medicaid policy, vital statistics, and youth education. Temporary Assistance for Needy Families legislation, which bankrolls such policies, addresses the correlation between poverty and single motherhood by trying to get mothers to marry: It aims to "end the dependence of needy parents on government benefits by promoting...marriage."[4]

Incentives to adopt promarriage policies have been effective. Since this legislation was enacted, a number of states have revisited no-fault divorce law, considering legislation to abolish it. Louisiana, Arizona, Arkansas have introduced "covenant marriage," an option imposing longer waiting periods, and in which "a no-fault divorce cannot be granted unless both parties agree...and no children are involved."[5] With "school-based marriage education" and "abstinence-until-marriage education," "states are also targeting the marriage message to youth."[6] States receiving abstinence education funding must provide educational programs adhering to "an abstinence-until-marriage message" as defined in the Social Security Act, teaching that abstinence is socially, psychologically, and medically beneficial, that "sexual activity outside the context of marriage is likely to have harmful psychological and physical effects."[7]

It might be argued that minimal marriage would not only end such marriage promotion, it will decrease "traditional" marriages and thereby exacerbate poverty. But "traditional" marriage promotion is an inefficient antipoverty program. Trying to address the poverty of single mothers through marriage is like trying to shove an escaped elephant into a cage it has outgrown. The conditions that, according to historian Stephanie Coontz, have led to higher rates of divorce and lower rates of marriage—women's economic independence, birth control, and the idea that marriage should be emotionally satisfying—are enduring.[8] At least one-third of U.S. children are now being reared outside marriage. The inefficiency of marriage promotion as an antipoverty program is even more obvious when one considers that many two-parent families are in poverty, and poorer families have less to divide on divorce.[9]

Furthermore, marriage promotion policy ignores sources of poverty in unrelated injustices. Justice as well as efficiency demands that society address economic disadvantage to caregivers, the drop in working-class real wages, racism and the legacy of slavery and Jim Crow, the effects of racial profiling, the lack of decent affordable housing, and the gendered division of labor. For example, as discussed in 5.iii, the African American Healthy Marriage Initiative targets African-Americans but seems to ignore extraordinarily high incarceration rates for African-American males. And marriage promotion seeks to alleviate female poverty through marriage rather than job training and subsidized child care. Indeed, its object is that poor women secure a breadwinner, not better-paid employment: A program funded under this legislation in Allentown, Pennsylvania, offered job training programs *to men only*.[10] Justice and efficiency require addressing root causes of poverty, such as unequal pay and racial discrimination.[11]

Another concern may be that minimal marriage will increase the number of single parents. Single parenting is correlated with poverty. But marriage promotion is a poor solution: It promotes female dependency, making women and children vulnerable. The economic costs of single parenting must be weighed with the detrimental effects of high-conflict and abusive marriages. Given widespread abuse and violence within marriage, and the additional harms of high-conflict marriages, women and children may often be better off outside marriage. Further, marriage promotion benefits only children whose parents marry. Benefits should be directed at children in poverty, not married parents. Minimal marriage, in contrast, would help single parents by increasing their marital options.

A more pressing concern is that, in an ideal liberal egalitarian state, minimal marriage would bring no health care entitlement or other financial benefits. But immediate abolition of marital health care, pension, and other benefits—with no alternative provision—would harm many. This might seem to pose a dilemma for liberals: Distributing health care and other benefits through marriage, as Card argued, unjustly excludes the unmarried and subsidizes the married at their expense. How can a transitional stage retaining benefit entitlements be justified? Why should single taxpayers or employees subsidize spousal health insurance and other benefits? In the case of dependency frameworks, the state can provide an answer, explaining why parental leave and other parental support do not discriminate against nonparents: Dependent children provide the state's future, and justice requires that children receive care. But why should a spouse who is capable of employment, but chooses not to work outside the home, receive financial benefits from the state or third parties?

A somewhat unsatisfactory response, considered already in Chapter 5.ii, is that while such benefits unjustly exclude the unmarried, providing health care or pensions unjustly to some comes closer to the universal provision that justice requires than unjustly not providing them at all. A transitional stage in which minimal marriage continues to carry such benefits would continue to exclude some unjustly, but it would help many others. This reflects the compromises that implementing ideal theory demands.

But we can give a more satisfactory answer as to why such benefits should be maintained for some time. First, the state has induced reliance on these benefits. People, and not only economically dependent wives, have made choices on their basis, and it would be unjust—tantamount to a violation of contract—to remove them. Entitlements are not fixed a priori, but are constructed through law and policy.

A second response applies specifically to dependent wives: Because their choices have been shaped in a system of amatonormative, patriarchal, and *state-sponsored* oppression, protecting women against the effects of these choices is a matter of rectification. These women might have been better off had they been encouraged to seek economic independence, not dependence; but given that the state has incentivized and promoted them into dependent marriage, it owes them rectificatory compensation. Given that, as late as 2001, some abstinence-education curricula have taught children gender-structured domestic roles (see Chapter 5.i), a long transition will be required to outlast the effects of state-sponsored gender hierarchy and amatonormativity.

These reasons also justify extending such benefits to minimal marriages, even when they do not involve dependent wives. Imagine that Anna receives health care entitlements through her current marriage. If she cannot receive this benefit in a new minimal marriage with members of her care network, her choice to leave her current marriage and enter the new one is unduly restricted—unduly in light of the state's role in inducing reliance and shaping her choices through amatonormative pressure. (My point, to be clear, is not that Anna's choice was politically unfree due to such pressures, but rather that the state owes her compensation for having unjustly sponsored discriminatory role pressures. It ought not to have interfered with her choices in this way.) Had she not been induced to rely on marriage to provide this benefit, she might have sought to be able to provide it for herself, and hence be able to enter the new marriage without losing healthcare. These are reasons of justice to extend the benefits throughout minimal marriage, not only to current recipients like Anna, but to the next generation, who have begun to form their preferences in light of existing structures.

While minimal marriage is not any more of an anti-poverty program than marriage promotion, it would benefit the worst-off more by making benefits more widely available. Current marriage promotion aims to increase women's economic dependence on men and so may exacerbate abuse. In contrast, minimal marriage, assuming that for a transitional period it will offer benefits such as healthcare, allows women more marriage options and thus greater bargaining power.

II. PROPERTY AND DIVORCE

Marriage reform must create good exit options. Exit options affect whether the outcome is just, when a marriage ends—whether the resulting situation comports with equality—and they affect justice within a marriage while it endures—as we saw in Chapter 5.1, lack of exit options facilitates abuse as well as power inequality. The need to ensure good exit options is challenging for minimal marriage because, in an ideal society, minimal marriage would not include default marital property arrangements that protect dependent spouses on divorce. The reason for this is that the law, recognizing the diversity of relationships in society, cannot assume a dependency relationship between married people. But property division and alimony or spousal support is the main means of assuring that economically dependent wives have good exit options. However, I argue that these protections be removed from marriage and replaced with universal default rules.

Minimal marriage would contractualize property arrangements, meaning that spouses could determine property division on divorce through individual contract. However, some feminists have argued against contractualizing marital property because marital property law protects women. As discussed in Chapter 5.1, Okin documented how women become economically vulnerable through marriage when they subordinate their economic independence to child care and household work. Such choices disadvantage women on divorce, and these disadvantages are compounded by the greater likelihood that children will remain with the mother after the divorce, bringing her greater financial costs. In light of these inequalities, Okin argues that in the transition to a gender-neutral society, divorce law protects economically vulnerable women in gender-structured marriages. Contractualizing marital property would eliminate such protections. Okin argues for a legal requirement that all spousal earnings be equally owned by both parties, and for mandatory alimony and property division on divorce. She argues that because the pattern of such choices systematically affects women, fair equal opportunity requires correcting the accruing disadvantages. In Rawls's later work, he too justifies spousal support and property division by appeal to the political value of women's equality in structuring family law.[12]

Other feminists have pointed out that, given existing social inequalities, women are not in a fair bargaining position to negotiate marriage contracts. Martha Minow and Mary Lyndon Shanley write that

> one of John Stuart Mill's great insights in *The Subjection of Women* was his observation that the decision to marry for the vast majority of women could scarcely be called "free." Given women's low wages, scarcity of jobs, and lack of opportunity for higher or even secondary education, marriage was for them a "Hobson's choice": that or none. Even the "I do" of someone very much in love and desirous of marriage does not in-and-of-itself guarantee freedom.[13]

Mill's insight suggests that given background inequalities, social disempowerment, and limited alternatives, contract does not assure women's free, in the sense of unconstrained, consent. If a woman's male partner earns more and has greater social power (by virtue of gender role hierarchy), and both expect him to be the primary breadwinner, a woman settling a marriage contract may be pressured to agree to terms she does not want: the higher-earning and more socially powerful party will have greater bargaining power. Freedom of contract is compatible with pressure to make disadvantageous choices. Nor, as Minow and Shanley point out, does prenuptial contract address dependencies arising within marriage over time. Insofar as women are likely to become economically vulnerable in marriage, they will be better protected economically by mandatory property division and alimony than by contractualization.

These concerns may justify a transitional stage retaining alimony, on liberal principles of equal opportunity, and for the reasons given in the last section for retaining benefits (the points regarding induced reliance and compensation apply here). But while mandatory alimony and property division address the inequities arising from gender-structured marriage, they do not address social pressures and gender roles that create these inequities. Furthermore, by assuming economic dependency in marriage, law may encourage women to become dependent.

There are other weaknesses to relying on alimony to protect the vulnerable. One concerns efficiency. The amount of money received and the percentage who receive it are particularly low for poor women. Marriage contracts, particularly alimony provisions, have tended to be less well-enforced than other contracts.[14] Also, mothers earn less than childless women ("mothers earn about 70 percent of the mean wages of men, and childless women earn 80 to 90 percent"), so pursuing policies targeted to the worst-off like raising the minimum wage, providing daycare, and Anne Alstott's "caretaker resource account" would help the worst-off more than alimony.[15]

There is also a problem regarding the grounds for interpersonal obligation in mandatory alimony.[16] Addressing systematic gender discrimination in employment, wages, and social pressures through alimony risks injustice to individual men. If the reason for alimony is equal opportunity, why should individual men be held responsible for the inequities of the social system? This is especially pertinent because the husbands of the neediest women are likely to be poor themselves. Mandatory alimony based on equal opportunity needs to be sensitive to the position of both parties. However, in nonideal circumstances, the balance of reasons may favor burdening a well-off husband with the costs of his ex-wife's job training over allowing her to enter poverty.

But if overall justice does require such transfers, then default rules governing property division on exit from financially dependent relationships can be enacted independently from marriage.[17] Separating such rules from marriage would extend protection to those outside marriage. If the rationale of property division is protecting the vulnerable against inequalities arising in relationships, there is no reason to limit protection to the married. The duration of the relationship, the extent of the dependency, the increase in economic inequality, and so on, are more relevant to determining whether support is owed (but not gender, for reasons I make clear below). Enacting default rules addressing inequalities within financially enmeshed intimate relationships does not assume dependency in marriage, but applies directly to cases of dependency. Separating such rules from marriage law may gradually alter the expectation that women make themselves dependent in marriage.

Such default rules would apply involuntarily. This allows the separation of minimal marriage rights and financial obligations suggested at the end of Chapter 7.iii. Minimal marriage entitlements will be voluntary—voluntary entry will be efficient because people will be motivated to apply for these entitlements as the need arises. Support obligations, however, would be imposed by default, so that they would protect vulnerable members of unregistered relationships. This would offer exit options from unmarried economically dependent relationships as well as dependent marriages.

The worry might arise that imposing such default rules involuntarily would interfere with freedom of contract and fail to treat adults as responsible for their choices. If a woman, due to religious views or her lower earning capacity, wishes to make a "vulnerability contract" in which she cedes rights to support while planning to forgo paid work, should such a contract be enforced when parties separate?

Should women's choices to prioritize child care over paid work be treated as private choices for the costs of which they are solely responsible? Can parties opt out of default rules?

Liberal egalitarianism does not require unregulated free contract and so can admit involuntary mechanisms to protect against dependency. Provisions preventing contracts from eventuating in one party's impoverishment are compatible with liberal egalitarianism. Freedom of contract is not a basic liberty, and the difference principle restricts it.[18] Default rules can be justified, as Rawls suggests, by political values such as women's equality.

But default rules can also be justified by other legal mechanisms, many of which already exist in law. Rather than enacting specific laws for relationships, it might be possible to address dependency through general principles derived from contract law. Induced reliance might require that when one party makes herself dependent on another while reasonably relying on his continued support, he is obligated to aid her in becoming self-sufficient if the arrangement ends. Fineman argues for abolishing marriage and shifting relations now governed by marriage to contract, labor, and tort law. (Spouses are still exempt from U.S. labor law protections, despite the fact that they may work for one another.) Fineman argues that compensation for contributions to the other party's career might be justified by appeal to mechanisms independently available in law: "the interests of a cohabitant who contributed to the accumulation of wealth for the other, even if she did not have a contract, would be protected to some extent by default and equity rules. The general regulatory rules found in equity (such as unjust enrichment or constructive trust), partnership, and labor law could provide rules for decisions in disputes involving sexual affiliates."[19] Default rules might be justified through independently justified legal principles (thus obviating the need for specifying gender).

Applying these general provisions might be even fairer than a law targeted at dependency. Rules correcting economic dependency might not compensate the unpaid labor supplied by "traditional" wives. But provisions inherent in contract can. Support liability on grounds of opportunities forgone and contributions to the other's career might be justified by appeal to induced reliance and verbal contracts. Fineman also suggests that abolishing marriage would actually expand the possibilities of legal recourse under tort and criminal law; she envisions new tort law addressing harms that occur between sexual intimates. But this would also be compatible with minimal marriage.

Property division and support are crucial to provide exit options from marriage. The threat of losing benefits, such as health care and pensions, can also constrain exit; for this reason, I argued in the last section that such benefits be retained for a transitional period. While these benefits can constrain the choice to stay married, removing the benefits actually reduces options overall. Extending them to minimal marriage increases women's marriage options and hence their bargaining power

A final note: As discussed in Chapter 2, the more restrictive the exit options, the more pressure to maintain a marital commitment. It might thus be thought that protecting exit options would reduce commitment to marriage. But, as argued there, commitment to abusive or exploitative relationships should not be protected. Moreover, internal commitment is not guaranteed by external pressures. Marriage may be a poor precommitment strategy, encouraging emotional laziness. Protecting exit options might improve marriages by giving spouses reason to keep each other happy—a husband who knows his wife can leave will be more motivated to share in domestic labor, for instance. Ensuring adequate exit options protects women and children, but it may also improve marriages.

III. POLYGYNY

Gender-structured polygyny presents another challenge for liberal feminism. It is important to be clear on terminology. Polygamy includes both polygyny—one husband and multiple wives—and polyandry—one wife and multiple husbands. Polygamy may be seen, as Emens suggests, as a type of polyamory, but polyamory takes many additional forms, ranging from a small interconnected group to a molecular structure with multiple nonoverlapping relationships to the "V" or spoke structure typical of polygyny (in which the husband is the center and maintains a separate, exclusive relationship with each wife).

Polygyny presents a problem because, as Thom Brooks reports, women in polygynous marriages suffer low self-esteem, depression, and lower marital satisfaction, at a higher rate than women in monogamous marriages.[20] (Because my argument for allowing suboptimal parenting structures in Chapter 6.iii applies here, I set aside effects on children that do not violate justice.) Andrew March questions these data; indeed, we should keep in mind that correlation is not causation. It is possible for polygyny to benefit women, as Elizabeth Joseph, a working lawyer and polygynous wife, claims. Joseph praises the arrangement in feminist terms as building strong relationships between women and providing a way to share domestic labor (albeit with the other sister wives, not the husband!), which, in her case, facilitates combining motherhood and a law practice.[21] And egalitarian or non-gender-structured polygyny involving a group of bisexual women and one man, on an equal footing, is possible.

However, if egalitarian forms or cases such as Joseph describes are relatively rare, polygyny creates an apparent tension for liberal feminists. This is because political liberalism requires, as I argued in Chapter 7.ii, recognizing the variety of different relationship forms if any are recognized. For the same reasons that the liberal state should not discriminate between same-sex and different-sex marriages, it should not discriminate between monogamous or polygynous, polyandrous, or polyamorous marriages.[22] But if polygyny does harm women, this seems to present a dilemma for liberal feminism. One response, suggested by John Rawls, is to argue that polygyny conflicts with the political value of women's equality and so there is public reason against it.[23] However, this strategy faces a weakness.

The problems attributed to polygyny are all also problems of patriarchal monogamous marriage! If the choice to enter polygyny is said to be unfree due to social pressure and coercion, this can be said of monogamous marriage. John Stuart Mill said as much: "[I]t must be remembered that this relation [polygyny] is as much voluntary on the part of the women concerned in it, and who may be deemed the sufferers by it, *as is the case with any other form of the marriage institution*; and however surprising this fact may appear, it has its explanation in the common ideas and customs of the world, which, in teaching women to think marriage the one thing needful, make it intelligible that many a woman should prefer being one of several wives, to not being a wife at all."[24] If polygyny is said to harm women, this can also be said of gender-structured male-female monogamous marriage and cohabitation.[25] Although polygyny may, as Brooks claims, be correlated with greater harms than monogamy is, the gap may disappear if we focus on monogamy in small patriarchal religious communities such as those within which polygyny tends to be located in the United States. In any case, as Susan Maushart reports, women in monogamous marriages suffer "more nervous breakdowns, inertia, loneliness, unhappiness with their looks; more insomnia, heart palpitations, nervousness, and nightmares; more phobias; more feelings of incompetence, guilt, shame, and low self-esteem" than unmarried women.[26]

By parity of reasoning then, this argument against polygyny suggests we should cease to recognize male-female monogamy. Brooks tries to bar this conclusion by arguing that polygyny is structurally inegalitarian as monogamy is not. But, first of all, in some communities—and in U.S. law within living memory—monogamy is structurally inegalitarian in its spousal roles, just as polygyny is: It gives the husband the dominant role. It might be said that not all monogamous marriage is patriarchal—but not all polygyny need be. In addition to cases such as Joseph's, egalitarian polygyny is possible.

Brooks gives two reasons for the claim that polygyny is structurally inegalitarian. First, it is asymmetrical in that the husband can bring a new wife into the marriage without other wives' consent: Only he "can choose who will join or leave the relationship through either marriage or divorce."[27] But in minimal marriage, the wives could legally take on other spouses, building a molecular structure. There is no legal asymmetry. Wives could choose to marry, or divorce, sister-wives. Brooks would presumably respond that they might not be empowered to do so in fact, despite having the legal right. But why not? If the answer is social pressure to marry and remain married, lack of exit options, or economic dependency, all of these features pertain to exclusive monogamy, in which a wife wanting to take on another spouse, or leave, may be constrained in doing so for these same reasons.

Second, Brooks argues that polygamy is structurally inegalitarian because it discriminates against gays and lesbians due to its gender-structured nature. However, as we have seen, many forms of relationship are possible. Minimal marriage allows all-women or all-men adult care networks or group marriages, or groups composed of lesbians, gays, and bisexuals. When all these options are on the legal table, the fact that some involve sex difference does not make their recognition discriminatory. Polygamy, like male-female monogamy, is only structurally discriminatory against gays and lesbians if same-sex marriage, including group marriage, is unavailable.

The problem with polygyny is not the form of relationship—as Joseph shows, the form itself can be relatively benign for women—but the injustices sometimes found in the community: Child abuse, underage marriage, lack of adequate education, social coercion, and indoctrination. However, the first three of these are crimes, and they can occur within monogamous marriage, too. Children should be adequately protected against abuse, and—legally—they should receive an adequate education. These problems should be dealt with through criminal law and social work, not by excluding this form of marriage. Furthermore, robust safeguards ensuring that consent is voluntary can be designed.[28]

Not only does denying marital status to polygyny treat polygynists unfairly (in the absence of compelling reason for differential treatment), but it threatens to deny recognition to polyamorous groups or care networks. It is not clear how these could be distinguished in law, except by specifying the polgynous structure. But as this structure can be benign, it would be more just to exclude specifically patriarchal or harmful marriages. But this leads back to the parity of reasoning argument against male-female monogamy—should all gender-structured marriages or marriages in which women suffer depression, and so on, be deprived of recognition? Should marriages within religious traditions that subscribe to gendered spousal roles be deprived of recognition? These consequences are simply illiberal. Law should not enforce such hierarchies, but it should not make marital recognition contingent on full egalitarianism between parties. Such choices between consenting adults should be respected.

There is a notable exception. In my view, law should interfere in family arrangements—whatever the form of the marriage—when they threaten children's developing self-respect. But given that children need continuity of care, that their self-respect may also depend on family pride, and that preventing certain parent-child communications is impossible while children remain with the parent, the balance of reasons suggests that protecting children's self-respect is best done through public education, of both children and prospective parents.

A liberal state should ensure education fosters children's developing self-respect and respect for others. Self-respect is a primary good, and respect for others contributes to state stability. The primary good status of care, and its connection to self-respect or self-esteem, also implies requiring relationship education. Teaching children that different relationships types exist and are treated equitably by the state protects the developing self-respect of children who are or will be sexual minorities as well as inculcating respect for difference. While parents in closed religious communities may protest, parental rights cannot allow deforming children's future autonomy and self-respect; religious freedom does not give the right to jeopardize "perhaps the most important primary good" (self-respect) or devastate children's life chances. Such education must give children knowledge and skills enabling them to depart from their closed religious communities.

Finally, in most U.S. states, individuals are free to cohabit polygynously anyway.[29] While critics charge that recognizing these arrangements as marriages will encourage them, increasing harms to women, it can be responded that recognizing polygyny would give multiple wives protective rights, such as alimony and property division on divorce. However, under minimal marriage, recognition would only give wives the more limited rights of minimal marriage; benefits would presumably be capped for efficiency, and spousal support and property division would apply independently under default rules, as discussed above.

In sum, the gravest harms associated with polygyny in closed religious communities should be addressed through education, robust consent procedures, and criminal law enforcement. Its other problematic features are not sufficiently different in kind from existing male-female monogamy to justify differential treatment. Finally, prohibiting, or failing to recognize, polygyny risks penalizing other, egalitarian, forms of group relationship. Even if, as Brooks claims, polyamory tends to patriarchal polygyny, there are still, as we have seen in Chapters 4 and 5, significant numbers of people in nonpatriarchal group relationships or networks requesting legal and social recognition.

IV. LIBERAL FEMINIST RESOURCES FOR NONIDEAL THEORY

The viability of a liberal feminist position on marriage is important because of the concerns of some feminists that liberal feminism is untenable. Catharine MacKinnon argues, repurposing Marx, that liberal freedoms protect patriarchal power: While they appear to have no gender bias, in fact they favor men. The supposedly neutral state is male.[30] In part, she means that laws are perverted in their application, as when, under antipornography laws, customs officers impound feminist books, but not violent pornography. But she also means that apparently gender-neutral laws are subtly discriminatory. Liberties are protected in exactly those areas that foster women's oppression: Freedom of speech protects pornography and hate speech; "privacy" protects unequal divisions of domestic labor, domestic violence, and exclusion of health coverage for abortion and contraception. The liberties are held equally, but in practice, their exercise systematically benefits men more. If ending oppression requires interference in areas protected by liberties of free speech, free association, freedom of conscience, and freedom of religion, then liberalism appears systematically unable to do so.

The state indeed has a double standard, when it refuses to "intervene" in parental teachings that degrade women while distributing abstinence curricula that interfere with other parents' egalitarian aspirations for their children; in defining allowed uses of "private" reproductive functions and contraception, while withholding funding from abortion and contraception due to their "private" nature. Marriage has been the primary means of constructing privacy oppressively, with its private sphere historically protected from justice, thereby facilitating rape, abuse, and exploitation. Theorists such as Rawls have continued to resist the full extension of liberal principles into the "private"; while he acknowledges that arrangements within the family should not issue from or lead to injustice, he also relegates the internal regulation of the family to "natural affection and goodwill" and suggests that parents have rights to infuse their children with gender-structured teachings.[31] Thus, feminists are right to be suspicious of a marriage law demarcating a "private" zone within which the state may capriciously intervene or not, or for the state to define who counts as a family and who does not.

These problems connect to the criticism of ideal theory. Liberal freedoms are derived in an idealized context, featuring idealized rational, autonomous agents, imagined under idealized circumstances. But, as exercised by actual agents who are imperfectly rational and subject to social pressures and constrained choices, these freedoms can contribute to oppressive outcomes. Actual injustices affect choices; the threat of stranger rape may lead women to choose monogamous relationships for perceived protection, workplace discrimination may make the choice to stay home easier, and the historical exclusion of women from certain fields may make those fields seem naturally masculine. Because liberal theory focuses on the individual in isolation, it fails to see how social structures may be systematically disempowering. While liberal egalitarianism can attend to economic inequalities between the worse-off and better-off, it does not track how these inequalities correspond to group membership on the basis of sex and race, or inequalities in power such as gendered inequalities in leadership roles.

Its inability to address inequalities between persons with unequal attributes is the basis of MacKinnon's criticism of the liberal conception of equality:

> It cannot recognize that every quality that distinguishes men from women is already affirmatively compensated in society's organization and values.... Men's physiology defines most sports, their health needs largely define insurance coverage, their socially designed biographies defined workplace expectations and successful career patterns, their perspectives and concerns define quality in scholarship, their experiences and obsessions define merit, their military service defines citizenship, their presence defines family.... For each of men's differences from women, what amounts to an affirmative action plan is in effect, otherwise known as the male-dominant structure and values of American society.[32]

Rawls's principle of fair equality of opportunity, for example, implies that men and women with similar abilities should have fair equal opportunity to access those positions: "[T]hose with similar abilities and skills should have similar life-chances."[33] But the principle does not correct for inequalities arising when boys and girls, differently encouraged by parents, teachers, peers, and society, develop different abilities.

Furthermore, liberalism protects choices that, as discussed in 5.i, systematically disadvantage women, such as the gendered division of domestic labor. Liberalism protects choices based on "adaptive preferences," those developed in an oppressive context and responsive to the conditions of oppression. Examples are women's preferences to give an inordinate amount of attention to their appearance, to be a nurse rather than a doctor, or to stay home with children rather than compete in the workplace. These preferences are as "authentic" as any, so that they are protected under liberalism, even though their effect may be to disadvantage women.[34] The feminist criticism might be restated thus: Although liberal egalitarianism has resources to extend protection to dependent wives and wives who can prove contributions to a husband's career, it fails, theoretically, to distinguish disadvantages resulting from oppression from disadvantages resulting from bad choices, laziness, and so on. It can thus not address oppression, because it reads its effects as "choices."

However, I have shown a number of ways in which liberalism can respond to these charges. Protections against the consequences of adaptive preferences can be justified as rectificatory compensation and under induced reliance when the state has itself supported those preferences and provided incentives to develop them, as it has in the oppression of women, nonwhites, and gays, lesbians, and bisexuals. While Rawls does not take rectification as a central topic of justice, there is no principled reason why a liberal egalitarian account of rectification could not be given. Furthermore, the argument that material caregiving is a primary good, and that the state should provide structures to protect it and those who do it, justifies dependency frameworks providing state support for caregivers and protecting their equal opportunity. Political liberalism, I have argued, requires such policies, which are also crucial to protect women. Finally, education must protect children's self-respect.

Liberalism can do much more to address oppression. Ideal theory itself, as the defense of minimal marriage shows, can prompt radical change by modeling how the world could be—if the state were truly neutral, or if we truly bargained as equals. Liberalism also has other resources for addressing oppression, which may guide minimal marriage law's implementation in a nonideal context.

First, Rawlsian liberalism requires nonideal circumstances to be considered at the legislative stage. Ideal legislators, only partly behind the veil of ignorance, can address real-world oppression. Legislators do not know their own positions, but know "general facts about their society," including facts about past and present oppression. They must also take into account *prospective* inequities. In framing legislation to implement the difference principle, "the full range of economic and social facts are brought to bear."[35]

Second, fair equal opportunity, implemented at this stage, can address ways in which the basic structure—including institutions of family and work—treats men and women differently. For example, employment practices penalize parents, and women bear the bulk of parenting, even if they have the same abilities and career aspirations as comparable males. Because "reproductive labor is socially necessary labor," parenting is part of the basic structure, to which the principles apply.[36] Fair equal opportunity implies that parents should be compensated, as with caregiver resource accounts, or employment be made more compatible with parenting, as through subsidized child care, and that men as well as women should be entitled to take parental leave.

Third, the first principle of justice requires that the social bases of self-respect should be distributed equally—indeed, they may be the most important primary good. This has tremendous implications. Racism, sexism, and other forms of discrimination undermine self-respect; even if adults can see themselves as free and equal citizens while inhabiting hierarchical roles in private, children cannot. Education protecting children's self-respect would include feminist and antiracist education teaching children their equality as citizens and bringing the wrongness of discrimination to light.[37]

Fourth, the requirements of rectification are also demanding. Major structures of oppression—sexism, racism, heterosexism, amatonormativity—have been constructed and enforced by the state. The state oppressed women by defining the private sphere and pressuring private choices. After World War II, propaganda encouraged women who worked outside the home during the war to quit their jobs and return home. Married women began to achieve full legal rights and to escape gendered legal responsibilities only in the 1970s. Current U.S. marriage promotion and abstinence-until-marriage education promote gender roles and amatonormativity. These policies clearly violate neutrality and public reason. For example, state media campaigns "extol the virtue of marriage" in Arkansas and Oklahoma; West Virginia provides cash payouts to married couples; and welfare workers are "encouraged to discuss marriage with their clients."[38]

Critics of liberal feminism allege that it cannot distinguish women's choices under oppression from other costly choices. But it can. Current distributions reflect past state injustice. What differentiates the "traditional" wife's choice from the beach bum's is the history of state incentives pressuring her to make that choice: Until the 1970s U.S. state law required wives to carry out domestic duties and defined them as "helpmeets"; earlier in the century, law allowed employers and educators to exclude women; federal monies still support curricula that teach gender stereotypes. Governments encroach on citizens' rights when they use their coercive power and authority to influence such choices, a fortiori when the pressures are inegalitarian. True, the choices made are politically free, but the state owes compensation for the costs incurred by women due to its unjust pressure to take on gender roles. The state is and has been instrumental in promoting oppressive norms and depriving women of full equal rights—as it has racial minorities, lesbians, gays, and bisexuals. It is not enough to repeal unjust laws or end patriarchal, heteronormative, and amatonormative propaganda—the state must provide compensation.

Given this history, it is proper for the state to use law to reform attitudes. In contrast, Tamara Metz, in her argument for abolishing marriage, defends a prohibition on state intervention aimed at affecting beliefs, as opposed to behavior. But, for example, civics education for schoolchildren justly attempts to affect beliefs about race, in part as compensation for past state racism. Where the state has sponsored racist beliefs, simply ceasing to do so without compensatory action aimed at correcting those beliefs is not fully just. By parity of reasoning, since the state has fostered discrimination against same-sex couples, polyamorists, group marriages, care networks, and friends, the state should compensate for such injustice by fighting discriminatory beliefs and attitudes—for example, by recognizing these relationships as marriage.

Finally, neutrality and public reason are powerful tools for reform. MacKinnon shows that the actual state is nonneutral and that false "neutrality" has served gender bias. Past non-neutrality requires rectification that corrects its costs. Thus, heterosexist curricula might be rectified through curricula treating all relationships equally, through providing support groups and apologies for those harmed by heterosexism, and so on. The proper implementation of neutrality and political liberalism would remedy bias by excluding as reasons for policy comprehensive doctrines that incorporate biased views. Taking political liberalism seriously in light of feminist social theory has far-reaching implications often unrecognized by liberals and feminists. It requires the state to root out its own sexist, heteronormative, and amatonormative assumptions. Minimal marriage is one example of the extensive change which that would require.[39]

V. CONCLUDING REMARKS

I want to conclude by emphasizing the feminist attractions of minimal marriage. Unlike current marriage, it involves informing prospective spouses of their rights, the terms of the agreement, and its implications. Arguably, equal opportunity and rectification for past discrimination require educating women about their potential economic vulnerability in gender-structured relationships. Information about the likely consequences of their choices might lead women to resist exploitative relationships.

Second, and more distinctively, minimal marriage gives women more marriage options, increasing their bargaining power. Along these lines, economist Gary Becker argued that polygamy, in a context of liberal rights, increases women's bargaining power.[40] His ideal models do not take account of the pressures on choice that affect women's bargaining power in a gender-structured society. However, the idea is more convincing with regard to minimal marriage: The increased marriage options of minimal marriage would open alternative, potentially more egalitarian, relationship models to women and therefore increase their bargaining power in negotiations with men.

Finally, minimal marriage denormalizes heterosexual monogamy as a way of life. In this respect, I consider my position responsive and sympathetic to lesbian and queer critiques of marriage such as Claudia Card's, Paula Ettelbrick's, and Drucilla Cornell's. By extending marriage to all caring relationships, minimal marriage affirms difference. It does not mark some relationships as "legitimate." Its rationale is to support the caring relationships individuals choose, not to distinguish among them. But minimal marriage will do more than abolishing marriage to combat amato- and heteronormativity because it makes new options salient.

This has a further implication. Social pressures surrounding different-sex monogamy contribute to women's economic vulnerability by promoting "traditional" wifehood. Minimal marriage removes state endorsement from "traditional" marriage, and over time this will change people's aspirations. I have drawn attention to how state marriage promotion reinforces oppressive social pressures; political liberalism, properly implemented, might combat them.

"Traditional" marriage promotion is problematic because it takes a single type of relationship as good for everyone. But my argument has suggested a need to recognize different kinds of caring relationships and secure their social bases. Policies supporting caring relationships extend to education, in order to support children's developing self-respect, to remedy the effects of discrimination, and to prepare children for diverse caring relationships as adults. They could also lead to policies supporting unpaid caregivers in the home. On my argument, care is a matter of justice within political liberalism, and this is perhaps the most powerful of the strategies surveyed here for making society fairer for women.

NOTES

Introduction

1. I use the term "heterosexual" only in contexts of critiques of heterosexism or hetero-sexual privilege.
2. On diverse marital practices, see Coontz, *Marriage*, and Fisher, *Anatomy*, Chapters 3 and 4. On proxy marriages, see Cott, *Public Vows*, pp. 151–155. On same-sex marriages, see Boswell, *Same-Sex Unions*, and James McGough, "Deviant Marriage Patterns in Chinese Society," in Sullivan, *Same-Sex Marriage*, pp. 24–28. On the Na, see Coontz, *Marriage*, pp. 32–33; cf. Eekelaar, *Family Law*, p. 1.
3. Augustine, "On Marriage and Concupiscence," Book I, Chapters 9 and 10, in *Anti-Pelagian Writings*; Aquinas, *Summa*, Supplement, Question 65.
4. Coontz, *Marriage*, pp. 106–7.
5. See Cott, *Public Vows*, Chapter 2.
6. Hegel, *Right*, §162, pp. 201–202. On medieval England, see Walker, "Widow and Ward"; see Coontz, *Marriage*, pp. 17–18 on excessive love, and Chapter 9 on the love revolution; cf. Shorter, *The Making of the Modern Family*.
7. Her speech at the 1851 Ohio Woman's Rights Convention is excerpted in Davis, *Women, Race*, p. 61. On Native American practices, see Cott, *Public Vows*, pp. 25–26.
8. Coontz, *Marriage*, Chapters 9 and 10; Okin, "Women and the Making of the Sentimental Family."
9. Mill, *Subjection*, p. 29.
10. On coverture, see Chapter 5.i in the present volume.
11. Shively, "Introduction," in Andrews, *Love, Marriage*, p. 1. See also Friedman, "Rights," p. 654; and Cott, *Public Vows*, pp. 47–52.
12. Morrison, *Beloved*, pp. xvi–xvii. See also Cott, *Public Vows*, pp. 33–35.
13. See Cott, *Public Vows*, pp. 81–93 (on the Freedmen's Bureau) and pp. 98–102 (on the post–Civil War proliferation of marriage bans) See also Wallenstein, *Tell the Court*. For racism and Canadian marriage law, see Dua, "Beyond Diversity."
14. On the history, see Cott, *Public Vows*, Chapter 5. On law, see Emens, "Monogamy's Law," fns. 51 and 158.
15. Sullivan, *Same-Sex Marriage*, pp. xxv–xxvi.
16. On illegitimacy, see Teichman, *Illegitimacy*, Chapter 8; and Shultz, "Contractual Ordering of Marriage," pp. 228–9. On criminal law, see Emens, "Monogamy's Law," fns. 49 and 50; see also Posner and Silbaugh, *A Guide to America's Sex Laws*, Chapters 7 and 8. The Supreme Court's 2003 ruling in *Lawrence v. Texas* presumably renders fornica-tion laws unconstitutional.
17. At the end of 2003, reported by the General Accounting Office. Dayna K. Shaw, Associate General Counsel, in a letter of January 23, 2004 to Bill Frist. The letter accompanies the 2004 GAO report, labeled "GAO-04–353R Defense of Marriage Act." See also Enclosure

I, "Categories of Laws Involving Marital Status," in a letter of January 31, 1997 by Barry R. Bedrick, Associate General Counsel, GAO, to Henry J. Hyde. The letter accompanies the 1997 GAO report, labeled "GAO/OGC-97-16 Defense of Marriage Act."

18. Case, "Marriage Licenses," pp. 1781, 1783.

19. Dean, "Gay Marriage," p. 112.

20. E.g. Kansas Code § 21-3517; Ohio Code §§ 2907.03. See Card, "Against Marriage." The 2003 Service Members Civil Relief Act allows the divorce deferral.

21. *Maynard v. Hill*, 125 U.S. 190, 211 (1888). See Metz, *Untying the Knot*, Chapter 4. See Freeman and Lyon, *Cohabitation*, pp. 184–189, for comparable statements in British law.

22. PRWORA, Title I, Section 101, Findings. Other findings (3–10) concern successful parenthood, collection of child support, increases in children receiving aid, increases in out-of-wedlock pregnancies, and negative consequences of out-of-wedlock pregnancy.

23. *Social Security Act*, Section 510 of Title V (my emphasis). See also Section 912 of the Personal Responsibility and Work Opportunity Reconciliation Act (H.R. 3734, 1996). Description of marriage promotion policies in this and the preceding paragraph is drawn from "State Policies to Promote Marriage," a 2002 report prepared for the U.S. Department of Health and Human Services. Available from the U.S. Department of Health and Social Services, or available online: http://aspe.hhs.gov/hsp/marriage02f/.

24. *Loving v. Virginia*, 388 U.S. 1 (1967).

25. A phrase found in Kipnis, *Against Love*, and Kingston, *Meaning*.

26. Cruz, "Just Don't"; Kaplan, "Intimacy and Equality"; Wedgwood, "Fundamental Argument"; Scott, "World without Marriage."

27. This section roughly follows the order of presentation in the history section of my *Stanford Encyclopedia* entry, "Marriage and Domestic Partnership."

28. Plato, *The Republic*, pp. 168, 178.

29. Plato, *The Republic*, pp. 157–181 (or Book V in this edition); Aristotle, *Complete Works, Politics*, Book I; quote from I.3 (1253b1); see Blustein, *Parents and Children*, pp. 31–46, for discussion.

30. On original sin, see Augustine, *City of God*, Book 14, Chapters 23–24. On lust in marriage and the goods of marriage, see Augustine, "On Marriage and Desire," Book I, Chapters 5, 8, 9, 10, 14–18, in *Answer to the Pelagians, II*; see also Augustine, "The Excellence of Marriage," in *Marriage and Virginity*. See Aquinas, *Summa*, Supplement 49, 1, "Of the Marriage Goods."

31. Capellanus, *On Love*, pp. 283, 151, 157, 283; in the Introduction, P. G. Walsh stresses that there is controversy as to how far *On Love*, and contemporary troubadours' tributes to adultery, portrayed actual mores as opposed to wishful thinking. For criticism of the widespread claim that the troubadours invented passionate love, see Fisher, *Anatomy*, pp. 49–51.

32. Abelard and Heloise, *Letters*, pp. 51–52.

33. Hobbes, *Leviathan*, Chapter XX, p. 152. See discussion in Okin, *Women in Western Political Thought*, pp. 197–199; Pateman, *Sexual Contract*, pp. 44–50.

34. Locke, *Two Treatises*, §77, 82; see Okin, *Women in Western Political Thought*, p. 197.

35. Astell, "Reflections upon Marriage," published 1700, in *Political Writings*, pp. 1–80; p. 18.

36. Kant *Metaphysics of Morals*, pp. 426–432, 494–496, 548–550, or Ak 6:276–284, 358–361, 424–426.

37. The derision includes a satirical poem by Brecht; see Brecht, "On Kant's Definition of Marriage in *The Metaphysic of Ethics*," *Poems*. See Herman, "Could It Be Worth Thinking about Kant on Sex and Marriage?" for the defense.
38. Hegel, *Right*, §75, p. 105; §40, p. 71; §163, p. 202.
39. Hegel, *Right*, §163A, p. 203; Hegel is attacking Schlegel, author of *Lucinde* (1799).
40. Wollstonecraft, *Vindications*, pp. 176, 286; fn. 1 on p. 176 notes that Defoe had also used the phrase in his *Conjugal Lewdness; or, Matrimonial Whoredom* (1727).
41. Mill, *Subjection*, p. 11.
42. Abbey and Den Uyl, "The Chief Inducement?" p. 39.
43. Andrews, *Love, Marriage*, p. 70. On the free love movement in practice, see Cott, *Public Vows*, pp. 68–72.
44. Goldman, "Jealousy," p. 215; de Cleyre, "They Who Marry Do Ill," in *Reader*, pp. 11–20.
45. Marx, "Communist Manifesto," pp. 157–186 in *Writings*, p. 173.
46. Engels, *Origin*, pp. 120, 128, 125.

Chapter 1

1. Forster, *Howard's End*, Chapter 2, p. 27. Much of this chapter revises my "Is Divorce-Promise-Breaking," published in *Ethical Theory and Moral Practice*.
2. Matthew 19:4–6.
3. Thanks to Jim Dwyer for this point.
4. "Vows" might be distinguished from promises; as Allen Habib draws the distinction in personal correspondence, "vows are private and non-social, while promises are social." Here, I ignore this distinction.
5. Adapted from Richard Ford's novel, *The Sportswriter*.
6. On the issue of who the recipient of the marital promise is, see Allen Habib, "Are Wedding Vows Promises to the Self?" (in circulation).
7. For an example, see Moller, "An Argument," p. 87.
8. See, e.g., Scanlon, *What We Owe*, pp. 311–314.
9. G. W. F. Hegel, *Right*, §164A, p. 205.
10. Kant, *Groundwork*, p. 54, or Ak. 4:399; but contrast his *Metaphysics of Morals*, p. 517, or Ak. 6:386.
11. On Gauguin, see Williams, *Moral Luck*. Williams calls considerations of value broader than moral permissibility and moral requirement "ethical."
12. Marcel and Albertine are characters in Marcel Proust's *In Search of Lost Time*.
13. For such a view, see Marquis, "What's Wrong."
14. See Mendus, "Marital Faithfulness," p. 244. Mendus argues that weddings vows do include unconditional promises to love unconditionally, and that the promise is analogous to a statement of intention. But a promise is not merely an expression of intention; it is the assumption of an obligation.
15. Moller, "An Argument," p. 85.
16. Isabel Archer is a character in Henry James's *The Portrait of a Lady*, Lambert Strether in James's *The Ambassadors*.
17. Cited in Coontz, *Marriage*, p. 15.
18. Thanks to Fiona Woollard for this point.
19. Cited in Wilson, "Can One Promise," p. 557.
20. See Deigh, "Promises"; Scanlon, *What We Owe*, pp. 295–296, 302, 304.

21. See Hobbes, *Leviathan*, Chapter XIV, para. 25, for a statement of this view.
22. See, e.g., Kekes, "Ought Implies," who worries that "ought-implies-within-one's-power" entails that sadists who cannot help their actions are not blameworthy. But if the sadist truly cannot control his actions, he is more like a robot than a moral agent. See also Stern, "Does 'Ought' Imply."
23. Wilson, "Can One Promise," p. 557.
24. Moller, "Marriage Commitment," p. 281.
25. The section title obliquely refers to a collection of Raymond Carver stories, *What We Talk about When We Talk about Love*.
26. Sartre, *Being*, p. 367, cited in Soble, *Structure*, p. 149.
27. Singer, *Nature*, p. 5.
28. See Jaggar, "Love and Knowledge"; Nussbaum, *Love's Knowledge*; Taylor, "Love."
29. Sartre, "Humanism," p. 44.
30. Landau, "An Argument," p. 477. See also Wilson, "Can One Promise," p. 557.
31. Liao, "The Idea of a Duty to Love," p. 9.
32. As I suggest above, there are other differences between love for adults and parental love for children. Adults, as moral agents, may act immorally in love-destroying ways; and not only do children need affection for their development, they are also dependent on their parents and so cannot easily seek affection elsewhere.
33. For the historical claims, see Coontz, *Marriage*; cf. Wilson, "Can One Promise."
34. Landau, "An Argument," pp. 476, 479.
35. See, e.g., Searle, *Expression*.
36. Wilson, "Can One Promise," p. 558.
37. Wilson, "Can One Promise," p. 562; see also p. 561.
38. Nietzsche, *Genealogy*, Second Treatise, 2, pp. 36–37. Thanks to Mark Migotti for pointing out this passage.
39. Kant, *Metaphysics of Morals*, p. 569, or Ak. 6:449.
40. See Anderson, "Prostitution," for discussion of sexual autonomy.
41. *Brides*, "In Your Own Words," http://www.brides.com/wedding-ideas/wedding-ceremonies/2006/11/in-your-own-words. (accessed June 12, 2011).

Chapter 2

1. This chapter's title was suggested by the title of a 1969 Bob Hope movie.
2. Mendus, "Marital Faithfulness," p. 247.
3. Landau, "An Argument," fn. 2 and p. 478.
4. The Oxford English Dictionary, e.g., draws this distinction. This distinction differs from that drawn by Brewer between "internalist" and "externalist" commitment in that, on my view, one can undertake a commitment privately; see Brewer, "Two Kinds."
5. See van Hooft, "Commitment," p. 456; and van Hooft, "Obligation, Character," p. 361. See also discussion in Calhoun, "Commitment," pp. 615–622: "Constitutive of any commitment is a stance of being prepared to maintain the commitment," p. 618.
6. See Brewer, "Two Kinds."
7. A phrase from T.S. Eliot's poem, "The Love-Song of J. Alfred Prufrock."
8. van Hooft, "Obligation, Character"; van Hooft, "Commitment," p. 456.
9. van Hooft, "Commitment," p. 455. He acknowledges that some commitments can be explicitly chosen but argues that this is not the case in love. Calhoun argues that completely nonvoluntary "commitments" "do not look much like commitments at all," but

rather like a different kind of motivation; commitment requires authorship. Calhoun, "Commitment," p. 617.

10. See, e.g., Mendus, "Marital Faithfulness."

11. This change could be construed as perceptual, as if commitment involves seeing things in the world differently from before; see Nussbaum, *Love's Knowledge*.

12. Calhoun, "Commitment," p. 619.

13. E.g., van Hooft, "Commitment," p. 456: Commitment is "an attitude which gives to its object a positive and practical importance which involves that object in one's own integrity." See also van Hooft, "Obligation, Character."

14. Calhoun, "Commitment," p. 615.

15. Calhoun, "Commitment," pp. 626–7.

16. Calhoun, "Commitment," p. 633.

17. Calhoun, "Commitment," pp. 636–641.

18. Mendus, "Marital Faithfulness," pp. 247, 250.

19. van Hooft, "Commitment," p. 454; see also p. 456.

20. van Hooft, "Commitment," p. 457; van Hooft also suggests that love-based commitments are exclusive on the basis of social practice. But this does not reflect the diversity of modern liberal societies, which include, for instance, polyamorists.

21. E.g., Scruton, *Sexual Desire*; Steinbock, "Adultery"; Martin, "Adultery."

22. E.g., Halwani, *Virtuous Liaisons*; Emens, "Monogamy's Law"; Barnhart and Barnhart, "Marital Faithfulness."

23. See Elster, *Ulysses and the Sirens*, and Elster, *Ulysses Unbound*, esp. pp. 1–20.

24. See the taxonomy of strategies in Elster, *Ulysses Unbound*, p. 6, and see p. 19.

25. This is a variation on the problem of skepticism with regard to other minds, explored in Cavell, *Pursuits*, as well as "The Avoidance of Love" in Cavell, *Must We*.

26. Cave proposes a "[rational] commitment conception of the marriage bond," as opposed to a contractual conception (his purpose is to make marriage amenable to the "contract-intolerant"), Cave, "Marital Pluralism," pp. 337. Unlike Cave's, my account integrates contractual obligations into rational commitment; I see those obligations as a way to carry out a commitment.

27. Elster, *Ulysses Unbound*, p. 13; see also p. 19.

28. Moller, "An Argument" and "Marriage Commitment."

29. Maushart, *Wifework*, p. 5; see also Okin, *Justice*; Card, "Against Marriage"; Chapter 5.i below.

30. Schelling, *Strategy*; on feminist uses of contract, see Cudd, "Rational Choice," and Hampton, "Feminist Contractarianism." Thanks to Tina Strasbourg for much discussion of this topic.

31. Cave, "Marital Pluralism." See also Card, "Against Marriage"; Andrews, *Love, Marriage*; Goldman, "Jealousy."

32. Cited in Elster, *Ulysses Unbound*, p. 81.

33. See Chapter 6.iii; the same trade-off applies in structuring divorce law to protect children, as (roughly) divorce benefits children in high-conflict marriages but harms children in low-conflict marriages.

34. Elster, *Ulysses Unbound*, p. 19.

35. Sartre, *Being*; see also Elster, *Ulysses Unbound*, p. 236.

36. Cited in Elster, *Ulysses Unbound*, pp. 13–14, fn. 31.

37. See Hegel, *Right*, §§158–181. Cf. Sandel, *Liberalism*, discussed in Chapter 4.iv, and Galston, *Liberal Purposes*, discussed in Chapter 6.iii. For general critical discussion, see Fineman, *Autonomy Myth*.

38. Bloom, *Closing*, pp. 118–9. Bloom excoriates, as itself symptomatic of social disintegration, the vernacular usage of the word "commitment," in a different sense from the way I use it here—as denoting an alternative to marriage.
39. FitzGibbon, "Marriage," p. 41.
40. FitzGibbon, "Marriage," p. 63.
41. See Kipnis, *Against Love*.
42. Mill, *Subjection*, p. 47. See also Okin, "*Political Liberalism*"; Young, "Mothers," responding to Galston's *Liberal Purposes*.
43. Okin, "*Political Liberalism*." On marriage as a school of injustice see Okin, *Justice*, pp. 97–101.

Chapter 3

1. U.S. Social Security Act, Title V, Section 510, under Section 912 of the Personal Responsibility and Work Opportunity Reconciliation Act (H.R. 3734, 1996).
2. U.S. Social Security Act, Title V, Section 510.
3. MacKinnon, *Feminism Unmodified*, p. 3.
4. MacKinnon, *Toward*, p. 124.
5. Kant's views on sex and marriage can be found in the *Metaphysics of Morals* (Ak 6:276–284, 358–361, 424–426, 469–473); the posthumously published *Lectures on Ethics* (Ak 27:48–52, 27:384–392); *Observations on the Feeling of the Beautiful and Sublime*, "Conjectural Beginning of Human History"; and *Anthropology from a Pragmatic Point of View* (Ak 7:303–311). Passages in this section reproduce in brief arguments made in Brake, "Justice and Virtue."
6. Two passages in Kant suggest such a principle: where he derives parental duty from creating a dependent being (*Metaphysics of Morals*, p. 495, Ak. 6:360) and where he says that unmarried sex is unjust because of women's special vulnerability (*Lectures*, p. 160, Ak. 27:390).
7. Kant, *Metaphysics of Morals*, p. 495, or Ak 6:359–360.
8. This is Herman's reconstruction of Kant. Conservative sexual moralists influenced by this vein of Kant's argument include Roger Scruton, John Finnis, and Karol Wojtya (better known as Pope John Paul II). Throughout, I am not trying to interpret Kant, but to give the strongest argument for marriage suggested by his writings.
9. Kant, *Lectures*, p. 156, or Ak. 27:384.
10. See Nussbaum, *Sex and Social*, Chapter 8.
11. Herman, "Could It Be," pp. 62-63.
12. Kant, *Lectures*, p. 158-159, or Ak. 27:388.
13. For further discussion, see Brake, "Justice and Virtue," which develops the arguments of this paragraph in greater detail.
14. Kant, *Metaphysics of Morals*, pp. 394–395, or Ak. 6:239.
15. Kant, *Metaphysics of Morals*, p. 394–395, or Ak. 6:239.
16. Finnis, "Good of Marriage," pp. 118, 109. Finnis relates this good to Aquinas's notion of marital *fides*. See also George, "Same-Sex"; Grisez, *Way of Lord*.
17. Finnis, "Good of Marriage," p. 102.
18. Finnis, "Good of Marriage," p. 127; cf. Anscombe, "You Can Have Sex without Children," in *Ethics, Religion, and Politics*, pp. 82–96, and George, "Same-Sex."
19. Finnis, "Good of Marriage," pp. 128–129.

20. Finnis, "Law, Morality," pp. 1066–1167.
21. Finnis, "Good of Marriage," p. 123
22. Macedo, "Homosexuality," p. 282.
23. Corvino, "Homosexuality," p. 512. See also Garrett, "Old Sexual Morality"; Buccola, "Finding Room," p. 337.
24. Garrett, "Old Sexual Morality."
25. Macedo, "Homosexuality," p. 276.
26. Corvino, "Homosexuality"; Macedo, "Homosexuality."
27. Macedo, "Homosexuality"; cf. Buccola, "Finding Room."
28. Mill, *Subjection*, pp. 22–23.
29. MacIntyre, *After*, p. 187.
30. Scruton, *Sexual Desire*, p. 326. Cf. Bayles, "Marriage, Love," p. 127.
31. Scruton, *Sexual Desire*, p. 337.
32. Scruton, *Sexual Desire*, pp. 358–359; cf. p. 356.
33. Passages in this and the next four paragraphs overlap with the discussion in my "Marriage, Morality," p. 246.
34. Scruton, *Sexual Desire*, p. 358.
35. Scruton, *Sexual Desire*, p. 359.
36. Scruton, *Sexual Desire*, p. 356.
37. Kipnis, *Against*; Fisher, *Anatomy*.
38. Bayles, "Marriage, Love," p. 127.
39. Scruton, *Sexual Desire*, p. 348.
40. See Goldman, "Plain Sex."
41. Scruton, *Sexual Desire*, pp. 344–346.

Chapter 4

1. While caring about is not always benign, here I use it to refer to a benign interest. See Held, *Ethics*, pp. 29–43, for discussion of the definition of "care."
2. Bowden, *Caring*; Held, *Ethics*. On care as emotion, see Nussbaum, *Sex and Social*, pp. 253–275.
3. Held, *Ethics*, p. 39.
4. See, e.g., Benhabib, *Situating the Self*; Held, "Non-Contractual Society"; Ruddick, *Maternal Thinking*, pp. 194 ff.
5. Noddings, *Caring*, p. 53.
6. Noddings, *Caring*, pp. 14, 16.
7. Ruddick, *Maternal Thinking*, p. 150.
8. Benhabib, *Situating the Self*, pp. 158–170.
9. See Held, *Ethics*, 48–49.
10. These points are made in Friedman, "Beyond Caring."
11. Kant wrote that only action motivated by duty has moral worth, so actions done from sympathetic motives alone have no moral worth; *Groundwork*, pp. 53–54. This brief discussion ignores the substantial literature on motivation.
12. Nussbaum, *Love's Knowledge*, Chapters 4 and 5, and pp. 148–149. On Nussbaum's view, James's novels are replete with examples of complex cases of moral judgments in intimate relationships.
13. McNaughton, *Moral Vision*, p. 62; cf. Nussbaum, *Love's Knowledge*.

14. Stanley Cavell writes of a modern difficulty in inhabiting public selves and engaging in the public sphere: We allow evil to happen by choosing to remain as audience and to conceal ourselves. See "The Avoidance of Love" in Cavell, *Must We*, esp. pp. 296, 333, 346, 349.

15. Rawls, *Theory*, pp. 473–475; Rawls, *Theory: Revised*, p. 414.

16. See Rawls, *Theory*, pp. 511–512.

17. Kipnis, *Against Love*, p. 3.

18. "Conjugonormativity" might better pick out the appropriate contrast, but it suggests that the privileged group is defined by legal marriage. However, unmarried cohabitants also benefit from such discrimination.

19. Rich, "Compulsory Heterosexuality"; Nielson, Walden, and Kunkel, "Gendered Heteronormativity," p. 288.

20. Nielson, Walden, and Kunkel, "Gendered Heteronormativity," p. 293, and p. 287, Table 1; cf. Warner, "Introduction."

21. Cagen, *Quirkyalone*, p. 14. Cagen does not fully reject amatonormativity because she theorizes that quirkyalones are single due to their romantic ideals—the right partner has not yet come along. She still assumes romantic love as a goal, although she rejects the invidious distinction between romantic love and friendship.

22. DePaulo, *Singled Out*, p. 209.

23. "51% of Women Are Now Living without Spouse," *New York Times*, January 16, 2007. (On February 11, 2007, a *Times* editorial—"Can a 15-Year-Old Be a 'Woman without a Spouse'?"—criticized the data but admitted that revised calculations still showed a slight majority of spouseless women. In Canada, according to Status of Women Canada, the percentage reached 52 percent in 2001.) See also "Married Couples Are No Longer a Majority, Census Finds," *New York Times*, May 26, 2011.

24. Demographic statistics tend to give the percentage of people married and unmarried, not of those living in adult care networks. Given that such networks are relatively culturally invisible, this lack of data is unsurprising.

25. See Emens, "Monogamy's Law," especially pp. 356, 303–330.

26. See "2 Kids + 0 Husbands = Family," *New York Times*, January 29, 2009; and "A New Trend in Motherhood," *New York Times*, May 17, 2009. Statistics Canada reports similar shifts.

27. Watters, *Urban Tribes*, pp. 38–39. Cagen makes and reports similar claims.

28. DePaulo, *Singled Out*, p. 133.

29. This editorial, published in the *Chicago Sun-Times* in 2004, is excerpted in DePaulo, *Singled Out*, p. 237; contrary to the stereotype of single women as lonely, DePaulo notes that of all older people, lifelong single women are by far the least likely to report feelings of loneliness, p. 206.

30. DePaulo, *Singled Out*, pp. 210–211.

31. DePaulo, *Singled Out*, pp. 81–84.

32. DePaulo, *Singled Out*, pp. 133, 239.

33. These examples are all taken from DePaulo, *Singled Out*, pp. 213–234.

34. Emens, "Monogamy's Law," pp. 310–332.

35. DePaulo, *Singled Out*, pp. 133, 116.

36. This and the following five paragraphs were prompted by discussion at the New Orleans Invitational Seminar in Ethics, hosted by The Murphy Institute at Tulane University,

March 19, 2010, especially Eric Cave's challenging comments on my paper, and tough questions from Janice Dowell, Dan Jacobson, and Doug Portmore.

37. See Cudd, *Analyzing Oppression*; Frye, *Politics of Reality*.

38. From Eric Cave's comments on my paper, "Friendship, Sex, Love, and Justice," presented at the New Orleans Invitational Seminar in Ethics, hosted by The Murphy Institute at Tulane University, March 19, 2010.

39. Fisher, *Anatomy*, p. 305. On "the four-year itch" and serial monogamy, see pp. 109–111, 115, and 152–154; on extramarital sex, see pp. 171–173; and on polygyny, see pp. 69–70.

40. Mill, *Subjection*, p. 29.

41. Rich, "Compulsory Heterosexuality"; cf. Card, "Against Marriage"; Parsons, "Fellowship": p. 400.

42. hooks, *Feminist Theory*, p. 151, cited in DePaulo, *Singled Out*, fn. to p. 147.

43. Parsons, "Fellowship," p. 393.

44. Kingston, *Meaning*, pp. 31, 47; cf. Kipnis, *Against*, and Mead, *Perfect*.

45. See Weiss, "Feminism"; cf. Benhabib, *Situating the Self*.

46. Benhabib, *Situating the Self*, p. 156, quoting Hobbes's "Philosophical Rudiments Concerning Government and Society"; cf. Held, "Non-Contractual Society."

47. Rawls, *Theory*, p. 130. See pp. 126–130 for his description of the circumstances of justice.

48. Sandel, *Liberalism*, p. 169. See also MacIntyre, *After*, pp. 244–251.

49. Sandel, *Liberalism*, p. 169. In fact, Rawls suggests that the internal life of the family should be regulated by affection, not the principles of justice, in "Idea," pp. 787–794.

50. Sandel, *Liberalism*, p. 33.

51. Okin, *Justice*, p. 26, and see also Chapter 2; cf. Okin, "Women."

52. Hume, *Enquiry*, p. 37.

53. Wollstonecraft, *Vindications*; Mill, *Subjection*; Okin, *Justice*.

54. Okin, *Justice*, p. 32; cf. Waldron, "When Justice."

55. Waldron, "When Justice," p. 627; Kleingeld, "Just Love?"

56. Tomasi, "Individual."

57. Hampton, "Feminist Contractarianism," p. 240; cf. Cudd, "Rational Choice."

58. Held, *Ethics*, p. 35.

59. Mahony, *Kidding*. Thanks to Tina Strasbourg for much discussion of these ideas.

60. Minow and Shanley, "Relational Rights," pp. 11–12; cf. Pateman, *Sexual Contract*. A further feminist worry is that such contracts will be exploitative; this is discussed in Chapters 7 and 8.

61. Weisbrod, "The Way," p. 778; cf. reservations in Kleingeld, "Just Love?"

62. Carbone, "Limits," p. 147; Shultz, "Contractual," p. 220.

63. These views about the roles of care and justice are developed in Held, *Ethics*; see esp. pp. 83–87.

Chapter 5

1. Passages in this and the following three chapters revise and in some cases reproduce passages in my "Minimal Marriage" (©2010 by the University of Chicago Press).

2. The Arkansas law was overturned April 7, 2011, by the State Supreme Court.

3. "Taking Marriage Private," *New York Times*, November 26, 2007.

4. Blackstone, *Commentaries*, Book 1, Chapter 15, Section 3. Coverture—derived from the Anglo-Norman French "feme covert"—was found throughout Europe. See Cott, *Public Vows*, pp. 11–12.

5. Norton, "A Letter to the Queen on Lord Chancellor Cranworth's Marriage and Divorce Bill," *Selected Writings*, pp. 8–13.

6. Mill, *Subjection*, Chapter 2.

7. Posner and Silbaugh, *Guide*, Chapter 2, "Marital Exemptions from Rape and Sexual Assault"; cf. Eskow, "Ultimate Weapon," p. 682.

8. See Weitzman, *Marriage*, Chapters 2 and 3; gender-based support was struck down by the Supreme Court in 1979 (p. 23) and "head and master laws" in the 1970s in the U.S. and Europe; see Coontz, *Marriage*, p. 255 and Cott, *Public Vows*, Chapter 7, esp. pp. 209–210.

9. Weitzman, *Marriage*, p. 338.

10. Quoted by Freeman and Lyon, *Cohabitation*, p. 32; see also p. 29.

11. Cited in Sachs and Wilson, *Sexism*, p. 149.

12. Weitzman, *Marriage*, p. 74; Maushart, *Wifework*, pp. 74–75; Cott, *Public Vows*, pp. 173, 186.

13. Dworkin, *Pornography*, pp. 19–20; compare Mill, *Subjection*, Chapter 1.

14. Cronan, "Marriage," p. 219.

15. Tjaden and Thoennes, "Extent," pp. 9–10. See Russell, *Rape*; Eskow, "Ultimate Weapon," p. 684; Bennice and Resick, "Marital Rape," p. 235. According to Bennice and Resick, literature in this area remains "sparse."

16. Tjaden and Thoennes, "Extent," p. iii.

17. Durose, et al., *Family Violence Statistics*, pp. 8, 1. According to this report, the rate of family violence fell from 5.4 victims in 1,000 persons over 12 years old in 1993 to 2.1 victims in 2002 (p. 10). Family violence as a percentage of all violence has remained stable.

18. Eskow, "Ultimate Weapon"; Bennice and Resick, "Marital Rape."

19. Tjaden and Thoennes, "Extent," p. 34.

20. Card, "Against Marriage"; Card, "Gay Divorce."

21. Eskow, "Ultimate Weapon," p. 688.

22. U.S. Department of Labor, "Women at Work," March 2011. http://www.bls.gov/spotlight/2011/women/ (accessed June 14, 2011). See also Alstott, *No Exit*, pp. 24–27.

23. Okin, *Justice*, pp. 157–159, and p. 137, cites studies showing correlations between power, exit options, and earnings in marriage. See also Maushart, *Wifework*.

24. Maushart, *Wifework*, pp. 10–11.

25. Maushart, *Wifework*, p. 5.

26. de Beauvoir, *Second Sex*, p. 425; cf. Firestone, *Dialectic*.

27. "The Content of Federally Funded Abstinence-Only Education Programs," prepared for Rep. Henry Waxman, United States House of Representatives, Committee on Government Reform—Minority Staff. December 2004, pp. ii, 17.

28. See Ferguson, "Gay Marriage"; Okin, *Justice*; Shanley, *Just Marriage*.

29. Pateman, *Sexual Contract*, p. 168; see also pp. 221–225. See also Fineman, *Neutered Mother*, Chapter 6; Metz, *Untying*; Scott, "World without Marriage"; and—on the gendered construction of marriage law—Cott, *Public Vows*, Chapter 7.

30. Cott, *Public Vows*, pp. 79–82.

31. Macedo, "Homosexuality."

32. Ettelbrick, "Since When"; Card, "Against Marriage." See also Warner, "Response."
33. Card, "Gay Divorce," 24.
34. Card, "Gay Divorce," p. 31.
35. Bolte, "Do Wedding Dresses"; Ferguson, "Gay Marriage"; Mayo and Gunderson, "Right."
36. Bolte, "Do Wedding Dresses"; Ferguson, "Gay Marriage"; Mayo and Gunderson, "Right."
37. Mohr, *Long Arc*, pp. 69 ff.; cf. Halwani, *Virtuous Liaisons*.
38. Mohr, *Long Arc*, 89; cf. Bolte, "Do Wedding Dresses" on "domestic partnerships"; see Scott, "World Without Marriage," on the legal arguments.
39. Calhoun, *Feminism*, p. 108; cf. Cott, *Public Vows*, pp. 79–82 and Chapter 5.
40. Ferguson, "Gay Marriage," p. 51; cf. Cornell, *At the Heart*; Bolte, "Do Wedding Dresses"; and Mayo and Gunderson, "Right."
41. Goldman, "Jealousy," p. 215.
42. Andrews, *Love, Marriage*, p. 6. See Cott, *Public Vows*, pp. 68–71, 107–109; cf. Cave, "Marital Pluralism."
43. Dua, "Beyond Diversity," p. 255; cf. Cott, *Public Vows*, pp. 25–26, 120–123.
44. Cott, *Public Vows*, pp. 40–46, 80–102.
45. Cable, *Old Creole Days*, p. 62.
46. Altman and Klinker, "Measuring the Difference"; see also Wallenstein, *Tell the Court*, Chapter 16, on reluctant compliance.
47. Sullivan, *Same-Sex*, p. xxv.
48. Collins, "It's All," p. 62; cf. Dua, "Beyond Diversity"; and Hoagland, "Heterosexualism."
49. Cott, *Public Vows*, pp. 4, 105–155.
50. hooks, *Feminist*; cf. Vanderheiden, "Why the State."
51. Collins, *Black Feminist Thought*, p. 119.
52. hooks, *Feminist*, p. 144; see also Collins, "It's All"; Vanderheiden, "Why the State"; Card, "Against Marriage."
53. On the inefficiency of such programs, see Chapter 6.iii and Chapter 8.i and Garrison, "Cooperative Parenting," pp. 268, 273–277: many causes contribute to poverty. According to Garrison, we "lack evidence" as to the long-term effects of Healthy Marriage Initiative programs, p. 274, and there is evidence that counseling "can produce harm as well as good," p. 275.
54. HMI Fact Sheets. Data collected in 2003. http://www.acf.hhs.gov/healthymarriage/about/factsheets.html (accessed June 14, 2011).
55. In the U.S. Census Bureau 2005 American Community Survey, 53% of American adults were married, with white adults at 56%, and Asian adults at 61%. One might infer that whites are in crisis compared with Asians. Indeed, Asians, who have the highest rates of marriage and lowest rates of divorce, were left out of the comparison in the AAHMI Fact Sheet.
56. Roundtable Report, "Why Marriage Matters," August 2003. http://www.acf.hhs.gov/healthymarriage/about/aami_report.htm (accessed June 14, 2011). See Garrison, "Cooperative Parenting," p. 274, at fn. 48.
57. State of the Union Address, January 20, 2004.
58. Hoagland, "Heterosexualism"; cf. Dua, "Beyond Diversity"; Butler, "Is Kinship."
59. McMurtry, "Monogamy," 595; cf. Pateman, *Sexual Contract*.

60. McMurtry, "Monogamy," 597.
61. Fineman, *Neutered Mother*.
62. Kipnis, *Against*, pp. 83, 93; cf. p. 36.
63. "Why are there so many single Americans?" *New York Times*, January 21, 2007.
64. Rawls, *Theory*, pp. 511–512; Nozick, *Anarchy*, p. 150.
65. Barbara Ehrenreich's *Nickel and Dimed*, an account of living as a Wal-Mart worker, a waitress, and a house cleaner makes such constraints vivid.
66. Garrison, "Cooperative Parenting," p. 274, fn. 49; she also points out that HMI initiatives have not been tested in the most at-risk demographics.

Chapter 6

1. Interviewed on *60 Minutes*, CBS, December 5, 2007, transcript, http://www.cbsnews.com/stories/2004/03/04/60minutes/main604060.shtml.
2. Mohr, *Long Arc*, p. 57.
3. Mercier, *Affidavit*.
4. Devlin, *Enforcement*, p. 13.
5. Devlin, *Enforcement*, p. 63.
6. Bolte, "Do Wedding Dresses."
7. Raz, *Morality*, pp. 162, 392–393; see Freeman, "Not Such"; Waldron, "Autonomy."
8. Macedo, "Homosexuality," p. 286.
9. See Rawls, *Political Liberalism*, pp. 212–254.
10. Dworkin, *Matter*, p. 191.
11. See Rawls, *Political Liberalism*, pp. 190–195; compare Rawls, *Theory*, p. 94, and Section 50. See also the critical discussion of variant neutrality principles in Sher, *Beyond*, Chapter 2.
12. Rawls, *Political Liberalism*, pp. 192–193.
13. See Raz, *Morality*, pp. 114–124; Wall, "Neutrality." See responses to Raz in Rawls, *Political Liberalism*, pp. 190–195, and Kymlicka, "Liberal."
14. Rawls, *Political Liberalism*, p. 252.
15. Sher, *Beyond*, p. 36. This exposition follows Sher at p. 28. Sher raises problems with defining "conception of the good" (pp. 37–43); but as judgments regarding sex and marriage are commonly given as examples of such conceptions, I set this aside for my purposes; see Rawls, *Theory*, p. 331; and Rawls, "Idea," p. 779.
16. See Rawls, *Political Liberalism*, p. 214. Rawls in *Theory*, and other neutral liberals (see Sher, *Beyond*, pp. 31–34), apply neutrality more extensively to all policy; in such theories I would not face the objection.
17. Rawls, "Idea," p. 779.
18. Rawls, "Idea," p. 788.
19. Rawls, *Political Liberalism*, p. 217.
20. Dworkin, *Matter*, p. 191; Rawls, *Theory*, p. 329.
21. Ackerman, *Social Justice*, p. 362.
22. Rawls, *Theory*, p. 331.
23. Munoz-Dardé, "John Rawls"; Okin, *Justice*; see discussion in Rawls, *Theory: Revised*, esp. p. 161. Rawls acknowledges that marriage law must be compatible with the principle of equal opportunity in Rawls, "Idea," pp. 787–794, but the implications of this are controversial; see Okin, "*Political Liberalism*."

24. Morse, "Unilateral," p. 75.
25. See Garrett, "History, Tradition." On diversity, see Coontz, *Marriage*, Chapter 2, and Chapter 4.iii above.
26. Mohr, *Long Arc*, Chapter 3; cf. Dean, "Gay Marriage."
27. Schaff, "Kant"; Wedgwood, "Fundamental Argument"; Wellington, "Why Liberals"; cf. Bolte, "Do Wedding Dresses."
28. Wedgwood, "Fundamental Argument," p. 233.
29. Wellington, "Why Liberals," p. 13.
30. Thanks to Eric Cave for suggesting this objection.
31. Wedgwood, "Fundamental Argument," p. 236. See also my Chapter 7.iii.
32. Mohr, *Long Arc*, p. 61; Calhoun, "Who's Afraid."
33. See Finnis, "Good of Marriage"; see Corvino, "Homosexuality," for discussion; see Emens, "Monogamy's Law," pp. 279–280.
34. Mohr, *Long Arc*; Wellington, "Why Liberals."
35. Rawls, "Idea," p. 779.
36. On Hawaii, see Nussbaum, *Sex and Social*, p. 205; see also Nussbaum, "Right," pp. 679–680. The quotation is from Bos and van Balen, "Children," p. 222. For more on harm-to-children arguments, see Cave, "Harm Prevention."
37. Galston, *Liberal Purposes*, pp. 283–289. Benefits of two-parent families are reported in Wax, "Traditionalism," p. 386.
38. Amato and Booth, cited in Garrison, "Cooperative Parenting," p. 266, at fn. 9. See also Amato, Loomis, and Booth, "Parental Divorce," which finds that children of high-conflict marriages benefit significantly from divorce, so effects of divorce are not simply "additive."
39. "Should Marriage Be Subsidized?" The Becker-Posner Blog, March 2007, http://www. becker-posner-blog.com/2007/03/index.html. June 14, 2011. Cf. Fineman, *Autonomy Myth*, p. 86. See also Young, "Mothers, Citizenship, and Independence."
40. On continuity of care, see Alstott, *No Exit*, pp. 15–20.
41. Russell, *Marriage*; Emens, "Monogamy's Law," pp. 336–337.
42. Rawls, "Idea," p. 788.
43. See Amato, Loomis, and Booth, "Parental Divorce," and Garrison, "Cooperative Parenting": Marriage matters less than conflict.
44. In Shanley, *Just Marriage*, p. 50.
45. Fineman, *Autonomy Myth*; Alstott, *No Exit*; LaFollette, "Licensing." Licensing would affect women disproportionately and risk unjust mistakes; thus the bar should be set low.
46. Fineman, *Neutered* and *Autonomy Myth*.
47. Butler, "Is Kinship," pp. 23–24.
48. Economist Gary Becker and legal theorist Richard Posner both express skepticism regarding the effectiveness of marriage promotion. "Should Marriage Be Subsidized?" The Becker-Posner Blog, March 2007, http://www.becker-posner-blog.com/2007/03/index.html (June 14, 2011).
49. James, *Bostonians*, p. 31 (Part One, Chapter IV).
50. See Jordan, "Is It Wrong," and replies in Beyer, "Public Dilemmas," and Boonin, "Same-Sex Marriage."
51. Beyer, "Public Dilemmas," and Boonin, "Same-Sex Marriage," use the interracial marriage example and respond to Jordan's attempt to stave it off; Schaff, "Kant." For Rawls's example of how a political liberal state would decide the controversial issue of abortion, see *Political Liberalism*, p. 243, fn. 32.

52. Vanderheiden, "Why the State."

53. Metz, *Untying*, p. 107. See also Scott, "World," pp. 545–554.

54. Early feminist arguments for contractualization are found in Weitzman, *Marriage*, and Shultz, "Contractual"; both retain a marriage contract, which sets out domestic aspirations as well as legally enforceable obligations.

55. See Weisbrod, "The Way."

56. For a dissenting view see Trainor, "State"; but there is no anomaly in allowing parties to make a contract which they can break with no penalty.

57. Kymlicka, "Rethinking," p. 88.

58. Okin, *Justice*, pp. 122–123; Sachs and Wilson, *Sexism*, p. 148; Pateman, *Sexual Contract*, p. 155; Kymlicka, *Rethinking*, p. 88.

59. Weisbrod, "The Way," pp. 779–780.

60. Sachs and Wilson, "Sexism," pp. 136, 80–85.

61. Maine, *Ancient*, p. 100.

Chapter 7

1. Part of this chapter substantially revises my article, "Minimal Marriage," published in *Ethics* (©The University of Chicago 2010). Revised passages from that article also appear in Chapters 5, 6, and 8. Thanks to the publishers for permission to reuse.

2. See Chapter 6.ii. On same-sex marriage see Schaff, "Kant," "Equal Protection"; Wedgwood, "Fundamental Argument"; Wellington, "Why Liberals"; cf. Buccola, "Finding Room." Neutrality also underlies the debate between Jordan, "Is It Wrong," Beyer, "Public Dilemmas," and Boonin, "Same-Sex Marriage."

3. The classic source is Hegel, *Right* §§75, 161A; for a more recent example, see Vodrasta, "Against Blackstone."

4. At the end of 2003, reported by the General Accounting Office. Dayna K. Shaw, Associate General Counsel, in a letter of January 23, 2004 to Bill Frist. The letter accompanies the 2004 GAO report, labelled "GAO-04–353R Defense of Marriage Act." See also Enclosure I, "Categories of Laws Involving Marital Status," in a letter of January 31, 1997 by Barry R. Bedrick, Associate General Counsel, GAO, to Henry J. Hyde. The letter accompanies the 1997 GAO report, labeled "GAO/OGC-97–16 Defense of Marriage Act."

5. Dean, "Gay Marriage," p. 112.

6. Case, "Marriage Licenses," pp. 1781, 1783.

7. See "State Policies to Promote Marriage," a report prepared for the U.S. Department of Health and Human Services, 2002.

8. Nathan McIntire, "Marrying for Money," *L.A. Weekly*, April 20–26, 2007, 26–27. Details can be confirmed on the Department of Defense website (http://www.dfas.mil/).

9. Both quotations from 1997 GAO report, Enclosure I. (See fn. 3 above.)

10. Coontz, *Marriage*, shows how this ideal developed over the last 150 years, how its flourishing in the 1950s and 1960s was exceptional, and how it fails to apply to large numbers of working-class families.

11. Den Otter, "Review," p. 133.

12. Case, "Marriage Licenses," p. 1773. Where caretaking is involved, privacy rights may protect caretaker autonomy; see Fineman, "Postscript," *Autonomy Myth*, and Brighouse and Swift, "Parents' Rights."

13. A similar argument against same-sex marriage insists that it entails recognizing polygamy, incest, and bestiality. For a response, see discussion in Chapter 6.ii and Corvino, "Homosexuality."

14. See Brighouse and Swift, "Parents' Rights."

15. Hartley and Watson, "Political," emphasize this aspect of Rawlsian political liberalism.

16. This is the conclusion of "Beyond Conjugality: Recognizing and supporting close personal adult relationships," a 2001 publication of the Law Commission of Canada, http://www.samesexmarriage.ca/docs/beyond_conjugality.pdf.

17. I draw on Rawls' statement of public reason in *Political Liberalism*, pp. 212–254, and "Idea."

18. Calhoun, "Who's Afraid," p. 1035.

19. Ettelbrick, "Since When"; Card, "Against Marriage"; Cornell, "The Public Supports of Love," in Shanley et al., *Just Marriage*, pp. 81–86.

20. On polyamory, see Emens, "Monogamy's Law"; Kipnis, *Against*; Cave, "Marital Pluralism."

21. See Cagen, *Quirkyalone*, p. 18: *Time* and *The Economist* reported in 2000 on the growing number of unmarried urbanites. See also DePaulo, *Singled*.

22. Wellington, "Why Liberals," reviews this literature at pp. 17ff. See Ettelbrick, "Since when."

23. hooks, *Feminist Theory*, pp. 133–146; cf. Collins, *Black*.

24. See Raz, *Morality*, pp. 161–162.

25. Sullivan, "Same-Sex," p. xxvi. Disapproval of interracial marriage continues at, according to Sullivan, "around 30 percent" (p. xxv). See Altman and Klinker, "Measuring the Difference."

26. Wall, "Neutrality." See also Raz, *Morality*, 117–124, and responses in Rawls, *Political Liberalism*, pp. 190–195, and Kymlicka, "Liberal."

27. Ackerman, *Social Justice*, p. 362.

28. Wedgwood, "Fundamental Argument," fn. 14; cf. Raz, *Morality*, pp. 307–313; Calhoun, "Commentary."

29. Rawls, *Theory*, p. 454

30. While Galston's influential version challenged neutrality, a neutrality-respecting argument focusing on stability can be made.

31. Okin, "*Political Liberalism*"; Mill, *Subjection*, Chapter 2.

32. Thanks to an anonymous reviewer for *Ethics* for this point.

33. Bennett, "Liberalism, Autonomy" and "Autonomy and Conjugal Love"; and Golash, "Marriage, Autonomy." See Maushart, *Wifework*, on women's autonomy. Okin, *Justice*; Shanley, *Just*; Metz, *Untying*; and Hartley and Watson, "Political" suggest an additional rationale, protecting caregivers; I discuss this in Chapter 8.ii.

34. Rawls, *Political Liberalism*, pp. 188, 180, 190.

35. Rawls, *Theory*, p. 92.

36. Rawls, *Political Liberalism*, p. 179.

37. Rawls, *Political Liberalism*, pp. 75–76; see also pp. 178–182, 187–190.

38. Rawls, *Political Liberalism*, pp. 75–76.

39. Rawls, *Theory*, Chapter 8. See also Alstott, *No Exit*.

40. Rawls, *Theory*, p. 440; see also 386.

41. For a survey of psychological benefits of relationships, see Perlman, "The Best"; Baumeister and Leary, "Need."

42. Doppelt, "Place"; Eyal, "Perhaps."
43. Dillon, "Self-Respect." Thanks to Cheshire Calhoun and audience members at the UBC Spring Colloquium, 2011, for questions on this point. The ensuing discussion also reflects the many helpful comments of participants in an online discussion on the PEA Soup blog (http://peasoup.typepad.com/peasoup/) and Calhoun's "Commentary." My strategy here has some similarities with Bennett's "Liberalism, Autonomy."
44. Perlman, "The Best," 11.
45. See Perlman, "The Best"; Baumeister and Leary, "Need." This discussion draws on empirical psychology, and so these claims are subject to further confirmation or disconfirmation from that field.
46. See Schwartz, "Moral"; Nagel, "Rawls." Kymlicka, "Liberal," responds.
47. Rawls, *Political*, p. 76; (my italics).
48. Baumeister and Leary, "Need," p. 497; Perlman, "The Best," p. 8.
49. Thanks to Clare Chambers for pressing me on this point.
50. The "representative legislator … does not know the particulars about himself," Rawls, *Theory*, p. 198; "general facts about their societies are made available to them but not the particularities of their own condition," p. 200. Compare Rawls, *Political Liberalism*, pp. 298, 338, 252.
51. E.g. Held, "Non-Contractual"; Held, *Ethics*, pp. 43, 80–85.
52. Fineman, *Autonomy Myth*; Pateman, *Sexual Contract*.
53. Metz, *Untying*, esp. pp. 126, 138, and Chapter 5. See also Brake, "Review," and den Otter, "Review."
54. Thanks to Clare Chambers for pressing me on this and the following points.
55. Nussbaum, "Right," p. 729.
56. On this point, see Wedgwood, "Fundamental"; Hartley and Watson, "Political."
57. Warner, "Response," p. 729.

Chapter 8

1. Rawls uses "ideal theory" in a narrower sense to refer to his assumption of strict compliance; see *Theory: Revised*, pp. 7–8. In the broader usage I follow Mills, "Ideal Theory," though he distinguishes different senses of ideal theory.
2. Mills, "Ideal Theory," p. 169.
3. Shiffrin, "Race," pp. 1645–6. She also notes that Rawls does not address discrimination on the basis of gender, sexual orientation, and disability.
4. "State Policies to Promote Marriage," p. 1; see Introduction, fn. 23. See also the 1996 U. S. Personal Responsibility and Work Opportunity Reconciliation Act (PRWORA), Title I, Section 101, Findings. TANF comes under PRWORA legislation.
5. "State Policies," p. 8. Georgia has similar legislation. Such legislation has been pending or under consideration in at least thirteen other states since 2001.
6. "State Policies," p. 22; in 2002, forty-nine states had accepted funding for abstinence-only education, although the number declined in subsequent years.
7. Social Security Act, Title V, Sec. 510.
8. Coontz, *Marriage*, Part Four; cf. Garrison, "Cooperative Parenting," p. 268.
9. Alstott, *No Exit*, p. 8; cf. Cave, "Harm Prevention"; Vanderheiden, "Why the State."
10. Legal Momentum, Annual Report 2005.

11. On the point that poverty is attributable to social problems other than divorce, see Okin, *Justice*; Vanderheiden, "Why the State"; Young, "Mothers"; Fineman, *Autonomy Myth*, Chapter 3.

12. Okin, *Justice*; cf. Rawls, "Idea," pp. 792–793.

13. Minow and Shanley, "Relational," p. 11, their citation of Mill omitted; cf. Shanley, *Just*; Pateman, *Sexual Contract*; Hartley and Watson, "Political."

14. See Shultz, "Contractual," pp. 232–240; Weitzman, "Marriage," pp. 1185, 1194–7.

15. Alstott, *No Exit*, p. 24.

16. Lucinda Ferguson, oral presentation, *Society for Applied Philosophy* annual conference, 2007.

17. Sunstein and Thaler, "Privatizing," p. 384; Stark, "Marriage," p. 1522, suggests precluding increases in economic inequalities during marriages.

18. See Rawls, *Theory: Revised*, pp. 53, 242; Rawls, "Idea," pp. 792–793.

19. Fineman, *Autonomy Myth*, p. 134.

20. Brooks, "Problem," pp. 111–112. See also May, "Liberal Feminism," for criticism of polygyny.

21. March, "Is There," pp. 258–259; Joseph is discussed in Emens, "Monogamy's Law," pp. 314–317, 332–334.

22. Calhoun, "Who's Afraid"; Mahoney, "Liberalism"; March, "Is There."

23. Rawls, "Idea," p. 779; Brooks, "Problem."

24. Mill, *On Liberty*, pp. 160–161 (my italics); see Baum, "Feminism."

25. See Chapter 5.1; Calhoun, "Who's Afraid"; Maushart, *Wifework*.

26. Maushart, *Wifework*, p. 5.

27. Brooks, "Problem," p. 116.

28. March, "Is There," p. 258.

29. March, "Is There," p. 266.

30. MacKinnon, *Toward*, pp. 161–162, see also 157–170, 195–214; and MacKinnon, *Feminism*.

31. Rawls, "Idea," p. 790.

32. MacKinnon, *Toward*, p. 224.

33. Rawls, *Theory: Revised*, p. 63.

34. In this paragraph I follow Levey, "Liberalism"; see also Walker, "Liberalism."

35. Rawls, *Theory*, pp. 199–200.

36. Rawls, "Idea," p. 788.

37. Rawls, "Idea," at pp. 787–794. See also Okin, *Justice*, and "*Political Liberalism*"; Nussbaum, *Sex and Social*, pp. 81–117.

38. "State Policies," p. 16.

39. Cf. Brake, "Rawls and Feminism."

40. See Becker, *A Treatise*, "Polygamy and Monogamy in Marriage Markets," pp. 80–107.

BIBLIOGRAPHY

Abbey, Ruth, and Douglas Den Uyl. "The Chief Inducement? The Idea of Marriage as Friendship." *Journal of Applied Philosophy* 18, no. 1 (2001): 37–52.

Abelard and Heloise. *The Letters of Abelard and Heloise*. Trans. Betty Radice. Ed. M. T. Clanchy. London: Penguin, 2003.

Ackerman, Bruce. *Social Justice in the Liberal State*. New Haven, CT: Yale University Press, 1980.

Almond, Brenda. *The Fragmenting Family*. Oxford: Oxford University Press, 2006.

Alstott, Anne. *No Exit: What Parents Owe Their Children and What Society Owes Parents*. Oxford: Oxford University Press, 2004.

Altman, Micah, and Phillip A. Klinker. "Measuring the Difference between White Voting and Polling on Interracial Marriage." *Du Bois Review* 3, no. 2 (2006): 299–315.

Amato, Paul R., Laura Spencer Loomis, and Alan Booth. "Parental Divorce, Marital Conflict, and Offspring Well-Being during Early Adulthood." *Social Forces* 73, no. 3 (1995): 895–915.

Anderson, Scott. "Prostitution and Sexual Autonomy: Making Sense of the Prohibition of Prostitution." *Ethics* 112, no. 4 (2002): 748–780.

Andrews, Stephen Pearl. *Love, Marriage, and Divorce, and the Sovereignty of the Individual*. Ed. Charles Shively. Weston, MA: M&S Press, 1975.

Anscombe, Elizabeth. *Ethics, Religion, and Politics: Collected Philosophical Papers*, vol. 3. Oxford: Blackwell, 1981.

Aquinas, Thomas. *Summa Theologiae*. Trans. English Dominicans. New York: Christian Classics, 1981.

Archard, David. *Children: Rights and Childhood*. London: Routledge, 1993.

———. *Children, Family and the State*. Burlington, VT: Ashgate, 2003.

Aristotle. *The Complete Works of Aristotle: The Revised Oxford Translation*. Ed. Jonathan Barnes. Princeton, NJ: Princeton University Press, 1984.

Arneson, Richard. "The Meaning of Marriage: State Efforts to Facilitate Friendship, Love, and Childrearing." *San Diego Law Review* 42 (2005): 979–1001.

Astell, Mary. *Political Writings*. Ed. Patricia Springborg. Cambridge: Cambridge University Press, 1996.

Augustine. *The City of God*. Trans. Philip Levine. Cambridge: Harvard University Press, 1966.

———. 1998, *Answer to the Pelagians, II: Marriage and Desire, Answer to the Two Letters of the Pelagians, Answer to Julian*, vol. I/24. Trans. Roland J. Teske. Ed. John E. Rotelle. Hyde Park, NY: New City Press.

———. 1999, *Marriage and Virginity: The Excellence of Marriage, Holy Virginity, the Excellence of Widowhood, Adulterous Marriages, Continence*, vol. I/9. Trans. Ray Kearney. Ed. David Hunter, John E. Rotelle, Hyde Park, NY: New City Press.

Barnhart, J. E., and Mary Ann Barnhart. "Marital Faithfulness and Unfaithfulness." *Journal of Social Philosophy* 4 (1973): 10–15.

Baum, Bruce. "Feminism, Liberalism, and Cultural Pluralism: J. S. Mill on Mormon Polygyny." *Journal of Political Philosophy* 5, no. 3 (1997): 230–253.

Baumeister, R. F., and M. R. Leary. "The Need to Belong: Desire for Interpersonal Attachments as a Fundamental Human Motivation." *Psychological Bulletin* 117 (1995): 497–529.

Bayles, Michael. "Marriage, Love, and Procreation." In *Philosophy and Sex*. 3rd ed. Ed. Robert Baker, Kathleen Wininger, and Frederick Elliston, 116–129. Amherst, NY: Prometheus Books, 1998.

Beauvoir, Simone de. *The Second Sex*. Ed. and trans. H. M. Parshley. New York: Vintage Books, 1989.

Becker, Gary. *A Treatise on the Family*, enlarged ed. Cambridge: Harvard University Press, 1993.

Benhabib, Seyla. *Situating the Self: Gender, Community and Postmodernism in Contemporary Ethics*. New York: Routledge, 1992.

Bennett, Christopher. "Liberalism, Autonomy, and Conjugal Love." *Res Publica* 9 (2003): 285–301.

———. "Autonomy and Conjugal Love: A Reply to Golash." *Res Publica* 12 (2006): 191–201.

Bennice, Jennifer, and Patricia Resick. "Marital Rape: History, Research, and Practice." *Trauma, Violence, and Abuse* 4, no. 3 (2003): 228–246.

Beyer, Jason A. "Public Dilemmas and Gay Marriage: Contra Jordan." *Journal of Social Philosophy* 33, no. 1 (2002): 9–16.

Blackstone, Sir William. *Commentaries on the Laws of England*. Oxford: Clarendon Press, 1765–1769.

Bloom, Allan. *The Closing of the American Mind*. New York: Penguin, 1987.

Blustein, Jeffrey. *Parents and Children: The Ethics of the Family*. Oxford: Oxford University Press, 1982.

Bolte, Angela. "Do Wedding Dresses Come in Lavender? The Prospects and Implications of Same-Sex Marriage." *Social Theory and Practice* 24, no. 1 (1998): 111–131.

Boonin, David. "Same-Sex Marriage and the Argument from Public Disagreement." *Journal of Social Philosophy* 30, no. 2 (1999): 251–259.

Bos, Henny M. W., and Frank van Balen. "Children in Planned Lesbian Families: Stigmatisation, Psychological Adjustment and Protective Factors." *Culture, Health & Sexuality* 10, no. 3 (2008): 221–236.

Boswell, John. *Same-Sex Unions in Premodern Europe*. New York: Vintage Books, 1994.

Bowden, Peta. *Caring: Gender-Sensitive Ethics*. New York: Routledge, 1997.

Brake, Elizabeth. "Rawls and Feminism: What Should Feminists Make of Liberal Neutrality?" *Journal of Moral Philosophy* 1, no. 3 (2004): 295–312.

———. "Justice and Virtue in Kant's Account of Marriage." *Kantian Review* 9 (2005): 58–94.

———. "Marriage, Morality, and Institutional Value." *Ethical Theory and Moral Practice* 10, no. 3 (2007): 243–254.

———. "Marriage and Domestic Partnership." In *The Stanford Encyclopedia of Philosophy*. Ed. Edward N. Zalta, Spring 2010. http://plato.stanford.edu/archives/spr2010/entries/marriage/.

———. "Minimal Marriage: What Political Liberalism Implies for Marriage Law." *Ethics* 120, no. 2 (2010): 302–337.

———. "Review of Tamara Metz, *Untying the Knot*." *Philosophy in Review* 30, no. 6 (2010): 418–421.

———. "Is Divorce Promise-Breaking?" *Ethical Theory and Moral Practice* 14 (2011): 23–39.

Brecht, Bertolt. *Poems 1913–1956*. rev. ed. Ed. John Willett, Ralph Manheim, Erich Fried. New York: Methuen, 1987.

Brewer, Talbot. "Two Kinds of Commitments (And Two Kinds of Social Groups)." *Philosophy and Phenomenological Research* 66, no. 3 (2003): 554–583.

Brighouse, Harry, and Adam Swift. "Parents' Rights and the Value of the Family." *Ethics* 117 (2006): 80–108.

Brooks, Thom. "The Problem with Polygamy." *Philosophical Topics* 37, no. 2 (2009): 109–122.

Buccola, Nicholas. "Finding Room for Same-Sex Marriage: Toward a More Inclusive Understanding of a Cultural Institution." *Journal of Social Philosophy* 36, 3 (2005): 331–343.

Butler, Judith. "Is Kinship Always Already Heterosexual?" *differences: A Journal of Feminist Cultural Studies* 13, no. 1 (2002): 14–44.

Cable, George Washington. *Old Creole Days*. Gretna, LA: Pelican, 2001.

Cagen, Sasha. *Quirkyalone*. New York: HarperCollins, 2006.

Calhoun, Cheshire. *Feminism, the Family, and the Politics of the Closet: Lesbian and Gay Displacement*. Oxford: Oxford University Press, 2003.

———. "Who's Afraid of Polygamous Marriage? Lessons for Same-Sex Marriage Advocacy from the History of Polygamy." *San Diego Law Review* 42 (2005): 1023–1042.

———. "What Good Is Commitment?" *Ethics* 119, no. 4 (2009): 613–641.

———. "Commentary on Elizabeth Brake's 'Minimal Marriage: What Political Liberalism Implies for Marriage Law.'" June 1, 2010. http://peasoup.typepad.com/peasoup/2010/06/ethics-discussions-at-pea-soup-elizabeth-brakes-minimal-marriage-what-political-liberalism-implies-f-1.html (accessed June 18, 2011).

Capellanus, Andreas. *Andreas Capellanus on Love*. Ed. and trans. P. G. Walsh. London: Duckworth, 1982.

Carbone, June. "The Limits of Contract in Family Law: An Analysis of Surrogate Motherhood." *Logos* 9 (1988): 147–160.

Card, Claudia. "Against Marriage and Motherhood." *Hypatia* 11, 3 (1996): 1–23.

———. "Gay Divorce: Thoughts on the Legal Regulation of Marriage." *Hypatia* 22, no. 1 (2007): 24–38.

Carver, Raymond. *What We Talk about When We Talk about Love*. New York: Vintage, 1989.

Case, Mary Anne. "Marriage Licenses." *Minnesota Law Review* 89 (2004–2005): 1758–1797.

Cave, Eric M. "Marital Pluralism: Making Marriage Safer for Love." *Journal of Social Philosophy* 34, no. 3 (2003): 331–347.

———. "Harm Prevention and the Benefits of Marriage." *Journal of Social Philosophy* 35, no. 2 (2004): 233–243.

Cavell, Stanley. *Pursuits of Happiness: The Hollywood Comedy of Remarriage*. Cambridge: Harvard University Press, 1981.

———. *Must We Mean What We Say?* updated ed. New York: Cambridge University Press, 2002.

Cleyre, Voltairine de. *The Voltairine de Cleyre Reader*. Ed. A. J. Brigati. Oakland, CA: AK Press, 2004.

Collins, Patricia Hill. *Black Feminist Thought: Knowledge, Consciousness, and the Politics of Empowerment*. New York: Routledge, 1991.

———. "It's All in the Family: Intersections of Gender, Race, and Nation." *Hypatia* 13, no. 3 (1998): 62–82.

Coontz, Stephanie. *Marriage: A History.* London: Penguin, 2006.

Cornell, Drucilla. *At the Heart of Freedom: Feminism, Sex, and Equality.* Princeton, NJ: Princeton University Press, 1998.

Corvino, John. "Homosexuality and the PIB Argument." *Ethics* 115 (2005): 501–534.

Cott, Nancy. *Public Vows: A History of Marriage and the Nation.* Cambridge: Harvard University Press, 2000.

Cronan, Sheila. "Marriage." In *Radical Feminism.* Ed. Anne Koedt, Ellen Levine, Anita Rapone, 213–221. New York: Quadrangle, 1973.

Cruz, David B. "'Just Don't Call It Marriage': The First Amendment and Marriage as an Expressive Resource." *Southern California Law Review* 74, no. 4 (2001): 925–1026.

Cudd, Ann. "Rational Choice Theory and the Lessons of Feminism." In *A Mind of One's Own*, 2nd ed. Ed. Louise Antony and Charlotte Witt, 398–417. Oxford: Westview Press, 2001.

———. *Analyzing Oppression.* New York: Oxford University Press, 2006.

Davis, Angela Y. *Women, Race & Class.* New York: Vintage Books, 1983.

Dean, Craig. "Gay Marriage: A Civil Right." *Journal of Homosexuality* 27, nos. 3–4 (1994): 111–115.

Deigh, John. "Promises under Fire." *Ethics* 112 (2002): 483–506.

Den Otter, Ronald. "Review of Tamara Metz, *Untying the Knot.*" *New Political Science* 33, no. 1 (2011): 131–134.

Denis, Lara. "From Friendship to Marriage: Revising Kant." *Philosophy and Phenomenological Research* 63, no. 1 (2001): 1–28.

DePaulo, Bella. *Singled Out: How Singles Are Stereotyped, Stigmatized, and Ignored, and Still Live Happily Ever After.* New York: St. Martin's Press, 2006.

Devlin, Patrick. *The Enforcement of Morals.* Oxford: Oxford University Press, 1965.

Dillon, Robin S. "Self-Respect: Moral, Emotional, Political." *Ethics* 107, no. 2 (1997): 226–249.

Doppelt, Gerald. "The Place of Self-Respect in a Theory of Justice." *Inquiry* 52, no. 2 (2009): 127–154.

Dua, Enakshi. "Beyond Diversity: Exploring the Ways in which the Discourse of Race Has Shaped the Institution of the Nuclear Family." In *Scratching the Surface.* Ed. Enakshi Dua and Angela Robertson, 237–259. Toronto: Women's Press, 1991.

Durose, Matthew R., et al. *Bureau of Justice Statistics, Family Violence Statistics: Including Statistics on Strangers and Acquaintances.* U.S. Department of Justice, NCJ 207846, 2005.

Dworkin, Andrea. *Pornography: Men Possessing Women.* New York: E.P. Dutton, 1989.

Dworkin, Ronald. *A Matter of Principle.* Cambridge: Harvard University Press, 1985.

Eekelaar, John. *Family Law and Personal Life.* Oxford: Oxford University Press, 2006.

Ehrenreich, Barbara. *Nickel and Dimed.* New York: Metropolitan Books, 2001.

Eliot, T.S. *The Waste Land and Other Poems.* Peterborough, Ontario: Broadview, 2011.

Elster, Jon. *Ulysses and the Sirens. rev. ed.* Cambridge: Cambridge University Press, 1984.

———. *Ulysses Unbound: Studies in Rationality, Precommitment, and Constraints.* Cambridge: Cambridge University Press, 2002.

Emens, Elizabeth F. "Monogamy's Law: Compulsory Monogamy and Polyamorous Existence." *New York University Review of Law and Social Change* 29 (2004): 277–376.

Engels, Friedrich. *The Origin of the Family, Private Property, and the State.* Ed. Eleanor Burke Leacock. New York: International, 1972.

Eskow, Lisa R. "The Ultimate Weapon? Demythologizing Spousal Rape and Reconceptualizing Its Prosecution." *Stanford Law Review* 48, no. 3 (1996): 677–709.

Ettelbrick, Paula. "Since When Is Marriage a Path to Liberation?" *Out/look: National Lesbian and Gay Quarterly* 6, no. 9 (1989): 14–17.

Eyal, Nir. "'Perhaps the Most Important Primary Good': Self-Respect and Rawls' Principles of Justice." *Politics, Philosophy & Economics* 4, no. 2 (2005): 195–219.

Ferguson, Ann. "Gay Marriage: An American and Feminist Dilemma." *Hypatia: A Journal of Feminist Philosophy* 22, no. 1 (2007): 39–57.

Fineman, Martha. *The Neutered Mother, the Sexual Family, and Other Twentieth Century Tragedies.* New York: Routledge, 1995.

———. *The Autonomy Myth: A Theory of Dependency.* New York: New Press, 2004.

Finnis, John. "Law, Morality, and 'Sexual Orientation.'" *Notre Dame Law Review* 69 (1994): 1049–1076.

———. "The Good of Marriage and the Morality of Sexual Relations: Some Philosophical and Historical Observations." *American Journal of Jurisprudence* 42 (1997): 97–134.

Firestone, Shulamith. *The Dialectic of Sex: The Case for Feminist Revolution.* New York: William Morrow, 1970.

Fisher, Helen. *Anatomy of Love: The Natural History of Monogamy, Adultery, and Divorce.* New York: W. W. Norton and Company, 1992.

FitzGibbon, Scott. "Marriage and the Good of Obligation." *American Journal of Jurisprudence* 47 (2002): 41–69.

Ford, Richard. *The Sportswriter.* New York: Vintage, 1986.

Forster, E. M. *Howard's End.* Ed. Alistair Duckworth. Boston: Bedford Books, 1997.

Freeman, Elizabeth. *The Wedding Complex: Forms of Belonging in Modern American Culture.* Durham, NC: Duke University Press, 2002.

Freeman, M. D. A. "Not Such a Queer Idea: Is There a Case for Same Sex Marriages?" *Journal of Applied Philosophy* 16, no. 1 (1999): 1–17.

Freeman, Michael, and Christina Lyon. *Cohabitation without Marriage.* Aldershot: Gower Publishing Company Limited, 1983.

Friedman, Lawrence. "Rights of Passage: Divorce Law in Historical Perspective." *Oregon Law Review* 63, no. 4 (1984): 649–669.

Friedman, Marilyn. "Beyond Caring: The De-Moralization of Gender." In *Science, Morality, and Feminist Theory.* Ed. Marsha Hanen and Kai Nielsen, *Canadian Journal of Philosophy* Supp. Vol. 13 (1987): 87–110.

Frye, Marilyn. *The Politics of Reality: Essays in Feminist Theory.* Trumansburg, NY: Crossing Press, 1983.

Galston, William. *Liberal Purposes.* Cambridge: Cambridge University Press, 1991.

Garrett, Jeremy. "History, Tradition, and the Normative Foundations of Civil Marriage." *The Monist* 91, nos. 3–4 (2008): 446–474.

———. "Why the Old Sexual Morality of the New Natural Law Undermines Traditional Marriage." *Social Theory and Practice* 34, 4 (2008): 591–622.

Garrison, Marsha. "Promoting Cooperative Parenting: Programs and Prospects." *Journal of Law and Family Studies* 9 (2007): 265–279.

George, Robert. "'Same-Sex Marriage' and 'Moral Neutrality.'" In *Homosexuality and American Public Life.* Ed. Christopher Wolfe, 141–153. Dallas: Spence, 2000.

Gilligan, Carol. *In a Different Voice.* Cambridge: Harvard University Press, 1993.

Golash, Deirdre. "Marriage, Autonomy, and the State: Reply to Christopher Bennett." *Res Publica* 12 (2006): 179–190.

Goldman, Alan. "Plain Sex." *Philosophy and Public Affairs* 6, no. 3 (1977): 267–287.

Goldman, Emma. "Jealousy: Causes and a Possible Cure." In *Red Emma Speaks: An Emma Goldman Reader*. Ed. Alix Kates Shulman, 214–221. Amherst, NY: Humanity Books, 1998.

Grisez, Germain. *The Way of the Lord Jesus*. Vol. 2, *Living a Christian Life*. Quincy, IL: Franciscan Press, 1993.

Halwani, Raja. *Virtuous Liaisons*. Peru, IL: Open Court, 2003.

Hampton, Jean. "Feminist Contractarianism." In *A Mind of One's Own*. Ed. Louise Antony and Charlotte Witt, 227–256. Oxford: Westview Press, 1993.

Hartley, Christie, and Lori Watson. "Political Liberalism, Marriage and the Family." *Law and Philosophy*, Online First, 6 September 2011.

Hegel, G. W. F. *Elements of the Philosophy of Right*. Ed. Allen W. Wood. Trans. H. B. Nisbet. Cambridge: Cambridge University Press, 1995.

Held, Virginia. "Non-Contractual Society: A Feminist View." In *Science, Morality, and Feminist Theory*. Ed. Marsha Hanen and Kai Nielsen, *Canadian Journal of Philosophy* Supp. Vol. 13 (1987): 111–37.

——. *The Ethics of Care: Personal, Political, and Global*. Oxford: Oxford University Press, 2006.

Herman, Barbara. "Could It Be Worth Thinking about Kant on Sex and Marriage?" In *A Mind of One's Own*. Ed. Louise Antony and Charlotte Witt, 49–67. Oxford: Westview Press, 1993.

Hoagland, Sarah Lucia. "Heterosexualism and White Supremacy." *Hypatia* 22, no. 1 (2007): 166–185.

Hobbes, Thomas. *Leviathan*. Ed. Michael Oakeshott. New York: Simon and Schuster, 1962.

hooks, bell. *Feminist Theory: From Margin to Center*. Boston: South End Press, 1984.

Hume, David. *An Enquiry Concerning the Principles of Morals*. London: Millar, 1751.

Jaggar, Alison. "Love and Knowledge: Emotion in Feminist Epistemology." *Inquiry: An Interdisciplinary Journal of Philosophy* 32 (1989): 151–76.

James, Henry. *The Bostonians*. New York: Thomas Crowell, 1979.

——. *The Ambassadors*. New York: Penguin, 1986.

——. *The Portrait of a Lady*. 2nd ed. New York: Norton, 1995.

Jordan, Jeff. "Is It Wrong to Discriminate on the Basis of Homosexuality?" *Journal of Social Philosophy* 26, no. 1 (1995): 39–52.

Kant, Immanuel, *Observations on the Feeling of the Beautiful and Sublime*. Trans. John T. Goldthwait. Berkeley: University of California Press, 1960.

——. "Conjectural Beginning of Human History." In *On History*. Ed. Lewis White Beck, 53–68. Indianapolis, IN: Bobbs-Merrill, 1963.

——. *Anthropology from a Pragmatic Point of View*. Trans. Mary Gregor. The Hague: Martinus Nijhoff, 1974.

——. *Groundwork of the Metaphysics of Morals*. Trans. Mary Gregor. In *Practical Philosophy*. Ed. Mary Gregor, 37–108. Cambridge: Cambridge University Press, 1996.

——. *The Metaphysics of Morals*. Trans. Mary Gregor. In *Practical Philosophy*. Ed. Mary Gregor, 355–588. Cambridge: Cambridge University Press, 1996.

——. *Lectures on Ethics*. Trans. Peter Heath. Ed. Peter Heath and J. B. Schneewind. Cambridge: Cambridge University Press, 2001.

Kaplan, Morris B. "Intimacy and Equality: The Question of Lesbian and Gay Marriage." *Philosophical Forum* 25, no. 4 (1994): 333–360.

Kekes, John. "'Ought Implies Can' and Two Kinds of Morality." *Philosophical Quarterly* 34, no. 137 (1984): 459–467.

Kierkegaard, Søren. *Either/Or*. Trans. Howard V. Hong and Edna H. Hong. Princeton, NJ: Princeton University Press, 1987.

Kingston, Anne. *The Meaning of Wife*. Toronto: HarperCollins, 2004.

Kipnis, Laura. *Against Love: A Polemic*. New York: Pantheon Books, 2003.

Kittay, Eva. *Love's Labor*. New York: Routledge, 1999.

Kleingeld, Pauline. "Just Love? Marriage and the Question of Justice." *Social Theory and Practice* 24, no. 2 (1998): 261–281.

Kymlicka, Will. "Liberal Individualism and Liberal Neutrality." *Ethics* 99, no. 4 (1989): 883–905.

———. "Rethinking the Family." *Philosophy and Public Affairs* 20, no. 1 (1991): 77–97.

LaFollette, Hugh. "Licensing Parents." *Philosophy and Public Affairs* 9, no. 2 (1980): 182–197.

Landau, Iddo. "An Argument for Marriage." *Philosophy* 79 (2004): 475–481.

Levey, Ann. "Liberalism, Adaptive Preferences, and Gender Equality." *Hypatia* 20, no. 4 (2005): 127–143.

Liao, S. Matthew. "The Idea of a Duty to Love." *Journal of Value Inquiry* 40 (2006): 1–22.

Locke, John. *Two Treatises of Government*. Ed. Peter Laslett. Cambridge: Cambridge University Press, 1988.

Lloyd, S. A. "Family Justice and Social Justice." *Pacific Philosophical Quarterly* 75 (1994): 353–371.

Macedo, Stephen. "Homosexuality and the Conservative Mind." *Georgetown Law Journal* 84 (1995): 261–300.

MacIntyre, Alasdair. *After Virtue*. London: Duckworth, 1985.

MacKinnon, Catharine A. *Feminism Unmodified: Discourses on Life and Law*. Cambridge: Harvard University Press, 1987.

———. *Toward a Feminist Theory of the State*. Cambridge: Harvard University Press, 1989.

Mahoney, Jon. "Liberalism and the Polygamy Question." *Social Philosophy Today* 23 (2008): 161–174.

Mahony, Rhona. *Kidding Ourselves: Breadwinning, Babies, and Bargaining Power*. New York: Basic Books, 1995.

Maine, Sir Henry. *Ancient Law*. London: J. M. Dent and Sons, 1917.

March, Andrew. "Is There a Right to Polygamy? Marriage, Equality, and Subsidizing Families in Liberal Political Justification." *Journal of Moral Philosophy* 8 (2011): 246–272.

Marquis, Don. "What's Wrong with Adultery?" In *What's Wrong?* Ed. Graham Oddie and David Boonin, 231–238. New York: Oxford University Press, 2005.

Martin, Mike W. "Love's Constancy." *Philosophy* 68, no. 263 (1993): 63–77.

———. "Adultery and Fidelity." *Journal of Social Philosophy* 25, no. 3 (1994): 76–91.

Marx, Karl. *Selected Writings*. Ed. Lawrence Simon. Indianapolis: Hackett, 1994.

Maushart, Susan. *Wifework: What Marriage Really Means for Women*. New York: Bloomsbury, 2001.

May, Simon. "Liberal Feminism and the Ethics of Polygamy." In *Exploding the Nuclear Family Ideal: For Better or Worse?* Ed. S. Chan and D. Cutas. London: Bloomsbury Academic, forthcoming 2012.

Mayo, David J. and Martin Gunderson. "The Right to Same-Sex Marriage: A Critique of the Leftist Critique." *Journal of Social Philosophy* 31, no. 3 (2000): 326–337.

McMurtry, John. "Monogamy: A Critique." *The Monist* 56 (1972): 587–599.

McNaughton, David. *Moral Vision: An Introduction to Ethics.* Oxford: Basil Blackwell, 1988.

Mead, Rebecca. *One Perfect Day: The Selling of the American Wedding.* New York: Penguin, 2007.

Mendus, Susan. "Marital Faithfulness." *Philosophy* 59 (1984): 243–252.

Mercier, Adèle. *Affidavit* for the petitioners to Ontario Superior Court of Justice in *Halpern et al.* and *Canada (Attorney General)*, Court files 684/00, 30/2001, Nov. http://www.ub.es/grc_logos/people/amercier/proof3.htm (accessed June 18, 2011).

——. "On the Nature of Marriage: Somerville on Same-Sex Marriage." *The Monist* 91, no. 3–4 (2008): 407–421.

Metz, Tamara. *Untying the Knot: Marriage, the State, and the Case for Their Divorce.* Princeton, NJ: Princeton University Press, 2010.

Mill, John Stuart. *On Liberty.* Ed. Gertrude Himmelfarb. London: Penguin, 1985.

——. *The Subjection of Women.* Ed. Susan Moller Okin. Indianapolis: Hackett, 1988.

Mills, Charles. "'Ideal Theory' as Ideology." *Hypatia* 20, no. 3 (2005): 165–184.

Minow, Martha, and Mary Lyndon Shanley. "Relational Rights and Responsibilities: Revisioning the Family in Liberal Political Theory and Law." *Hypatia* 11, no. 1 (1996): 4–29.

Mohr, Richard D. *The Long Arc of Justice: Lesbian and Gay Marriage, Equality, and Rights.* New York: Columbia University Press, 2005.

Moller, Dan. "An Argument against Marriage." *Philosophy* 78, no. 1 (2003): 79–91.

——. "The Marriage Commitment: Reply to Landau." *Philosophy* 80 (2005): 279–284.

Morrison, Toni. *Beloved.* New York: Alfred A. Knopf, 2004.

Morse, Jennifer Roback. "Why Unilateral Divorce Has No Place in a Free Society." In *The Meaning of Marriage.* Ed. Robert P. George and Jean Bethke Elshtain, 74–99. Dallas: Spence, 2006.

Munoz-Dardé, Veronique. "John Rawls, Justice *in* the Family, and Justice *of* the Family." *Philosophical Quarterly* 48, no. 192 (1998): 335–352.

Nagel, Thomas. "Rawls on Justice." *Philosophical Review* 82, no. 2 (1973): 220–234.

Nielson, Joyce, Glenda Walden, and Charlotte Kunkel. "Gendered Heteronormativity: Empirical Illustrations in Everyday Life." *Sociological Quarterly* 41, no. 2 (2000): 283–396.

Nietzsche, Friedrich. *On the Genealogy of Morality: A Polemic.* Trans. Maudemarie Clark, Alan Swensen. Indianapolis: Hackett Publishing, 1998.

Noddings, Nel. *Caring: A Feminine Approach to Ethics and Moral Education.* London: UCLA Press, 1984.

Norton, Caroline. *Selected Writings of Caroline Norton.* Ed. James O. Hoge and Jane Marcus. Delmar, NY: Scholars' Facsimiles and Reprints, 1978.

Nozick, Robert. *Anarchy, State, and Utopia.* New York: Basic Books, 1974.

Nussbaum, Martha. *Love's Knowledge.* Oxford: Oxford University Press, 1990.

——. *Sex and Social Justice.* Oxford: Oxford University Press, 1999.

——. "A Right to Marry." *California Law Review* 98, no. 3 (2010): 667–696.

Nussbaum, Martha, and David M. Estlund, eds. *Sex, Preference, and Family: Essays on Law and Nature.* Oxford: Oxford University Press, 1998.

Okin, Susan Moller. *Women in Western Political Thought.* Princeton: Princeton University Press, 1979.

———. "Women and the Making of the Sentimental Family." *Philosophy and Public Affairs* 11, 1 (1982): 65–88.

———. *Justice, Gender, and the Family.* New York: Basic Books, 1989.

———. "Political Liberalism, Justice, and Gender." *Ethics* 105 (1994): 23–43.

Parsons, Kate. "Subverting the Fellowship of the Wedding Ring." *Journal of Social Philosophy* 39, 3 (2008): 393–410.

Pateman, Carole. *The Sexual Contract.* Cambridge: Polity Press, 1988.

Perlman, Daniel. "The Best of Times, the Worst of Times: The Place of Close Relationships in Psychology and Our Daily Lives." *Canadian Psychology* 48, no. 1 (2007): 7–18.

Plato. *The Republic.* Trans. Desmond Lee. New York: Penguin, 1955.

Posner, Richard, and Katharine Silbaugh, *A Guide to America's Sex Laws.* Chicago: University of Chicago Press, 1996.

Rajczi, Alex. "A Populist Argument for Same-Sex Marriage." *The Monist* 91, nos. 3–4 (2008): 475–505.

Rawls, John. *A Theory of Justice.* Cambridge: Harvard University Press, 1971.

———. *Political Liberalism.* New York: Columbia University Press, 1993.

———. "The Idea of Public Reason Revisited." *The University of Chicago Law Review* 64, no. 3 (1997): 765–807.

———. *A Theory of Justice.* rev. ed. Cambridge: Harvard University Press, 1999.

Raz, Joseph. *The Morality of Freedom.* Oxford: Oxford University Press, 1986.

Rich, Adrienne. "Compulsory Heterosexuality and Lesbian Existence." *Signs: Journal of Women in Culture and Society* 5 (1980): 631–660.

Robson, R. "A Mere Switch or a Fundamental Change? Theorizing Transgender Marriage." *Hypatia* 22, no. 1 (2007): 58–70.

Ruddick, Sara. *Maternal Thinking.* London: The Women's Press, 1990.

Russell, Bertrand. *Marriage and Morals.* New York: Bantam Books, 1959.

Russell, Diana. *Rape in Marriage.* New York: Macmillan Press, 1990.

Sachs, Albie, and Joan Hoff Wilson. *Sexism and the Law.* Oxford: Martin Robertson, 1978.

Sandel, Michael. *Liberalism and the Limits of Justice.* Cambridge: Cambridge University Press, 1982.

Sartre, Jean-Paul. "The Humanism of Existentialism." In *Essays in Existentialism.* Ed. Wade Baskin, 31–62. New York: Citadel Press, 1947.

———. *Being and Nothingness.* Trans. Hazel E. Barnes. New York: Philosophical Library,1956.

Scanlon, T. M. *What We Owe to Each Other.* Cambridge, MA: Belknap Press, 1998.

Schaff, Kory. "Kant, Political Liberalism, and the Ethics of Same-Sex Relations." *Journal of Social Philosophy* 32, no. 3 (2001): 446–462.

———. "Equal Protection and Same-Sex Marriage." *Journal of Social Philosophy* 35, no. 1 (2004): 133–147.

Schelling, Thomas. *The Strategy of Conflict.* Cambridge: Harvard University Press, 1960.

Schlegel, Friedrich von. *Friedrich Schlegel's "Lucinde" and the Fragments.* Trans. and ed. Peter Firchow. Minneapolis: University of Minnesota Press, 1971.

Schwartz, Adina. "Moral Neutrality and Primary Goods." *Ethics* 83, no. 4 (1973): 294–307.

Scott, Elizabeth. "A World without Marriage." *Family Law Quarterly* 41 (2007): 537–566.

Scruton, Roger. *Sexual Desire.* London: The Free Press, 1986.

Searle, John. *Expression and Meaning.* Cambridge: Cambridge University Press, 1979.

Shanley, Mary Lyndon, et al. *Just Marriage.* Oxford: Oxford University Press, 2004.

Sher, George. *Beyond Neutrality: Perfectionism and Politics.* Cambridge: Cambridge University Press, 1997.

Shiffrin, Seana. "Race, Labor, and the Fair Equality of Opportunity Principle." *Fordham Law Review* 72 (2004): 1643–1675.

Shorter, Edward. *The Making of the Modern Family*. London: Collins, 1976.

Shrage, Laurie. *Moral Dilemmas of Feminism*. New York: Routledge, 1994.

Shultz, Marjorie. "Contractual Ordering of Marriage: A New Model for State Policy." *California Law Review* 70, no. 2 (1982): 204–334.

Singer, Irving. *The Nature of Love*. Vol. 1, *Plato to Luther*. 2nd ed. Chicago: University of Chicago Press, 1984.

Soble, Alan. *The Structure of Love*. New Haven: Yale University Press, 1990.

Stark, Barbara. "Marriage Proposals: From One-Size-Fits-All to Postmodern Marriage Law." *California Law Review* 89, no. 5 (2001): 1479–1548.

Steinbock, Bonnie. "Adultery." *QQ: Report from the Center for Philosophy and Public Policy* 6, no. 1 (1986): 12–14.

Stern, Robert. "Does 'Ought' Imply 'Can'? And Did Kant Think It Does?" *Utilitas* 16, no. 1 (2004): 42–61.

Stivers, Andrew, and Andrew Valls. "Same-sex marriage and the regulation of language." *Politics, Philosophy and Economics* 6, no.2 (2007): 237–253.

Sullivan, Andrew. *Same-Sex Marriage: Pro and Con*. rev. ed. New York: Vintage, 2004.

Sunstein, Cass, and Richard Thaler. "Privatizing Marriage." *The Monist* 91, nos. 3–4 (2008): 377–387.

Taylor, Gabriele. "Love." *Proceedings of the Aristotelian Society* 76 (1975–1976): 147–164.

Teichman, Jenny. *Illegitimacy*. Ithaca, NY: Cornell University Press, 1982.

Tjaden, Patricia, and Nancy Thoennes. "Extent, Nature, and Consequence of Intimate Partner Violence." Findings from the National Violence Against Women Survey, published by the U. S. Department of Justice, NCJ 183781, 2000.

Tomasi, John. "Individual Rights and Community Virtues." *Ethics* 101 (1991): 521–536.

Torcello, Lawrence. "Is the State Endorsement of Any Marriage Justifiable? Same-Sex Marriage, Civil Unions, and the Marriage Privatization Model." *Public Affairs Quarterly* 22, 1 (2008): 43–61.

Trainor, Brian. "The State, Marriage and Divorce." *Journal of Applied Philosophy* 9, no. 2 (1992): 135–148.

Vanderheiden, Steve. "Why the State Should Stay Out of the Wedding Chapel." *Public Affairs Quarterly* 13, no. 2 (1999): 175–190.

van Hooft, Stan. "Obligation, Character, and Commitment." *Philosophy* 63, no. 245 (1988): 345–362.

———. "Commitment and the Bond of Love." *Australasian Journal of Philosophy* 74, no. 3 (1996): 454–466.

Vodrasta, Stanley. "Against Blackstone and the Concept of Marriage as Contract." *Modern Schoolman* 81 (2004): 97–120.

Waldron, Jeremy. "When Justice Replaces Affection: The Need for Rights." *Harvard Journal of Law and Public Policy* 11, no. 3 (1988): 625–647.

———. "Autonomy and Perfectionism in Raz's *Morality of Freedom*." *Southern California Law Review* 62 (1988–1989): 1097–1152.

Walker, John D. "Liberalism, Consent, and the Problem of Adaptive Preferences." *Social Theory and Practice* 21, no. 3 (1995): 457–471.

Walker, Sue Sheridan. "Widow and Ward: The Feudal Law of Child Custody in Medieval England." In *Women in Medieval Society*. Ed. Susan Mosler Stuard, 158–172. Philadelphia: University of Pennsylvania Press, 1976.

Wall, Steven. "Neutrality and Responsibility." *Journal of Philosophy* 98, no. 8 (2001): 389–410.

Wallenstein, Peter. *Tell the Court I Love My Wife: Race, Marriage, and Law: An American History*. New York: Palgrave Macmillan, 2002.

Warner, Michael. "Introduction: Fear of a Queer Planet." *Social Text* 29 (1991): 3–17.

———. "Response to Martha Nussbaum." *California Law Review* 98, no. 3 (2010): 721–729.

Watters, Ethan. *Urban Tribes: Are Friends the New Family?* New York: Bloomsbury, 2003.

Wax, Amy. "Traditionalism, Pluralism, and Same-Sex Marriage." *Rutgers Law Review* 59, no. 2 (2006–2007): 377–412.

Wedgwood, Ralph. "The Fundamental Argument for Same-Sex Marriage." *Journal of Political Philosophy* 7, no. 3 (1999): 225–242.

Weisbrod, Carol. "The Way We Live Now: A Discussion of Contracts and Domestic Arrangements." *Utah Law Review* 2 (1994): 777–815.

Weiss, Penny. "Feminism and Communitarianism." In *Feminism and Community*. Ed. Penny Weiss and Marilyn Friedman, 161–186. Philadelphia: Temple University Press, 1995.

Weitzman, Lenore. *The Marriage Contract*. New York: Macmillan, 1981.

Wellington, Adrian Alex. "Why Liberals Should Support Same Sex Marriage." *Journal of Social Philosophy* 26, no. 3 (1995): 5–32.

Williams, Bernard. *Moral Luck*. Cambridge: Cambridge University Press, 1981.

Wilson, John. "Can One Promise to Love Another?" *Philosophy* 64 (1989): 557–563.

Wollstonecraft, Mary. *The Vindications: The Rights of Men, The Rights of Woman*. Ed. D.L. Macdonald and Kathleen Scherf. Peterborough, Ontario: Broadview, 1997.

Young, Iris Marion. "Mothers, Citizenship, and Independence: A Critique of Pure Family Values." *Ethics* 105 (1995): 535–556.

INDEX